# The English Electric Class 37

Co Co Diesel Electric Locomotives From Design to Demise

# The English Electric Class 37

Co Co Diesel Electric Locomotives From Design to Demise

**DAVID MATHER**

First published in Great Britain in 2025 by
Pen and Sword Transport
An imprint of
Pen & Sword Books Ltd.
Yorkshire - Philadelphia

Copyright © David Mather, 2025

ISBN 978 1 39903 326 8

The right of David Mather to be identified as author of this work has been asserted by him in accordance with the Copyright, Designs and Patents Act 1988.

A CIP catalogue record for this book is available from the British Library.

All rights reserved. No part of this book may be reproduced, transmitted, downloaded, decompiled or reverse engineered in any form or by any means, electronic or mechanical including photocopying, recording or by any information storage and retrieval system, without permission from the Publisher in writing. No part of this book may be used or reproduced in any manner for the purpose of training artificial intelligence technologies or systems.

Typeset in Palatino by SJmagic DESIGN SERVICES, India.

The Publisher's authorised representative in the EU for product safety is Authorised Rep Compliance Ltd., Ground Floor, 71 Lower Baggot Street, Dublin D02 P593, Ireland.
www.arccompliance.com

For a complete list of Pen & Sword titles please contact

PEN & SWORD BOOKS LIMITED
George House, Beevor Street, Off Pontefract Road, Hoyle Mill, Barnsley, South Yorkshire, England, S71 1HN.
E-mail: enquiries@pen-and-sword.co.uk
Website: www.pen-and-sword.co.uk

or

PEN AND SWORD BOOKS
1950 Lawrence Rd, Havertown, PA 19083, USA
E-mail: uspen-and-sword@casematepublishers.com
Website: www.penandswordbooks.com

# CONTENTS

Acknowledgements & thanks ................................................................................................. 6

Foreword .................................................................................................................................. 7

| Chapter 1 | Background and the quest for Standardisation ........................................... 8 |
| Chapter 2 | The Development of the Class 37 Locomotives ......................................... 10 |
| Chapter 3 | Locomotive Histories ..................................................................................... 13 |
|  | Pre-TOPS Days ............................................................................................... 13 |
|  | Sub-class variations post TOPS .................................................................... 16 |
|  | Sub-class 37/0 ................................................................................................ 17 |
|  | Sub-class 37/3 ................................................................................................ 56 |
|  | Sub-class 37/4 ................................................................................................ 64 |
|  | Sub-class 37/5 .............................................................................................. 101 |
|  | Sub-class 37/7 .............................................................................................. 135 |
|  | Sub-class 37/9 .............................................................................................. 150 |
|  | Sub-class 97/3 .............................................................................................. 152 |
| Chapter 4 | Class 37s in Colour ..................................................................................... 156 |
| Appendix 1 | Technical Data ............................................................................................ 203 |
| Appendix 2 | Liveries ........................................................................................................ 205 |
| Appendix 3 | Regional variations .................................................................................... 207 |
| Appendix 4 | Rail Freight Logos ...................................................................................... 208 |
| Appendix 5 | Where are they now? (correct to July 2024) ............................................ 209 |
|  | Bibliography ................................................................................................ 212 |

# ACKNOWLEDGEMENTS & THANKS

For my wife Mair whose continued support has as always proved invaluable. Thanks also to my late friend Rick Ward and to Jonathan Allen for permissions to reproduce their images, along with the several other fellow enthusiasts whose work is included.

Special thanks also to:

Web masters for: Six Bells Junction (Gary Thornton: sixbellsjunction.co.uk]
The Class 37 Locomotive Group (Mick Parker: class37lg.co.uk]

for permission to use material from their excellent web sites.

Images are copyright of the author unless credited otherwise.

# FOREWORD

When I was growing up in Bolton in the 1950s, steam was still king. The railway from Manchester Victoria through my hometown went on to join the West Coast Main Line at Euxton Junction south of Preston and carried a seemingly endless stream of passenger, parcels and freight trains in both directions. By the 1960s the wholesale replacement of steam traction was well underway, though the goods sidings around Bolton's Trinity Street station still echoed with the sounds of busy little former Lancashire & Yorkshire Railway (L&YR) 0-4-0 and 0-6-0 saddle tanks rearranging the lines of wagons for Class 3F 0-6-0 freight locos to take them on their way.

Introduced in the 1890s, these and other 'workhorses' would soon be no more. On the adjacent running lines, Stanier's 'Black 5s' and '8Fs' hurried past, they too destined all too soon for the cutter's torch. Already diesel multiple units (dmu) were becoming commonplace on local services, BR, Beyer-Peacock and Sulzer 'Type 2' diesel locos were taking over freight duties and the English Electric (EE) 'Type 4' (later denoted as the Class 40) was muscling in on longer distance passenger trains. Into this mix came the EE 'Type 3', now known to all as Class 37, built from 1960. Little did we know that this design would achieve so much and survive for so long. The 309 locomotives outshopped from EE's works at Newton-le-Willows and Darlington would prove so versatile and dependable that they would outlive many of the more powerful and 'glamorous' constructions which would follow. Over the years they have benefitted from several modifications, carried numerous liveries and visited virtually every corner of the network. This book lists all 309 class members by sub-class and presents a representative selection of examples in greater detail, describing their histories and achievements from delivery through working life to, for those lucky few, preservation, up to July 2024, accompanied by photographs from my collection and those of fellow enthusiasts.

David Mather
York.

## Chapter 1
# BACKGROUND AND THE QUEST FOR STANDARDISATION

The devastation caused to Britain's transport system by the Second World War together with the severe backlog of maintenance which had built up necessitated not only the nationalisation of the railways but also the formulation of a strategic plan to modernise and re-equip the railway network. In 1948 the Railway Executive set up a committee to report on the economic balance between steam, diesel, electric and gas turbine locomotives and in 1951 it recommended large scale trials with main-line diesel and electric locos. Passenger and, arguably more importantly, freight haulage was losing money in competition with road and air traffic. Something had to be done and quickly. Experience gained with diesel traction overseas, notably in North America might have proved valuable to the British Transport Commission (BTC) in its search for replacements for the ageing steam fleet but established designs from abroad were ignored. Capital investment in British industry was urgently needed to support the skilled workforce crying out for orders and the pressure to 'buy British' was such that large scale importation of diesel locomotives was politically unacceptable. The review ordered by the government resulted in the report entitled 'Modernisation and Re-equipment of the British Railways', more commonly known as the 'Modernisation Plan'. Announced in 1955, its aim was to bring the railways up to date and in so doing eliminate the growing financial deficit. It was envisaged that this would be achieved in less than ten years by the electrification of the main lines, replacing steam traction with a modern diesel fleet, the introduction of new passenger and freight rolling stock, widespread re-signalling and track renewal, the closure of some unprofitable lines and the introduction of an automated freight handling system centred on large freight marshalling yards.

The replacement of almost 1,500 steam locomotives built between 1948 and 1953, not forgetting the large number of earlier designs still in service throughout the country, would require a major diesel locomotive building programme to be undertaken and the Modernisation Plan called for the introduction of some 2,500 mainline locomotives within the ensuing ten years. The responsibility for overseeing this massive regeneration project (as well as similar modernisation programmes involving road haulage, bus transport, docks and shipping, waterways, tramways and several allied operations) was shouldered by the BTC, created under the Transport Act of 1947. The operations involving the railways were to be administered by the Railway Executive under the business name British Railways (BR).

Initially the Modernisation Plan had encompassed a pilot scheme in which planned new diesel designs would be evaluated over a period of three years and the most appropriate would be commissioned. Continuing financial problems forced the BTC to modify and accelerate its planned programme of commissioning designs for new diesel locomotives, abandoning the pilot scheme and basing their decisions on engineering judgements together with knowledge of the reliability of the products of the various bidding companies and any experience of operating in other countries. The Commission was specifically concerned to limit the number of locomotive types and that orders should be based primarily on the reliability issue while demonstrating as much standardisation in production as possible. The pressure to 'buy British' had previously created a more open-ended bidding process which resulted in numerous manufacturers producing a wide variety of designs, some of which proved unreliable and did not survive the steam locomotives they were meant to replace. The requirement for standardisation in the design of the new diesel locomotives was addressed in a report to the Commission 'Main-Line Diesel Locomotives: Limitation of Variety', published in 1957 and formed the basis of the planned introduction of the new types of diesel-electric locomotives. A further report in 1960, 'Standardisation of Main-Line Diesel Locomotives', provided specific recommendations as to how variety should be limited in order to achieve the required standardisation and concluded that, for political reasons, only British firms should be invited to quote for and produce the 'Standard Types', while at the same time allowing that BR or any other designated contractor should build the locomotives to the accepted designs.

These recommendations were accepted by the Technical Committee of the BTC and were subsequently included in the 1961 and 1962 building programmes. Agreement was reached on the specifications and sourcing of the first four (later increased to five) main-line diesel-electric types, with EE and Brush supplying the majority, though it should be remembered that by the early 1960s a considerable number of such locos were already in service. Yet even at this stage it was becoming clear that the aim of increasing BR's profitability was not being achieved as the locos delivered to date failed to live up to expectations, with less than acceptable availabilities often blamed on their steam heating boilers. Competition from the newly opened M1 Motorway (without speed limits), the first section from St Albans to Dunchurch near Rugby having been opened in 1959, and express bus services between London and the Midlands increased pressure on BR to improve journey speeds. By 1963, all the main line diesel locos chosen by BR had been ordered, the British Railways Board (BRB) had replaced the BTC and Dr Beeching's plan for the reorganisation of the railways was published.

The five diesel 'Types' established by the Modernisation Plan were:

Type 1: Locos of 1,000 brake horse power (bhp) or below

Type 2: Locos between 1,001 and 1,499bhp

Type 3: Locos between 1,500 and 1,999bhp

Type 4: Locos between 2,000 and 2,999bhp

Type 5: Locos of 3,000bhp or more.

The mid-power Type 3 diesel locomotive classification consisted of four designs built between 1957 and 1965 which later became known as Classes 31, 33, 35 and 37. Class 31 (Brush Type 2, previously Class 30) consisted of 263 locos built by Brush Traction between 1957 and 1962. Class 33 (known as BRCW Type 3 or Cromptons) were ninety-eight locos built by the Birmingham Carriage and Wagon Company between 1960 and 1962. Class 35 (the Hymeks) consisted of 101 locos built by Beyer Peacock (Hymek) Ltd between 1961 and 1964 while Class 37 (EE Type 3) was by far the largest class in this power range comprising 309 locomotives built by EE between 1960 and 1965. By the end of 1964, diesel traction accounted for just under 50 per cent of BR's traffic, with electric power taking 37 per cent and steam down to only 13 per cent.

# Chapter 2
# THE DEVELOPMENT OF THE CLASS 37 LOCOMOTIVES

The contract to build the BR Class 37 locomotives was awarded to the English Electric Company Limited (EE) which had a proud history of building railway locomotives dating back into the 1920s as well as being heavily involved in aviation and heavy armaments such as tanks. After the Second World War the company had moved into the aviation business proper and quickly established themselves as technological pacesetters. Their reputation was such that an initial order for forty-two units was placed on 27 January 1959 (EE Order No. CCL 1031) even though there had been no prototype for evaluation, but the success of earlier designs such as the EE Type 4s (BR Class 40) built from 1958 and the EE Type 2s (BR Class 23) built in 1959 was enough to secure the work. The design of the Class 40s, considered the pride of BR's early diesel fleet, strongly influenced that of the Class 37s and subsequent orders would bring the fleet total to 309 locomotives by 1965. Intended as a 'mixed traffic' design, having the benefit of train-heating boilers and a maximum

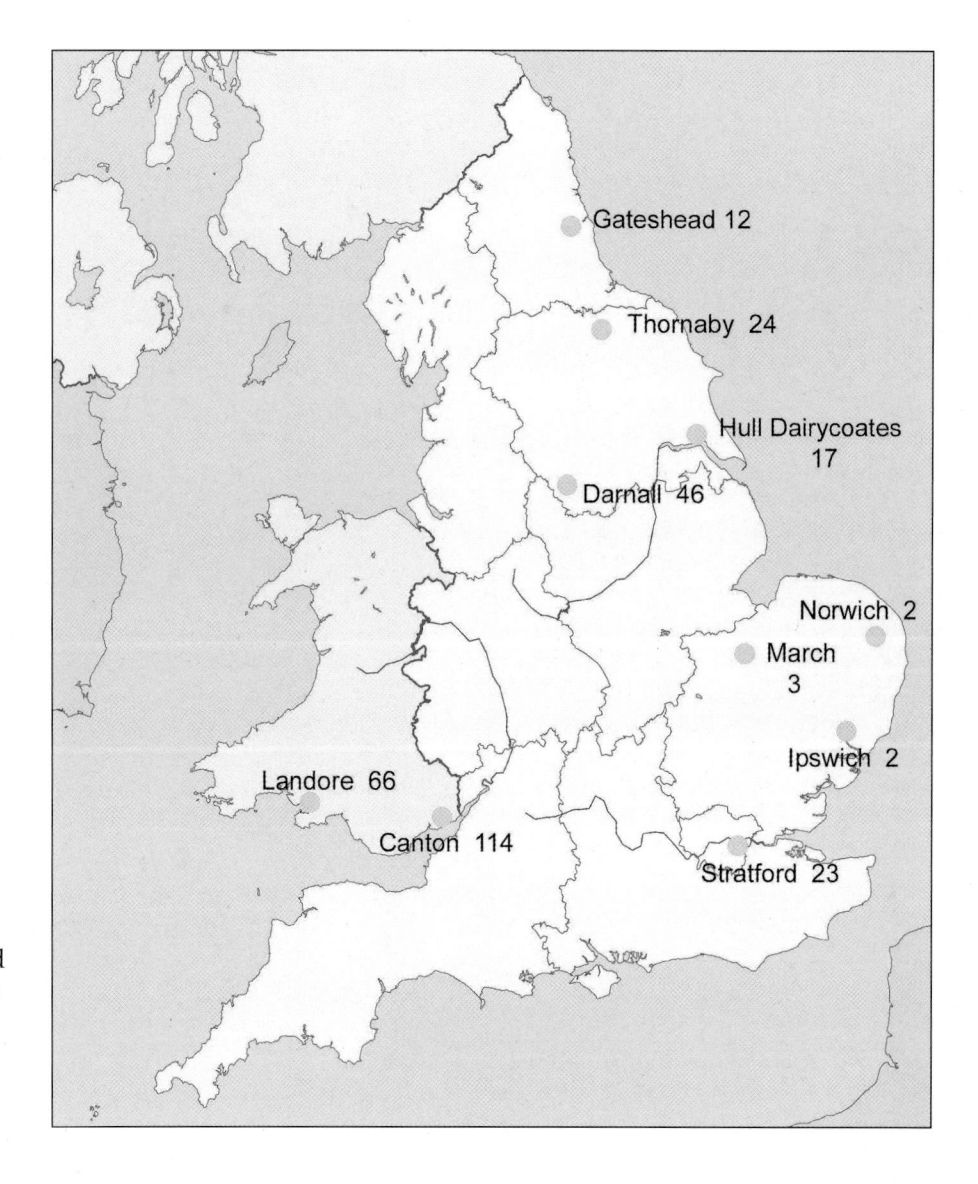

**Upon their** completion, the Depots receiving the 309 locomotives (with total first allocation) were as shown.

speed of 90mph (145km/hr) made them suitable for express passenger work. They could also be worked in multiple with most other EE diesel locos of Types 1-4 which had a 'blue star' coupling code. They would be lighter and more efficient than the Class 40s with a high power to weight ratio making them also ideal for use on routes governed by weight restrictions. They were built at EE's Vulcan Foundry in Newton-le-Willows, Lancashire (now Merseyside) and by Robert Stephenson and Hawthorns (RSH) of Darlington, which had become part of EE in 1955. A total of 242 of the 309 originated from Vulcan Foundry with the remaining 67 locos being from RSH. The first was delivered in November 1960 and the last in November 1965. In June 1965, Western Region staged high-speed trials with their new Class 37 diesel electric locos numbers D6881 and D6882, demonstrating their potential on the fast route between Paddington and the south west. With Route Availability (RA) 5 they would handle virtually all the locomotive-hauled services on the West Highland Line, the lines north of Inverness, those into East Anglia and in parts of Wales. (RA is based on axle-load and Network Rail currently states RA5 is for locos with an axle-load of up to 19.0 tonnes)

**Class 37 General** description and components.

## Class 37 Drawings

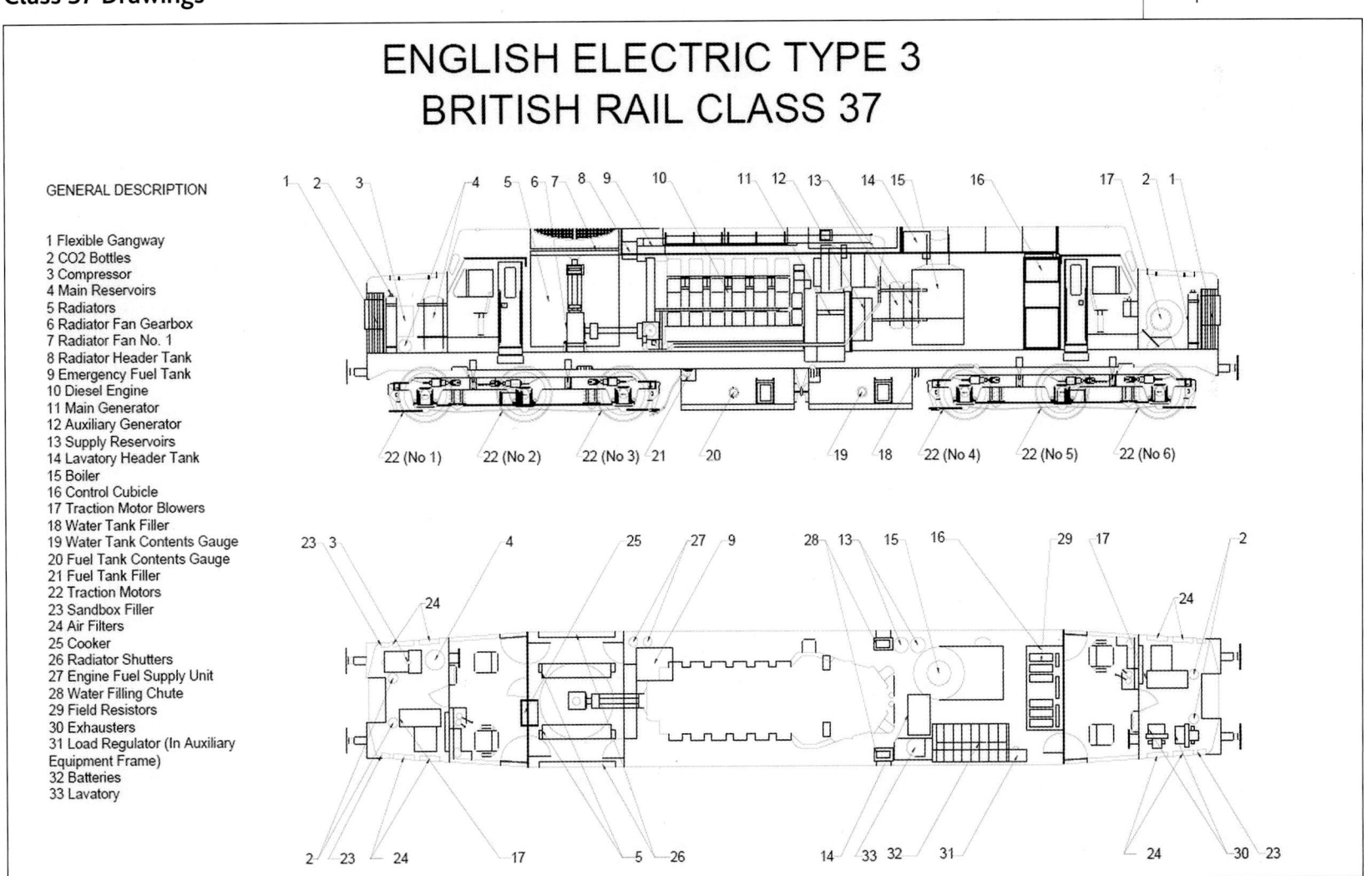

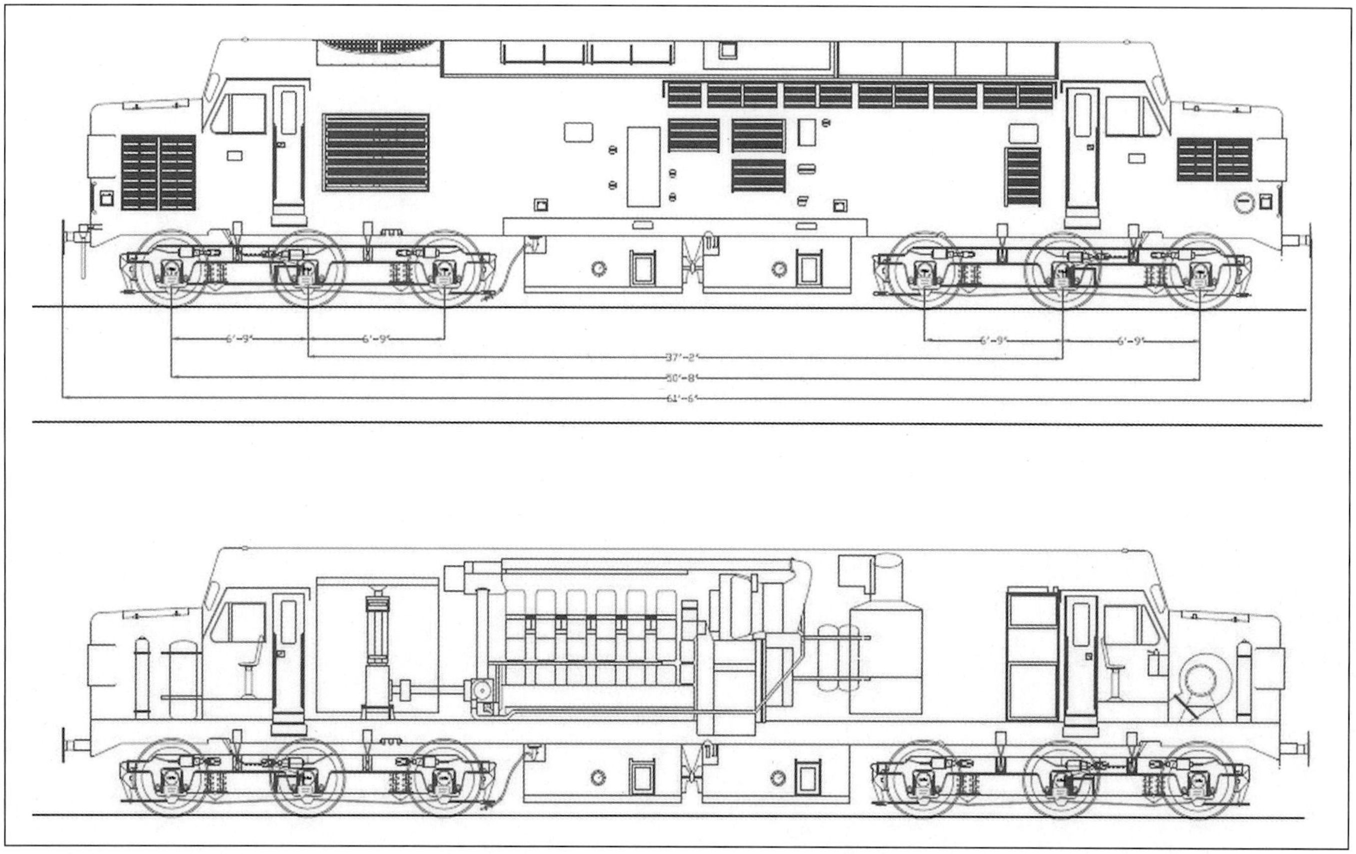

**12** • THE ENGLISH ELECTRIC CLASS 37: CO CO DIESEL ELECTRIC LOCOMOTIVES FROM DESIGN TO DEMISE

**Class 37 Plan,** side view.

**Class 37 Noses.**

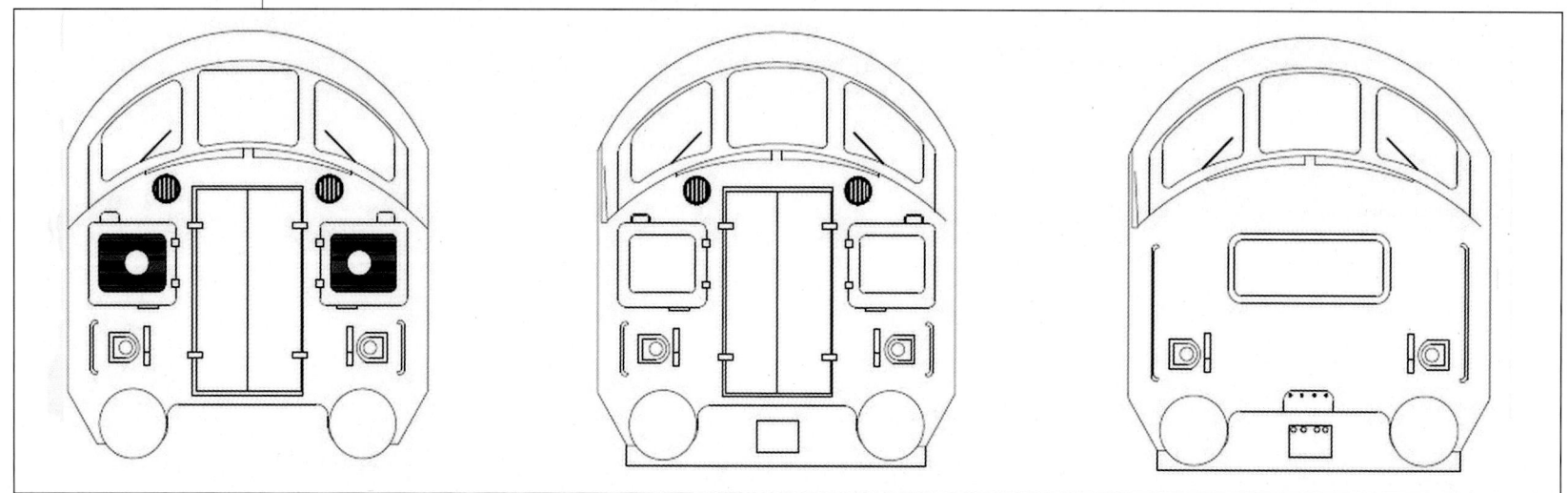

The original locos featured their four-digit train head code displayed in boxes either side of a pair of doors, later to be replaced by 'domino' style dots as shown above left. These were later plated over with opaque lenses fitted as shown above middle. This arrangement was replaced in later locos by a single central display box with no 'nose-doors', above right. (*Class 37 drawings, courtesy Mick Parker, The Class 37 Locomotive Group*).

# Chapter 3
# LOCOMOTIVE HISTORIES

**Pre-TOPS Days**

The first example was completed in November 1960 and numbered D6700. From the outset she was earmarked for preservation as part of the National Collection and following her successful inspection and trials at Doncaster Works the first orders were soon on their way to Stratford MPD in East London, other Eastern Region Depots and later to Dairycoates MPD in Hull where they quickly proved their worth and took over steam services in their respective regions. The pioneering batch of forty-two, numbered D6700–41 was soon followed by Order No. CCM 1114 on 5 February 1960, before the last of the first batch had been delivered and consisted of a further thirty-seven locos, twenty-seven of which would be built at Vulcan Foundry (numbers D6742–68) and ten (numbers D6769–78) by RSH. These in turn were followed by Order No. CCN 1239, placed on 27 April 1961 for seventeen more from RSH, numbered D6779–95. The next order, number CCP 1267 from Vulcan Foundry for twenty-three locos to be numbered D6796–6818 was placed on 13 December 1961 and completed the first set of 119 which were characterised by a divided head-code box showing two digits either side of a pair of doors. The fifth batch, Order No. CCP 1304 was placed in July 1962 for a further 100 locos of which sixty (numbers D6829–58, D6869–78 and D6899–6918) would be from Vulcan Foundry and forty (numbers D6819–28, D6859–68 and D6879–98) from RSH. These and subsequent locos would be distinguishable by having a centrally placed head-code box and horns on the roof. A period of eighteen months would pass before the penultimate batch of twenty locos were ordered from Vulcan Foundry as Order Number CCR 1320 in January 1964 (numbers D6919–38) to be followed in February of that year by Order Number CCS 1362 for the final seventy from the same source (numbers D6939–99 and D6600–08).

The success of the design drew the attention of the Western Region where their potential to replace steam on heavy coal trains in the South Wales valleys was attractive and as early as March 1963 Cardiff Canton had its first consignment with both builders continuing to supply locomotives for these duties and for the equally demanding Ebbw Vale iron ore trains. By 1964, the Western Region alone was operating some 100 examples and soon was conducting high speed tests with locos in multiple between Paddington and the West Country where speeds in excess of 100mph (161km/h) were recorded. Others were out-based to Bromsgrove on the London Midland Region to serve as bankers on the testing climb to Blackwell, the Lickey Incline. In June 1965 EE supplied its 2,000th diesel engine BR, a feat which no other company had achieved to one railway, thus creating a new world record. The last loco in the class of 309 examples arrived at Doncaster from the Newton le Willows plant in November 1965

All the locos were built to the Co-Co wheel arrangement system which has two six-wheeled bogies with all axles powered, with a separate traction motor per axle. Locomotive length is 61ft 6ins (18.8m). Fuel capacity is 1,690 gal (7,683 litres). The driving wheel diameter is 3ft 7ins (1092mm) and the loco weight was 102 to 108 tonnes. The engines fitted were EE 12-cylinder 12CSVT of 1,750bhp at 800rpm giving a maximum tractive effort of 55,500lb. Transmission is by six EE axle-hung nose-suspended traction motors. They were designed for a maximum speed of 90mph (145km/h) and with an RA of 5. This is a relatively low loading considering the size and power of the locomotive and has allowed them to operate virtually throughout the network including on many lines with weight restrictions. The ability of EE to use standard components across a range of classes kept the price per unit down to a very acceptable £83,000. Considering their many attributes, it is unsurprising that they achieved such success and longevity as they became a familiar sight over the length and breadth of the country and formed the main motive power for Inter-City services in East Anglia where they took charge of services from Liverpool Street to Norwich. Though the more powerful Class 47s would take over these heavy workings in later years, the 37s would continue to dominate on trains to Cambridge and onwards to Kings Lynn as well as on the Harwich line where steam-heated coaching stock was still in everyday use in the late 1970s. These Eastern Region locos were based at March, Ipswich and Norwich as well as at Stratford. They also performed well on secondary and inter-regional services including in Scotland where they worked on both passenger and goods workings on the West Highland lines as well as on heavy freight turns in the Borders, Clyde and Forth areas. At the other end of the UK, they could be seen in Cornwall with china clay workings. A number were allocated to Special Projects and forty were sent to France during 1999 to aid construction work on the TGV Sud extension from Valence to Marseilles and in 2002 fourteen others were despatched to Spain for similar duties. Now, over sixty years after their introduction, many are still in everyday use, having recorded the highest availability of any diesel electric loco ever built and demonstrating, if proof were needed, their claim to be the most ubiquitous of diesel locomotive designs.

Prior to the introduction of BR's Total Operations Processing System (TOPS) in the 1970s, the locos carried the number allocated to them on their release from the builder, though as time progressed and steam traction disappeared the need for 'D' for Diesel became unnecessary and was removed.

**At Doncaster** in 1969 is D6735 (*Rick Ward*)

**D6735 (37035)**
Released by EE Vulcan Foundry as D6735, Works Number EE/VF2898/D614 on 17 April 1962 and allocated to Hull Dairycoates.

Final depot: Stewarts Lane, 10/95.

Name carried: None.

Status: Cut up by C.F. Booth, Rotherham, 1/00

**D6814 (37114)**
Released by EE Vulcan Foundry as D6814, Works Number EE/VF3243/D768 on 20 February 1963 and allocated to Darnall.

Final depot: Toton, 5/07.

Names carried: *Dunrobin Castle*, 6/85–3/93; *City of Worcester*, 5/93.

Status: Cut up at EMR, Kingsbury, 1/08.

**D6910 (37210, 37693)**
Released by EE Vulcan Foundry as D6910, Works Number EE/VF3388/D854 on 26 November 1963 and allocated to Landore.

Final depot: Toton, 5/07.

Name carried: *Sir William Arrol*, 3/90–7/93.

Status: Cut up at EMR, Attercliffe, 5/11.

**D6993 (37293)**
Released by EE Vulcan Foundry as D6993, Works Number EE/VF3553/D982 on 1 July 1965 and allocated to Canton.

Final depot: Toton, 5/07.

Name carried: None.

Status: Cut up by C.F. Booth, Rotherham, 2/09.

**At Wakefield** Kirkgate with a freight on 26 June 1964 is D6814. (*Ben Brooksbank*)

**In BR** green with full yellow front ends hauling a freight at Swansea East Dock in April 1967 is D6910. (*Hugh Llewelyn*)

**Taking her** freight through Newport South Wales on 26 July 1966 is D6993, later renumbered to 37293.

### Sub-class variations post TOPS

The 309 locomotives built between 1960 and 1965 were originally numbered D6700 to D6999 and D6600 to D6608. Their livery was plain green with a grey roof, BR crest and a small yellow warning panel which was sometimes applied during a works visit. By the end of the 1960s, the yellow warning was extended to the full height of the nose. As the years rolled by, the green livery was replaced with BR Blue and the yellow extended further to form a full yellow nose. With the introduction of TOPS in the 1970s, all locos would be renumbered with an identifier which began with the class, followed by the unique engine number, starting with xx001, where xx is the class. Sub-classes would be indicated by the first digit of the individual number. By the middle of the 1970s, most locos had been allocated their TOPS number in the series 37001 to 37299 (formerly D6700 to D6999) and 37300 to 37308 (formerly D6600 to D6608), though complications did arise relating to some of this latter batch, as explained below. Class leader D6700 was identified as a candidate for preservation as part of the National Collection to be housed at the National Railway Museum in York and renumbered to 37119 instead of D6819, which became 37283, the number intended for D6983 which was unfortunately an early casualty, being withdrawn and subsequently scrapped when barely a year old following a fatal accident in December 1965, after being in collision with Class 47 number D1671 *Thor* which had been derailed due to a landslip near Bridgend in South Wales.

D6983 was the first EE Type 3 to be withdrawn and as a result, the only locomotive in the entire class not to receive a TOPS number. The remains of both locomotives were sold to local scrap merchants, R.S. Hayes, and cut up the following year, the 37 having only been released from Vulcan Foundry in May 1965.

The Class 37's capability to handle both freight and passenger trains was apparent from an early stage but as high-volume block freight for heavy industry became more prevalent during the 1970s, the sight and sound of a pair of 'Growlers' working in tandem became the norm in many parts of the country. The practice of running two locomotives coupled together and under the control of one driver, known as multiple-unit train control, required the operating system of each locomotive to be compatible. Locomotives capable of working together in this way can be identified by their Coupling Code, usually indicated on the front of each locomotive by a coloured geometrical shape. The Coupling Code for Class 37s is Blue Star, indicating an electro-pneumatic system of coupling. Several other classes of diesel locomotives operated with this Coupling Code including Classes 33, 40, 44, 45 and 46. Eastern Region passenger trains operating out of London Liverpool Street continued to be predominantly the responsibility of single Class 37s and by the mid-1980s the fleet had become almost as ubiquitous as the legendary Stanier 'Black 5s' before them.

Many of the early batches, that is most of those in orders placed before January 1964, were fitted with steam-heating boilers, also known as steam generators, which produced low pressure steam from a feed-water supply tank which was heated by the loco's diesel fuel and passed on through a system of pipes to heat the passenger carriages along the length of the train. By the mid-1980s, it was decided to refurbish the entire class by replacing generators with alternators and providing lower-geared bogies. The extensive refurbishment programme undertaken during the 1980s, necessitated as a result of the class having been chosen as BR's 'standard' Type 3 design following the withdrawal of many Type 2 and other Type 3 locomotives, involved a heavy overhaul designed to extend their working life into the 1990s and beyond. The refurbishment programme was curtailed in 1988 after 135 locos had been modified, leaving a number of re-geared bogies which were fitted to modified bodies creating sub-class 37/3. Most of this work was carried out at British Rail Engineering's Crewe Works and resulted in the formation of a number of sub-classes. The sub-classes created were:

37/0     Those locos left unmodified after other sub-classes had been formed.
37/3     Locos re-bogied at various depots but otherwise not refurbished. Numbered in the range between 37310 and 37384.
37/4     Locos refurbished and rewired with Brush alternator and electric train heating (ETH) fitted in place of steam heating.

| | |
|---|---|
| | Given numbers between 37401 and 37431. |
| 37/5 | Locos refurbished and rewired as 37/4 but without ETH. Numbered between 37501 and 37669. |
| 37/6 | Included twelve locos further modified from 37/5 intended to haul overnight international trains operated by Eurostar (service never introduced). Locos therefore remained within sub-class 37/5. |
| 37/7 | Locos refurbished, rewired with modified gearing and extra ballast added for heavy freight work in the coal and metals sectors. Numbered between 37701 and 37899. |
| 37/9 | Locos refurbished, rewired, new engines, bogies and extra ballast weight added for use in the BR heavy metals sector. Given numbers 37901 to 37906. Numbers 37901-4 were fitted with Brush traction motors and Mirrlees engines while 37905 and 37906 received GEC traction motors and Rushton engines. |
| 97/3 | Four former Class 37/0 locos modified to be compliant with the European Rail Traffic Management System (ERTMS), numbered 97301 to 97304. Initially intended for use on the Cambrian lines they also work charter trains, infrastructure support and monitoring trains, Royal Trains and other special workings. |

In the early 1990s Class 37 withdrawals began in response to a decline in freight traffic and the introduction of Class 60 and later Class 66 locomotives.

**Sub-class 37/0**
Considering the large number of locomotives in the Class, it is not surprising that many variations occurred even within sub-classes. The distinctive feature within sub-class 37/0, which originally covered all 309 locos built, related to the head-code box in which the train reporting number or head-code was displayed. The first 119 locos built had a 'split' head-code box separated by a pair of doors incorporated into the nose to permit crews to access the train heating boiler of the second locomotive when two were running coupled together while the train was in motion. The doors were rarely used and were unpopular as they caused draughts in the cab, so much so that many were later welded shut. Each member of the pair of boxes would display two digits of the four-digit head-code. This arrangement was replaced in later locos by a single central display box with no 'nose-doors'. The head-code display was later replaced by the 'domino style' marker dots and in due course plated over with opaque lenses fitted. Later locos also differed in having the horns located on the cab roof rather than incorporated into the nose of the loco as had previously been the case.

**Class details as built**
(see also Appendix 1)
Engine type: EE 121CSVT
Wheel arrangement: Co-Co
Weight: 102 to 108 tonnes
Length: 61ft 6ins (18.75m)
Horsepower: 1750
Power at rail (hp): 1250
Tractive Effort: 55,500lb (245kN)
Brake force: 50 tonnes
Maximum speed: 90mph (145km/h) later reduced to 80mph (129km/h)
Number of traction motors: 6
Brake type: vacuum (dual brakes fitted from 1970s)
Fuel capacity: 1690 gallons (7683 litres)
RA: 5

The locomotives which remained in Class 37/0 were numbered between 37001 and 37308, though complications arose which led to repeated renumbering, including:

**D6971** became 37271 in March 1974 but was later modified and renumbered to 37418 from 15 November 1985

**D6603** became 37303 in March 1974 but was then renumbered to 37271 from 26 January 1986 and then modified and again renumbered to 37333 from 26 July 1994.

**D6972** became 37272 in March 1974 then 37431 from 18 April 1986

**D6604** became 37304 from March 1974 then 37272 from 19 January 1989, only to be later modified and renumbered to 37334.

**D6973** became 37273 in March 1974 then 37410 from 26 September 1985

**D6606** became 37306 in April 1974 then 37273 from 17 February 1989.

**D6974** became 37274 in March 1974 then 37402 from 19 July 1985 while D6608 became 37308 in March 1974 then 37274 from 1 February 1989 only to be renumbered back to 37308 again from 5 August 2000.

The remaining five members of the batch originally numbered D6600 to D6608 had a more straightforward transition to their new sub-classes:

**D6600** became 37300 in November 1973, then 37429 (sub-class 37/4) from 13 March 1986.

**D6601** became 37301 in March 1974, then 37412 (sub-class 37/4) from 22 October 1985.

**D6602** became 37302 in March 1974, then 37416 (sub-class 37/4) from 30 October 1985.

**D6605** became 37305 in March 1974, then 37407 (sub-class 37/4) from 7 August 1985.

**D6607** became 37307 in March 1974, then 37403 (sub-class 37/4) from 28 June 1985.

But for the majority remaining in sub-class 37/0 the transition from their BTC number to their TOPS number was more logical, see Table 1.

Numbers 37300–37305 and 37307 were renumbered to 37429, 37412, 37416, 37333, 37334, 37407 and 37403 respectively, though they all remained in sub-class 37/0 as not modified. 37306 was renumbered to 37273 and 37308 remained as such.

**37003 (D6703, 37003, 37360, 37003)**
(See also 37003 in Class 37s in Colour)
Released by EE Vulcan Foundry as D6703, Works Number EE/VF2866/D582 on 28 December 1960 and allocated to Stratford.

Final depot: Doncaster, 3/94.

Names carried: *First East Anglian Regiment*, 4/63–9/63; *Tiger Moth*, 10/89; *Dereham Neatherd High School 1912–2012*, 7/12.

## Table 1. Sub-class 37/0 locos, including those returned from other sub-classes

### 37/0

| | | | |
|---|---|---|---|
| D6603: 37333 | D6770: 37070 | D6840: 37140 | D6920: 37220 |
| D6604: 37334 | D6771: 37071 | D6841: 37141 | D6921: 37221 |
| D6708: 37008 | D6772: 37072 | D6842: 37142 | D6922: 37222 |
| D6710: 37010 | D6773: 37073 | D6844: 37144 | D6923: 37223 |
| D6711: 37011 | D6774: 37074 | D6846: 37146 | D6925: 37225 |
| D6712: 37012 | D6775: 37075 | D6852: 37152 | D6927: 37227 |
| D6713: 37013 | D6777: 37077 | D6853: 37153 | D6929: 37229 |
| D6719: 37019 | D6778: 37078 | D6854: 37154 | D6930: 37230 |
| D6723: 37023 | D6779: 37079 | D6856: 37156 | D6932: 37232 |
| D6725: 37025 | D6780: 37080 | D6858: 37158 | D6935: 37235 |
| D6726: 37026 | D6783: 37083 | D6862: 37162 | D6938: 37238 |
| D6729: 37029 | D6787: 37087 | D6865: 37165 | D6940: 37240 |
| D6731: 37031 | D6788: 37088 | D6874: 37174 | D6941: 37241 |
| D6732: 37032 | D6792: 37092 | D6875: 37175 | D6942: 37242 |
| D6735: 37035 | D6795: 37095 | D6878: 37178 | D6944: 37244 |
| D6737: 37037 | D6796: 37096 | D6884: 37184 | D6945: 37245 |
| D6738: 37038 | D6797: 37097 | D6885: 37185 | D6948: 37248 |
| D6740: 37040 | D6798: 37098 | D6888: 37188 | D6950: 37250 |
| D6742: 37042 | D6799: 37099 | D6890: 37190 | D6951: 37251 |
| D6743: 37043 | D6800: 37100 | D6891: 37191 | D6952: 37252 |
| D6745: 37045 | D6804: 37104 | D6894: 37194 | D6954: 37254 |
| D6746: 37046 | D6806: 37106 | D6896: 37196 | D6955: 37255 |
| D6747: 37047 | D6807: 37107 | D6897: 37197 | D6959: 37259 |
| D6748: 37048 | D6808: 37108 | D6898: 37198 | D6960: 37260 |
| D6751: 37051 | D6809: 37109 | D6901: 37201 | D6961: 37261 |
| D6754: 37054 | D6810: 37110 | D6903: 37203 | D6962: 37262 |
| D6755: 37055 | D6811: 37111 | D6907: 37207 | D6963: 37263 |
| D6757: 37057 | D6813: 37113 | D6909: 37209 | D6964: 37264 |
| D6758: 37058 | D6814: 37114 | D6911: 37211 | D6973: 37273 |
| D6759: 37059 | D6816: 37116 | D6912: 37212 | D6975: 37275 |
| D6762: 37062 | D6700: 37119 | D6913: 37213 | D6978: 37278 |
| D6763: 37063 | D6831: 37131 | D6914: 37214 | D6980: 37280 |
| D6765: 37065 | D6833: 37133 | D6915: 37215 | D6993: 37293 |
| D6766: 37066 | D6837: 37137 | D6916: 37216 | D6994: 37294 |
| D6768: 37068 | D6838: 37138 | D6918: 37218 | D6998: 37298 |
| D6769: 37069 | D6839: 37139 | D6919: 37219 | D6608: 37308 |

Status: Preserved by the Class 37 Locomotive Group, operational on the Mid Norfolk Railway, 2/09; temporarily renumbered to 37360 for their 50th Anniversary Gala, 9/10; renumbered back to 37003, 9/11; Operational with UK Leasing from 6/23.

**37004 (D6704)**
Released by EE Vulcan Foundry as D6704, Works Number EE/VF2867D583 on 6 January 1961 and allocated to Stratford. Final depot: Motherwell, 10/93.

Name carried: *Second East Anglian Regiment*, 4/83–5/83.

Status: Cut up at MC Metals, Glasgow, 6/96.

Notable movements:
Appearances in her long career included in the mid-1960s in charge of the Harwich Boat Train which ran from Manchester Piccadilly via Sheffield, Retford, Gainsborough, Lincoln, Sleaford, Spalding and March to Harwich Parkeston Quay. It was well known for including elderly LNER Gresley teak-bodied buffet cars painted in BR blue and grey livery. Regular passenger work continued into the late 1960s before a transfer to Thornaby saw her more involved with freight duties in the Yorkshire and North East areas. She featured in the Crewe Works Open Day held on 22 September 1979 before her transfer back to Stratford after which she appeared regularly on passenger services between London Liverpool Street and Cambridge, Kings Lynn, Lowestoft and Norwich in the early 1980s, as well as a brief period in charge of trains between Yarmouth and Birmingham New Street in September 1983.

In the mid-1980s, her transfer to Gateshead saw her involved with Freightliner and other express freight work before a move back to Stratford renewed her acquaintance with the line to Norwich. A move to Scotland in the early 1990s saw her take charge of sections of the Anglo-Scottish trains from Euston between Edinburgh and Inverness, often in partnership with sister loco 37251. She featured on the Scottish Railway Preservation Society's charter 1Z09 between Stirling, Edinburgh and Carlisle on 12 June 1993 before being employed on week-end work for ScotRail and then going into storage pending final withdrawal.

**37008 (D6708, 37008, 37352)**
Released by EE Vulcan Foundry as D6708, Works Number EE/VF2871/D587 on 10 February 1961 and allocated to Ipswich.

Final depot: Tinsley, 5/87.

Name carried: *Hornet*, 10/91–2/92.

Status: Cut up by M.R.J. Phillips at Crewe, 7/96

**37010 (D6710)** (See also 37010 in Class 37s in Colour)
Released from EE Vulcan Foundry as D6710, Works Number EE/VF2874/D590 on 24 February 1961 and allocated to Stratford. Final depot: Barrow Hill, for HNRC, 8/06.
Name carried: None.

Status: Cut up by C.F. Booth, Rotherham, 7/07.

Notable movements:
Early passenger work included at the head of trains out of London Liverpool Street to Ipswich, Cambridge and Norwich and while in the north to Manchester and Newcastle, often being observed at York. Freight and parcels workings also occupied her in the early 1980s, heading trains from the Midlands, the North West and Yorkshire. Following her Last Classified Repair in August 1984 and subsequent transfer to Gateshead she worked between Newcastle and York in October 1985 and then into Scotland between Edinburgh and Carstairs later that month. She then moved south again and spent much of 1986 operating between Bristol Temple Meads and Taunton before her E Exam.

Her time at Bristol involved extensive passenger workings in the Exeter area and during the 1990s she was involved with charter specials including for Pathfinder Railtours on 12 October 1991, 'The Wye Knott', Hereford to Carlisle via Crewe and the S&C, hauling the return from Carlisle to Hereford. On 27 April 1996 she hauled the Hertfordshire Rail Tours charter 'The Tinsley Humper & Pennine Perambulator' originating at London King's Cross, with sister loco 37372 from Nottingham Trowell Junction and as far as milepost 138 near Blackwell, where unfortunately she failed, to be replaced by 47704. On 17 August 1996 she was in charter action again, this time for Pathfinder Railtours and 'The Crewe–Chester Flyer', when with 37042 she handled the section between the start at Exeter St Davids and Chester. Class 31s numbers 31201 and 31233 headed the middle section between Chester and Crewe before the 37s took over again for the return to Exeter. Some freight work occupied her during the later years of the 1990s before her brief move to France in 1999, but after her return she became redundant, was withdrawn from stock and stored. A reprieve seemed possible in August 2006 when she was re-registered for Network Rail but this came to nothing and she was scrapped the following year.

**37011 (D6711)** (See also 37011 in Class 37s in Colour)
Released from EE Vulcan Foundry as D6711, Works Number EE/VF2875/D591 on 3 March 1961 and allocated to Stratford.

Final depot: Eastfield, 10/82.

Name carried: None.

Status: Cut up by J. Rollason, Wellington, 8/89.

Notable movements:
While at Stratford she was employed on passenger services out of London Liverpool Street to East Anglia as well as passenger and freight north to Yorkshire. After a series of moves between depots during the 1960s and early 1970s, it was her transfer to March Depot in August 1972 which heralded a period of great activity, both passenger and freight, the former including a return to her earliest days out of Liverpool Street to Kings Lynn, Norwich, Ipswich or Cambridge and freight workings often to the railway recycling centre at Whitemoor or parcels trains to Cambridge or Peterborough. This continued through to early 1981 and also included involvement in what is believed to be the first Class 37-hauled passenger train into Cornwall, on 14 April 1979. This was F+W Railtours' 'The Pixieland Express' which ran between Cheltenham Spa, Gloucester, Bristol Temple Meads, Penzance and Newquay. The initial leg to Bristol was taken by 37011 and 37276 with the remainder including the return being handled by classmates 37084, 37178 and 37279.

Her transfer to Scotland in June 1981 saw her working passenger services north from Glasgow including to Dundee, Perth, Oban, Fort William and Mallaig, and while at Inverness Depot to Wick and Kyle of Lochalsh. When transferred back to Eastfield in October 1982, her busy passenger schedule continued including rugby 'extras' between Glasgow and Edinburgh in early 1984 in addition to reinstating her previous duties. During 1986, she was also involved with charter 'specials' including for the Scottish Railway Preservation Society's railtour on 16 August between Dundee and Mallaig, and on 18 October between Glasgow, Aberdeen and Edinburgh. Her demise was perhaps inevitable after she was damaged by a runaway

**Stabled at** York MPD on 3 September 1980 is 37011 with Class 45 45006 *Honourable Artillery Company* alongside.

dmu set in January 1987 and subsequently stored before being moved to Crewe Works where she was on display at the Open Day on 4 July 1987. There she stayed until being scrapped in August 1989.

**37012 (D6712)**
Released from EE Vulcan Foundry as D6712, Works Number EE/VF2873/D589 on 10 March 1961 and allocated to Stratford.

Final depot: Doncaster, 6/99.

Name carried: *Derwent*, 9/89–11/90.

Status: Cut up at McIntyre's scrapyard, Beeston, 8/03.

**37013 (D6713)**
Released by EE Vulcan Foundry as D6713, Works Number EE/VF2876/D592 on 20 March 1961 and allocated to Stratford.

Final depot: Doncaster, 10/99

Name carried: *Vampire*, 11/89.

Status: Cut up at EMR Kingsbury, 2/07.

**37019 (D6719)** (See also 37019 in Class 37s in Colour)
Released by EE Vulcan Foundry as D6719, Works Number EE/VF2882/D598 on 27 June 1961 and allocated to Stratford.

Final depot: Immingham, 1/95

Name carried: None

Status: Cut up at Sims Metal UK Ltd. 7/04

**37023 (D6723)**
Released by EE Vulcan Foundry as D6723, Works Number EE/VF2886/D602 on 20 July 1961 and allocated to March.

**At Haymarket** during 1988 is 37012 *Loch Rannoch* (*Rick Ward*)

Final depot: Kingmoor, 11/05.

Names carried: *Stratford*, 11/91–1/94; *Stratford TMD Quality Approved*, 2/94.

Status: Privately preserved and operational on the Pontypool & Blaenavon Railway where she was fitted with a refurbished power unit during 8/23.

**37025 (D6725)** (See also 37025 in Class 37s in Colour)
Released from EE Vulcan Foundry as D6725, Works Number EE/VF2888/D604 on 31 August 1961 and allocated to Stratford.

Final depot: Doncaster, 2/99.

Name carried: *Inverness TMD Quality Approved*, 3/94–6/99.

Status: Preserved by the Scottish 37 Group, Bo'ness, 8/00; On hire to Colas Rail Freight, 4/16. Operational on the Bo'ness & Kinneil Railway from 5/22.

Notable movements:
Early passenger work mainly involved working out of London Liverpool Street with services to East Anglia until her move north in 1981 saw her taking trains from Glasgow to Dundee, Oban and Mallaig and then from Inverness to Wick, Thurso and Kyle. Scottish duties would occupy her until her transfer to Bescot in May 1995 when for a short time she worked trains to Holyhead from Birmingham International and from Crewe. Briefly employed by English, Welsh & Scottish freight (EWS) before being condemned, her rescue and move back to Scotland led to her employment on the heritage Bo'ness & Kinneil Railway until January 2009. After a very brief stay as a guest on the Keighley & Worth Valley Railway (K&WVR) in June of that year, often seen in partnership with sister loco 37682, she moved back to Bo'ness until June 2015 when she was on the

move again, this time to grace the East Lancashire Railway (ELR) with her appearance during July, then back to base at Bo'ness until January 2016.

Back to England she worked from Birmingham Washwood Heath followed by allocation to Colas Rail Freight in April 2016, involved with Network Rail Engineering Trains before being a frequent performer at the head of charter 'specials' between June 2017 and May 2019. These included for the Scottish Railway Preservation Society, 'The Far North Explorer', Edinburgh to Thurso and Wick and return with 37421 on 2 to 4 June 2017, 'The Blackpool Excursion' on 1 July 2017 with 37217 and 'Routes & Branches, Neilstone or Bust', Bo'ness to Edinburgh and Glasgow and return with 37403 *Isle of Mull* and 37703 on 1 and 2 June 2018.

This was followed from August 2019 to February 2020 working for Transport for Wales on the Rhymney Valley Line to Cardiff Queen Street, then after some time at Barrow Hill Depot between September 2021 and May 2022 she moved back to Bo'ness to continue her life in preservation. On 29 October 2023 she featured hauling trains double-headed with 37403 *Isle of Mull* during a 'Class 37 Running Day' on that railway.

**37026 (D6726, 37026, 37320)**
Released by EE Vulcan Foundry as D6726, Works Number EE/VF2889/D605 on 8 September 1961 and allocated to Stratford.

Final depot: Doncaster, 5/96.

Names carried: *Loch Awe*, 10/81–7/86; *Shap Fell*, 7/86–5/88.

Status: Cut up at Wigan CRDC, 7/00.

**37029 (D6729)** (See also 37029 in Class 37s in Colour)
Released by EE Vulcan Foundry as D6729, Works Number EE/VF2892/D608 on 3 October 1961 and allocated to Stratford.

Final depot: Kingmoor, 12/06.

Name carried: None.

Status: Privately preserved and operational on the Epping Ongar Railway from 10/10.

**37031 (D6731)**
Released by EE Vulcan Foundry as D6731, Works Number EE/VF2894/D610 on 23 October 1961 and allocated to Hull Dairycoates.

Final depot: Canton, 10/93.

Name carried: None.

Status: Cut up by M.R.J. Phillips at Cardiff Canton, 5/97.

**At Oban** during the summer of 1985 are 37026 *Loch Awe* and 37081 *Loch Long*. *(Jim Carter)*

**Working on** the K&WVR on 15 August 1998 is 37029. *(Douglas Todd)*

## Locomotive Histories • 23

**Approaching Keighley** station on the Worth Valley line on 2 August 1998 is 37029 led by 37609. (*Douglas Todd*)

**37032 (D6732, 37353, 37032)** (See also 37032 in Class 37s in Colour) Released by EE Vulcan Foundry as D6732, Works Number EE/VF2895/D611 on 9 March 1962 and allocated to Hull Dairycoates

Final depot: Tinsley, 5/92.

Name carried: *Mirage,* 10/92–3/94.

Status: Preserved and operational on the North Norfolk Railway from 9/94.

**37035 (D6735)** (See D6735 in Pre-TOPS Days)
Released by EE Vulcan Foundry as D6735, Works Number EE/VF2898/D614 on 17 April 1962 and allocated to Hull Dairycoates.

Final depot: Stewarts Lane, 10/95.

Name carried: None.

Status: Cut up BY C.F. Booth, Rotherham, 1/00.

**37037 (D6737, 37321)**
Released by EE Vulcan Foundry as D6737, Works Number EE/VF2900/D616 on 4 May 1962 and allocated to Hull Dairycoates.

Final depot: Doncaster, 7/99; France, 8/99–8/00; Wigan CRDC for disposal, 8/00.

Names carried: *Gartcosh,* 7/86–5/92; *Loch Treig,* 8/05.

Status: Barrow Hill, for preservation, 1/04; South Devon Railway, 6/04; Reinstated into traffic as a Private Owner Diesel Locomotive (PODL), 5/08; Operational on the South Devon Railway from 9/13.

**37038 (D6738)**
Released by EE Vulcan Foundry as D6738, Works Number EE/VF2901/D617 on 11 May 1962 and allocated to Hull Dairycoates.

Final depot: Kingmoor, 5/03.

Name carried: None.

Status: Currently (from 7/22) at Barrow Hill allocated to Harry Needle Railroad Company (HNRC), stored locomotives.

**37040 (D6740)**
Released by EE Vulcan Foundry as D6740, Works Number EE/VF2903/D619 on 1 June 1962 and allocated to Hull Dairycoates.

**Shunting wagons** at Buckfastleigh, South Devon Railway, on 5 November 2011 in preparation for scheduled engineering work is 6737 (37037). (*Geoff Sheppard*)

Final depot: Doncaster, 2/00.

Name carried: None.

Status: Cut up by C.F. Booth, Rotherham, 4/06.

**37042 (D6742)** (See also 37042 in Class 37s in Colour)
Released by EE Vulcan Foundry as D6742, Works Number EE/VF3034/D696 on 15 June 1962 and allocated to Darnall.

Final depot: Toton, 5/07.

Name carried: None.

Status: Privately preserved on the Eden Valley Railway, Cumbria from 4/11. Under restoration, 5/24.

**37043 (D6743, 37043, 37354)**
Released by EE Vulcan Foundry as D6743, Works Number EE/VF3035/D697 on 22 June 1962 and allocated to Darnall.

Final depot: Doncaster, 1/00.

Name carried: *Loch Lomond*, 10/81–6/86.

Status: Cut up at McIntyre's scrapyard, Beeston, 5/03.

Nameplate of 37043.

**37045 (D6745, 37045, 37355)**
Released by EE Vulcan Foundry as D6745, Works Number EE/VF3037/D699 on 6 July 1962 and allocated to Darnall.

Final depot: Thornaby, 3/94.

Name carried: None.

Status: Cut up by HNRC at Toton, 11/03.

**37046 (D6746)**
Released by EE Vulcan Foundry as D6746, Works Number EE/VF3038/D700 on 13 July 1962 and allocated to Darnall.

Final depot: Toton, 5/07.

Name carried: None.

Status: Cut up at C.F. Booth, Rotherham, 9/09.

**37047 (D6747)**
Released by EE Vulcan Foundry as D6747, Works Number EE/VF3039/D701 on 20 July 1962 and allocated to Darnall.

Final depot: Toton, 5/07.

Name carried: None.

Status: Cut up at EMR Kingsbury, 5/08

**37048 (D6748)**
Released by EE Vulcan Foundry as D6748, Works Number EE/VF3040/D702 on 10 August 1962 and allocated to Darnall.

Final depot: Toton, 3/94.

Name carried: None.

Status: Cut up at Toton, 4/03

**37051 (D6751)**
Released by EE Vulcan Foundry as D6751, Works Number EE/VF3043/D705 on 31 August 1962 and allocated to Darnall.

Final depot: Kingmoor, 11/05.

Name carried: *Merehead*, 5/96.

Status: Cut up at Sims Metal UK Ltd. Newport, 1/08

**37054 (D6754)**
Released by EE Vulcan Foundry as D6754, Works Number EE/VF3046/D708 on 19 September 1962 and allocated to Darnall.

Final depot: Doncaster, 4/99.

Name carried: None.

Status: Cut up at Motherwell, 9/03

**37055 D6755)**
Released by EE Vulcan Foundry as D6755, Works Number EE/VF3047/D709 on 21 September 1963 and allocated to Thornaby.

Final depot: Toton, 5/07.

Name carried: *Rail Celebrity*, 11/95.

Status: Cut up at EMR, Kingsbury, 4/08

**37057 (D6757)**
Released by EE Vulcan Foundry as D6757, Works Number EE/VF3049/D711 on 6 October 1962 and allocated to Thornaby.

Final depot: Derby RTC, 2/16.

Names carried: *Viking*, 11/89–2/96; renamed *Viking*, 4/96; *Barbra Arbon*, 7/21.

Status: Operational for Colas Rail Freight from 7/20.

**37058 (D6758)**
Released by EE Vulcan Foundry as D6758, Works Number EE/VF3050/D712 on 10 October 1962 and allocated to Thornaby.

# Locomotive Histories • 25

In EWS livery at Barrow Hill on 23 August 2008 is 37057. The livery was based on that of its original parent company Wisconsin Central, established in 1995. The English, Welsh & Scottish brand was launched in April 1996 and by April 1997 it controlled ninety per cent of the UK rail freight market. In November 2007 it was bought by the German train operator Deutsche Bahn and in 2009 it was rebranded as DB Schenker. (*Hugh Llewelyn*)

Final depot: Toton, 5/07.

Name carried: None.

Status: Cut up at C.F. Booth, Rotherham, 4/09.

**37059 (D6759)** (See also 37059 in Class 37s in Colour)
Released from EE Vulcan Foundry as D6759, Works Number EE/VF3051/D713 on 12 October 1962 and allocated to Thornaby.

Final depot: Kingmoor, 2/05.

Name carried: *Port of Tilbury*, 9/88–1/95.

Status: Operational with Locomotive Services Ltd (LSL) at Crewe Diesel, 7/22. Transferred to Barrow Hill for use by HNRC, 1/24.

Notable movements:
Her early years involved freight workings in the Yorkshire and north-east areas, work which would continue when she was transferred to Stratford and to March in 1971 and 1972 respectively. It would not be until 1980 that regular passenger duties would come her way, first in the Newcastle area then more regularly out of London Liverpool Street to Harwich, Kings Lynn, Norwich and Cambridge during 1982 and 1983. There then followed a period of more widespread mainline activity, including on 3 August 1983 in charge of a BR 'Merrymaker Special' excursion from Coventry to Largs, working between Polmadie and Largs and the return between Polmadie and Carlisle. On 29 August she was at the head of 1Z09, Nelson to Largs 'Additional' between Polmadie and Largs and the return to Burnley. This was followed on 17 March 1984 by 1Z37 the Severnside Railtours Swansea to Middlesbrough 'Tyne Tees Explorer', being in charge between Eaglescliffe and Middlesbrough coupled with 37095.

Passenger work was to become her main occupation during the 1980s with duties taking her to destinations throughout the north of England and into Scotland. Her transfer to Tinsley in 1987 saw her combine both freight and passenger work but her move to Inverness heralded her conversion to full-time passenger duties. This would involve the Scottish sections of for example Euston to Aberdeen trains, taking over at Edinburgh to double-head the train to its destination often with sister loco 37156 or 37063 or the Euston to Inverness services, taking over at Glasgow Central. Her move south again to Immingham from January 1993 brought this kind of work to an abrupt end, with freight turns resuming, though occasional appearances on charters did add variety and after her time on Nuclear Traffic in Cumbria more of this 'special' work would come her way.

She appeared at 'Eastleigh 100' Open Day on 24 May 2009 then followed a series of celebrity appearances heading such trains as Spitfire Railtours' 'The Broadsman', Crewe–Norwich–Holt–Norwich–Crewe on 24 April 2010. Following this on 22 May 2010 came 12D Railtours' 'The Solway Viking', Workington–York via the Tyne Valley, and return. Then on 18 August 2011, 1Z97 Aberystwyth to Durham and return, 37059 coupled with 37218 from Crewe to Durham and return. Next on 25 April 2015, Pathfinder Railtours' 'The Devon Explorer', Crewe to Melton Mowbray by way of Exeter St Davids and return, coupled with 37605 throughout. Charity Railtours' 'The Four Triangles' followed, running from Crewe by means of a complex route to Norwich and London Euston on 9 May, with 37509 involved with 37606 in the early stages and with 37419 *Carl Haviland* later. Then a few days as a guest on the North Norfolk Railway in June 2015 and in May 2016 on the Wensleydale Railway in North Yorkshire.

The summer of 2017 saw her next 'special' dates when on 24 June she headed the first of several charters for Pathfinder Railtours, 'The Mazey Day Cornishman', from Worcester Shrub Hill to Penzance and return. On 28 July she was in action again with 'The Buffer Puffer 14.0', from Eastleigh to London Euston, top & tail with 37069 throughout followed the next day by 'The Buffer Puffer 15.0' from London Euston to Eastleigh, again in co-operation with 37069. In the spring of 2018 she continued her work for Pathfinder Railtours by heading 'The Heart of Wales Wanderer' from Eastleigh to Shrewsbury and return, once again coupled with 37069 throughout. Her final celebrity outings were in the summer of 2019 with first 'The Yorkshire Explorer' on 8 June, Taunton to Leeds and return coupled with 37038 throughout, then 'The Mazey Day Cornishman' on 29 June from Tame Bridge Parkway to Penzance and return coupled with 37218. For this charter the 37s had been called in to replace the unavailable 'Deltic' number D9009 *Alycidon*. After several years in the limelight it was then business as usual for 37059 until in February 2022 she was deregistered and stored by Direct Rail Services (DRS) for disposal, but a new era beckoned when she was moved to Crewe Diesel Depot to re-enter service with LSL. She appeared as a guest at the ELR Summer Diesel Gala in 2023, operating with their own 37109 and transferred to Barrow Hill for HNRC in January 2024.

### 37062 (D6762)

Released by EE Vulcan Foundry as D6762, Works Number EE/VF3054/D716 on 26 October 1962 and allocated to Thornaby.

Final depot: Tinsley, 7/87.

Name carried: None.

Status: Cut up at Vic Berry's scrapyard, Leicester, 4/90.

### 37063 (D6763)

Released by EE Vulcan Foundry as D6763, Works Number EE/VF3055/D717 on 2 November 1962 and allocated to Thornaby.

Final depot: Doncaster, 9/98.

Name carried: None.

Status: Cut up by HNRC at EMR, Kingsbury, 12/01.

### 37065 (D6765)

Released by EE Vulcan Foundry as D6765, Works Number EE/VF3057/D719 on 14 November 1962 and allocated to Thornaby.

Final depot: Toton, 5/07.

Name carried: None.

Status: Cut up at EMR, Kingsbury, 12/07.

### 37066 (D6766)

Released by EE Vulcan Foundry as D6766, Works Number EE/VF3058/D720 on 16 November 1962 and allocated to Thornaby.

Final depot: Doncaster, 4/96.

Name carried: *Valient*, 11/89–7/90.

Status: Cut up at Crewe Adtranz, 8/97.

**37068 (D6788, 37068, 37356)**

Released by EE Vulcan Foundry as D6768, Works Number EE/VF3060/D722 on 23 November 1962 and allocated to Thornaby.

Final depot: Barrow Hill, for HNRC, 2/05.

Name carried: *Grainflow*, 9/87–11/95.

Status: Cut up by C.F. Booth, Rotherham, 8/05.

**37069 (D6769)**

Released by EE RSH as D6769, Works Number EE/RSH3061/8315 on 17 July 1962 and allocated to Thornaby. Final depot: Kingmoor, 9/04.

Name carried: *Thornaby TMD*, 9/86–5/92.

Status: Stored for disposal by DRS at Kingmoor, 5/23; Offered for sale, 9/23; Transferred to Leicester for EuroPhoenix Locomotives UK, 1/24.

Notable movements:
Her close association with Thornaby Depot was apparent from the start with most of her work during her first twenty years being in the northeast of England though the 1980s saw her increasingly employed on a variety of passenger services outside of this area. These included heading trains out of London Liverpool Street and from Paddington to the Midlands. Back in the north she took trains out of Edinburgh to Carstairs and worked with services in the Aberdeen area until transferring to Cardiff Canton in the early 1990s to work with Trainload Metals. Her time in South Wales was short however, as her next move to Inverness Depot involved passenger work again mainly between Inverness and Edinburgh or Aberdeen and then on to Motherwell Depot where she was employed on similar duties, often in tandem with sister loco 37073 or 37087 which would continue into the mid-1990s.

A period working passenger services between Birmingham or Crewe to Holyhead in 1998 was followed by her move to Toton Depot for EWS in whose employ she would continue after her return from France until after an overhaul at Brush Traction in Loughborough her transfer to DRS at Carlisle involved her joining the Sellafield Pool in 2003. She was a guest at Carlisle Kingmoor Open Day on 11 June 2005 which heralded her induction into the 'charter specials' ranks where she appeared on 22 March 2008 with 37423 heading the Dumbarton to Oban section of Stobart Rail Tours' 'The Easter West Highlander', originating at London King's Cross. On 23 May 2009 in partnership with 37602 she took Spitfire Railtours' 'The Wessexman' from Crewe to Weymouth and return, followed on 17 and 18 July, again for Spitfire Railtours' 'The West Highlander' Preston to Fort William and Mallaig and back. Same operator again on 29 May 2010 this time with the Crewe to Pwllheli and return legs of 'The Prisoner' coupled with 37218. Classmates 37685 and 37706 were also involved in the tour originating and finishing at Preston.

After a period in store she was reinstated into DRS Nuclear Traffic duties in 2015 before resuming her 'tours' with Pathfinder Railtours' 'The Evening Lark/Night Owl/Round Robin' event of 31 March and 1 April 2017. This involved working between Derby, Crewe, Matlock and Long Marston in combination with classmate 37716. Pathfinder Railtours were the operators again on 28 and 29 July when she headed their 'Buffer Puffer' tours with 37059 and yet again on 10 February 2018 with 'The Blue Boys Ribble Rouser', taking the section from Eastleigh to Nuneaton and return with 37609, the whole tour going on to Preston Docks. A week later and she was in action with the same operator again for 'The Pennine Pathfinder', Gloucester to Carlisle and return with 37259 throughout and once more on 24 March with 'The Heart of Wales Wanderer' with 37059 from Eastleigh to Shrewsbury then into Wales to mark the 150th anniversary of the 'Heart of Wales' line before returning to Eastleigh. On 26 May 2018 she was reunited with 37259 for Retro Railtours' 'The Retro Bath Centurion & Retro Salisbury Cathedral Belle' from Huddersfield to Bath and Salisbury via Crewe and return.

A break from tour duties allowed her to appear on display at Crewe Gresty Bridge Open Day on 21 July 2018 before resuming her work for Pathfinder Railtours in 2021 with 'The Blue Boys Merrymixer', Eastleigh to Crewe on 7 August,

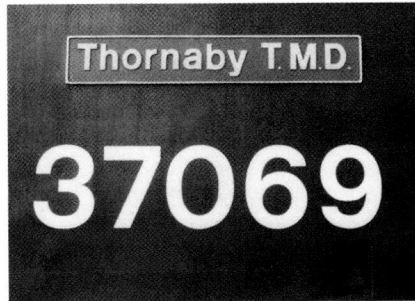

**Nameplate of** 37069.

taking the Bescot to Crewe section with 37716 and finally 'The Cambridge & Norfolk Explorer' from Eastleigh on 14 August with 37402 throughout. Following a period working Departmental trains with 37422 or 37424 for Network Rail to and from Stowmarket during September and in October 2021 she joined the DRS Stored Locomotives Pool. In January 2024 she transferred to Leicester for EuroPhoenix.

**37070 (D6770)**
Released by EE RSH as D6770, Works Number EE/RSH3062/8316 on 17 August 1962 and allocated to Thornaby.

Final depot: Toton, 3/94.

Name carried: None.

Status: Cut up by HNRC at Toton, 7/04.

**37071 (D6771)**
Released by EE RSH as D6771, Works Number EE/RSH3063/8317 on 22 August 1962 and allocated to Thornaby.

Final depot: Doncaster, 10/00

Name carried: *British Steel Skinningrove*, 9/85–3/87.

Status: Cut up by C.F. Booth, Rotherham, 10/05.

**37072 (D6772)**
Released by EE RSH as D6772, Works Number EE/RSH3064/8318 on 4 September 1962 and allocated to Thornaby.

Final depot: Doncaster, 9/98.

Name carried: *Venom*, 11/89–7/90.

Status: Cut up by HNRC at EMR, Kingsbury, 10/04.

**37073 (D6773)**
Released by EE RSH as D6773, Works Number EE/RSH3065/8319 on 10 September 1962 and allocated to Thornaby.

Final depot: Doncaster, 10/02.

Names carried: *Tornado*, 11/89–7/91; *Fort William/An Gearasdan*, 3/94–6/99

Status: Cut up by I. Riley Engineering at Bury, 4/03.

**37074 (D6774)**
Released by EE RSH as D6774, Works Number EE/RSH3066/8320 on 17 September 1962 and allocated to Thornaby.

Final depot: Doncaster, 4/04.

Name carried: None.

Status: Cut up by C.F. Booth at Rotherham, 11/05.

**37075 (D6775)**
Released by EE RSH as D6775, Works Number EE/RSH3067/8321 on 24 September 1962 and allocated to Thornaby.

Final depot: Thornaby, 3/94.

Name carried: None.

Status: Preserved by the Class 37 Locomotive Group, 8/99; Owned and operational on the K&WVR.

**37077 (D6777)**
Released by EE RSH as D6777, Works Number EE/RSH3069/8323 on 12 October 1962 and allocated to Thornaby.

Final depot: Toton, 5/07.

Names carried: *British Steel Shelton*, 9/85–7/87; *Hurricane*, 10/89–8/90.

Status: Cut up by C.F. Booth, Rotherham, 1/10.

**37078 (D6778)**
Released by EE RSH as D6778, Works Number EE/RSH3070/8324 on 29 October 1962 and allocated to Thornaby.

**At Haworth** Yard, K&WVR on 9 November 2014 is 37075.

Final depot: Motherwell, 12.93.

Name carried: *Teesside Steelmaster*, 7/84–2/87.

Status: Cut up at EMR, Kingsbury, 2/04.

**37079 (D6779, 37079, 37357)** See also 37079 in Class 37s in Colour

Released by EE RSH as D6779, Works Number EE/RSH3206/8325 on 6 November 1962 and allocated to Hull Dairycoates.

Final depot: Toton, 5/96.

Name carried: *Medite*, until 1/00.

Status: Cut up at EMR, Kingsbury, 8/08.

Notable movements:
Her early years were typical of her class in that her time was shared between passenger and freight duties. On 4 August 1979 she headed the Norwich to Sheffield section of a Yarmouth to Manchester Piccadilly express, while on 5 July 1980 she dad charge of a service from Glasgow Queen Street to Scarborough and on 31 July 1983 a charter for the British Rail Staff Association between Bridlington and Wolverhampton. At this time she was also occupied with freights from locations as diverse as Parkeston in Essex, Crewe or Sunderland as well as Class 1 passenger services from London Liverpool Street and Crewe. During the mid-1980s passenger work became more dominant, with trains north of Carlisle to Carstairs, Glasgow and Edinburgh while stabled at Motherwell shed during July 1984 and then between Scarborough and Newcastle and in August between Sheffield and Blackpool.

She would be busy mainly with Class 1 passenger services for the remainder of the 1980s, reaching such destinations as Bristol, Cardiff, Morpeth, Edinburgh, Inverness and Fort William. This continued into the 1990s with freights adding variety. On 25 May 1992 she appeared at Melton Mowbray Rail Open Day and on 15 November of the same year she was involved with DC Tours' 'The West of England Coalpower' which ran from Waterloo to Exeter and return. From that time freight became her mainstay again when not in store, though she was still called upon to head the occasional 'special' including on 31 May 1997 1Z58 Carlisle to Luton between Turner's Lane Junction near Wakefield and Doncaster, then on 1 November 1997 Pathfinder Railtours' 'The Blackpool Illuminator/Nor'West Thunderbolt', a charter from Cardiff to Blackpool and return where she was coupled with classmate 37140. On 13 and 14 June 1998 she operated a number of passenger runs between Crewe and Bangor and then Crewe to Chester and Holyhead and return after which she went into store for EWS as unserviceable. After several years during which preservation was a possibility, she was eventually scrapped in August 2008.

**Approaching York** at York Yard North on a snowy 11 February 1978 with a south bound freight is 37079, later to be renumbered to 37357.

**37080 (D6780)**
Released by EE RSH as D6780, Works Number EE/RSH3207/8326 on 14 November 1962 and allocated to Hull Dairycoates.

Final depot: Doncaster, 12/95.

Name carried: None.

Status: Cut up by M.R.J. Phillips at Canton, 6/97.

**37083 (D6783)**
Released by EE RSH as D6783, Works Number EE/RSH3210/8329 on 5 December 1962 and allocated to Hull Dairycoates.

Final depot: Immingham, 7/91.

Name carried: None.

Status: Cut up by Raxstar, Immingham, 4/00.

Notable movements:
Early duties in Yorkshire and the northeast combined both passenger and freight work, ranging from trans-Pennine services between York and Manchester, trips to the Yorkshire coast at Hull and Scarborough and East Coast Main Line (ECML) duty to Newcastle. Her transfer to March in 1972 brought with it the opportunity to work the boat train between Harwich Parkeston Quay and Manchester Piccadilly and also London Liverpool Street to Cambridge services, duties which would continue into the late 1970s, after which she was transferred to Thornaby and then on to Healey Mills. She was employed as station pilot at Manchester Victoria for a time in early 1984 but she was always a much travelled loco, being allocated to passenger trains out of such diverse locations as Bristol, Nottingham, York, Carlisle and Edinburgh during the 1980s and early 1990s, always interspersed with freight work and the occasional tour such as Regional Railways 'Settle & Carlisle Special' between Leeds and Carlisle on 27 December 1991, working with 37071 and 47479 for the outward leg only. Some freight work continued into the mid-1990s but after that she went into store and was eventually scrapped in April 2000.

**37087 (D6787)**
Released by EE RSH as D6787, Works Number EE/RSH3214/8333 on 31 December 1962 and allocated to Gateshead.

Final depot: Kingmoor, 2/05.

Names carried: *Vulcan*, 11/89–4/90; *Vulcan Avro B1 & B2*, 5/03; *Keighley & Worth Valley Railway*, 6/08.

Status: Cut up by C.F. Booth, Rotherham, 3/13.

**37088 (D6788, 37323)**
Released by EE RSH as D6788, Works Number EE/RSH3215/8334 on 13 January 1963 and allocated to Gateshead.

Final depot: Doncaster, 5/96.

Name carried: *Clydesdale*, 7/86–9/99.

Status: Cut up by C.F. Booth, Rotherham, 10/02.

**37092 (D6792)**
Released by EE RSH as D6792, Works Number EE/RSH3219/8338 on 13 February 1963 and allocated to Gateshead.

Final depot: Doncaster, 3/00.

Name carried: None.

Status: Cut up at T.J. Thomson's scrapyard, Stockton, 10/01.

**37095 (D6795)**
Released by EE RSH as D6795, Works Number EE/RSH3222/8342 on 8 March 1963 and allocated to Gateshead.

Final depot: Doncaster, 9/98.

Name carried: *British Steel Teesside*, 9/85–3/87.

Status: Cut up by HNRC at Carnforth, 2/05.

**37096 (D6796)**
Released by EE Vulcan Foundry as D6796, Works Number EE/VF3225/D750 on 30 November 1962 and allocated to Darnall.

Final depot: Tinsley, 5/87.

Name carried: *Spitfire*, 9/89–9/91.

Status: Cut up by MC Metals, Glasgow, 9/91.

Notable movements:
Her career being largely dominated by working out of depots in Yorkshire and the northeast it is no surprise that during the 1960s and '70s she could turn up on passenger duty anywhere from Ipswich and Lincoln to Derby, Wakefield and Sheffield, west to Manchester and north through York to Darlington, Sunderland, Newcastle and beyond. By the late 1970s she might be seen working out of London Liverpool Street on services to Cambridge or Kings Lynn and her move to Gateshead depot involved her on occasional trains from Edinburgh. In 1981 while stabled at Worcester she found employment on banking duty on the Lickey Incline between Bromsgrove and Blackwell but by mid-1982 she was back in the south on trains into East Anglia. Passenger work continued to be her main employment throughout the

1980s and she could be deployed anywhere between Bristol and Aberdeen, working Class 1 or Class 2 trains as required. By the late 1980s she was more in demand for freight duties though some passenger work continued until being consigned to storage from 29 September 1989, soon to be sent for scrapping.

**37097 (D6797)**
Released by EE Vulcan Foundry as D6797, Works Number EE/VF3226/D751 on 7 December 1962 and allocated to Darnall.

Final depot: Doncaster, 1/99.

Name carried: *Old Fettercairn*, 5/07.

Status: Preserved and operational on the Caledonian Railway, Brechin from 7/03.

**37098 (D6798)**
Released by EE Vulcan Foundry as D6798, Works Number EE/VF3227/D752 on 12 December 1962 and allocated to Darnall.

Final depot: Immingham, 9/97.

Name carried: None.

Status: Cut up by HNRC at Old Oak Common, 5/02.

**37099 (D6799, 37324)** (See also 37099 in Class 37s in Colour)
Released by EE Vulcan Foundry as D6799, Works Number EE/VF3228/D753 on 14 December 1962 and allocated to Darnall.

Final depot: Doncaster, 3/96.

Names carried: *Clydebridge*, 7/86; renamed *Clydebridge*, 9/00; *Merl Evans 1947–2016*, 12/16.

Status: Operational with Colas Rail Freight from 3/16. Based at Derby working test trains.

**37101 (D6801, 37345)** (See sub-class 37/3, 37345)

**37104 (D6804)** (See also 37104 in Class 37s in Colour)

Released by EE Vulcan Foundry as D6804, Works Number EE/VF3233/D758 on 11 January 1963 and allocated to Darnall.

Final depot: Immingham, 1/94.

Name carried: None.

Status: Cut up by Raxstar, Immingham, 4/00.

Notable movements:
Passenger duties in her early years whilst based in Yorkshire and the northeast involved workings from Sheffield to the Midlands and

**At Derby** on 7 August 1985 is 37101.

**At Carlisle** during the 1980s are 37104 and 37209. (*Rick Ward*)

Lancashire and between York and Scarborough. Her move to Stratford in the late 1980s saw her employed heading passenger trains in East Anglia when not on Freightliner duty and when transferred to Cardiff Canton in 1989 she was equally at home in this 'mixed traffic' role. During her times at Immingham she might also be used on passenger turns from Leeds to Carlisle and between Carlisle and Newcastle. By January 1994 when she was in store there it seemed she would soon be no more, but she was returned to traffic at Immingham in February 1996 and again in August 1997 after another period in store. Her working days were finally over when she was stored for component recovery by EWS in September 1998 until finally being scrapped.

### 37106 (D6806)
Released by EE Vulcan Foundry as D6806, Works Number EE/VC3235/D760 on 18 January 1963 and allocated to Darnall.

Final depot: Toton, 11/98.

Name carried: None.

Status: Cut up at Wigan CRDC, 8/00.

### 37107 (D6807)
Released by EE Vulcan Foundry as D6807, Works Number EE/VF3236/D761 on 23 January 1963 and allocated to Darnall.

Final depot: Doncaster, 6/96

Name carried: *Fury*, 11/89–11/90.

Status: Cut up at Wigan CRDC, 12/98.

### 37108 (D6808, 37325, 37108)
Released by EE Vulcan Foundry as D6808, Works Number EE/VF3237/D762 on 25 January 1963 and allocated to Darnall.

Final depot: Bescot, 3/96.

Name carried: *Lanarkshire Steel*, 8/86–2/92.

Status: Preserved by the Type 3 Traction Group, Carnforth, 4/00; Moved to Crewe Heritage Centre, 9/10. Moved by road to Nottingham Transport Heritage Centre, (Great Central Railway [GCR], Nottingham), 4/24.

Notable movements:
Her early days in Yorkshire were taken up with the usual mix of local freight and passenger services from the Sheffield area. On 24 June 1973 she had charge of a BR Day Excursion from Barnsley to Blackpool and throughout the 1970s it was passenger duty which occupied most of her schedule. Her transfer to Eastfield in 1978 continued this pattern with her taking services primarily from Glasgow to such destination as Dundee, Fort William, Mallaig and Oban, work which would occupy her until late 1985 when she was used repeatedly on 'Test Train' duties from Crewe Works to Llandudno Junction and to Rhyl. Her transfer to Motherwell in June 1988 led to more freight work, notably iron ore workings from British Steel at Ravenscraig in combination with one and sometimes two classmates.

Her return to Tinsley in November 1991 heralded a return to passenger services interspersed with freight, including Freightliner on the ECML and passenger in the Liverpool and Manchester area.

**Near Aviemore** on 5 July 1978 is 37108, heading the 12.35 Inverness to Edinburgh service. She was later renumbered to 37325 in July 1986 and then back to 37108 in September 1989 as not converted. (*Jonathan Allen*)

On 2 October 1993 she featured on Pathfinder Railtours' 'The Neath Navigator' charter from Preston to Cwmgwrach and return, in the company of classmates 37068, 37704 and 37889. Between then and September 1996 she had charge of several Class 1 passenger services visiting such diverse locations as Cardiff, Llandudno, Birmingham, Stockport, Penrith and Carlisle before being put into store by EWS and later rescued to be privately preserved at Crewe Heritage Centre during 2010 where she underwent restoration into BR green livery. In April 2024, now fully operational she was transferred to the Nottingham Transport Heritage Centre, the northern terminus of the heritage GCR (Nottingham).

**37109 (D6809)** (See also 37109 in Class 37s in Colour)
Released by EE Vulcan Foundry as D6809, Works Number EE/VF3238/D763 on 1 February 1963 and allocated to Darnall.

Final depot: Toton, 5/07.

Name carried: None.

Status: Preserved and operational on the ELR, Bury from 11/07.

Notable movements:
A much-travelled loco being engaged on all manner of duties including express passenger, football specials and freight of every kind. Her transfer to March depot led to a period of regular passenger work out of London Liverpool Street which occupied her until the mid-1980s when she was transferred north spending a short time in Yorkshire working out of Sheffield and York before continuing on to Scotland for more passenger duties, first in the Glasgow, Dundee and Edinburgh areas and then into the Highlands for passenger and freight work. This lasted until 1989 when she was moved south again and her role was extended to heading occasional charter specials. These included on 19 September 1993 for the Newport Open Day Committee, their special train from Newport to Ebbw Vale Steelworks and return, working 'top & tail' with classmate 37174. On 25 September 1999 she was in sole charge of Tractor Tours' 'The Last Chance', from Finsbury Park to Sheffield, Bradford and Hull before returning to King's Cross. The new millennium saw an increase in this type of work with Pathfinder Railtours' 'The Soton Vinegar' Derby to Southampton Central on 14 September 2002, the legs between Derby and Gloucester and Westbury to Derby, again working with 37174. On 1 March 2003 she was paired with 37216 for Past Time Rail's 'The Spinnin' State VI', London Euston to Preston and return, handling the sections between Euston and Bescot Goods Loop and then the return from Birmingham International to Euston.

The year 2004 was busy with Pathfinder Railtours' 'The Lord of the Isles', a four-day tour from Swindon to Inverness and Kyle of Lochalsh and return, with her involved with 37174 and 37401 for the sections from Carlisle northwards and return. On 15 June she headed the V.S.O.E. 'British Pullman' from London Victoria to Portsmouth Harbour and return with 37174 and 37401. Next came Pathfinder Railtours' 'The Industrial Invader' on 18 September, Crewe to Whatley Quarry and return, working with 37047, 37410 and 37418 and finally on 2 October 2004 Pathfinder Railtours' 'The Settle & Carlisle Railway', Bristol Temple Meads to Carlisle via the WCML, Carlisle to Hellifield by the S&C and then on to Warrington to return to Bristol, for most of the tour in the company of 37047.

Her purchase by the ELR saw her begin regular work over their lines from March 2008 until going on loan to the Mid Norfolk Railway on 24 and 25 September 2010. Back to the ELR, then her next visit was to the Churnet Valley Railway from 26 November 2010 to 26 March 2011, then it was back home to the ELR again until 2013 when she was briefly loaned to the Nene Valley Railway (NVR) in May then for a longer period to the Severn Valley Railway (SVR) from June to October. After returning home again she was kept busy there until October 2014 when she was again loaned out to the SVR. ELR duties continued until 10 October 2019 when she was moved by road to the NVR to work until returning, again by road ten days later. She is now fully occupied on ELR services and was on duty during their Diesel Gala held from 29 June to 1 July 2024, working with visiting sister loco 37425.

**37110 (D6810)**
Released by EE Vulcan Foundry as D6810, Works Number EE/VF3239/D764 on 4 February 1963 and allocated to Darnall.

Final depot: Tinsley, 3/93.

Name carried: None.

Status: Cut up by Raxstar at Immingham MPD, 5/00.

**37111 (D6811, 37111, 37326)**
Released by EE Vulcan Foundry as D6811, Works Number EE/VF3240/D765 on 8 February 1963 and allocated to Darnall. Final depot: Doncaster, 3/96.

Names carried: *Loch Eil Outward Bound*, 4/85–7/86; *Glengarnock*, 7/86.

Status: Cut up by EMR, Kingsbury, 7/03.

Notable movements:
During her early years in Yorkshire she was occupied mainly with coal workings and occasional passenger services out of Sheffield, though she did have charge of a Sheffield to Rhyl charter on 23 June 1968 with sister loco D6807 and over the following years became much more sought after for passenger duties. Her move to Stratford in 1973 led to work out of London Liverpool Street to East Anglia and after being returned to Tinsley in 1976 she headed Class 1 trains in that area. On 29 October 1977 she was involved with the LCGB charter 'The Hadrian Railtour' which ran from Blackpool through Hellifield to Carlisle by the S&C, then to Newcastle, York and Blackburn by way of Copy Pit to Preston and back to Blackpool. Her move to Scotland early in 1978 led to extensive passenger workings north of Glasgow with services to Dundee, Inverness, Oban, Fort William and Mallaig dominating her schedule until 1991. During this time she was called upon for charter work including on 16 April 1983 1Z37, a BR 'Merrymaker' excursion from Peterborough to Fort William, Mallaig and return when she was in charge between Fort William and Mallaig.

On 1 June 1985 she was in action for the SLOA rail-tour 'The West Highlander' which originated at Edinburgh and travelled to Oban, Crianlarich, Fort William and Mallaig. Again she headed the section between Fort William and Mallaig, this time with classmate 37081. Later that year on 5 October she took the initial leg of 1Z47, the BR 'TayRail' excursion from Arbroath to Fort William, leading from Arbroath to Cowlairs West Junction. Then occasional freight once again came into play for a short time when allocated to Rail Freight at Eastfield and Trainload Petroleum at Immingham but transferring back to Scotland first to Inverness in January 1993 and then Motherwell from October that year involved her working passenger trains once more, now for Regional Railways, ScotRail.

From November 1994 until May 1995 whilst at Motherwell she was regularly called into action to take over Anglo-Scottish express services having originated at London Euston, which she and a classmate would take forward from Edinburgh to their destination of Aberdeen or Inverness. All this came to an end when she was transferred south to England once more, first in May 1995 to Bescot and shortly afterwards into store, spending time at Toton and Barrow Hill between 1997 and 2001 before being sent to Kingsbury for scrapping.

**37112 (D6812, 37510)** (See also 37510 in sub-class 37/5)
Released by EE Vulcan Foundry on as D6812, Works Number EE/VF3241/D766 on 13 February 1963 and allocated to Darnall. Final depot: Doncaster, 3/16.

Name carried: *Orion*, 12/19.

Status: Operational with the Rail Operations Group from 1/20, based at Barrow Hill Roundhouse.

**37113 (D6813)**
Released by EE Vulcan Foundry as D6813, Works Number EE/VF3242/D767 on 15 February 1963 and allocated to Darnall.

Final depot: Motherwell, 3/94.

Name carried: *Radio Highland*, 9/89–8/95.

Status: Cut up by MC Metals at Portobello Yard, Edinburgh, 8/95.

**37114 (D6814)** (See D6814 in Pre-TOPS Days)

**37116 (D6816)**
Released by EE Vulcan Foundry as D6816, Works Number EE/VF3245/D770 on 1 March 1963 and allocated to Darnall. Final depot: Doncaster, 12/01.

Names carried: *Comet*, 11/89–1/96; *Sister Dora*, 2/96.

Status: Preserved on the Chinnor & Princes Risborough Railway, 2/07; Reinstated into traffic as a PODL, 1/14, allocated to Colas Rail Freight, operational from 10/15.

Notable movements:
Although freight dominated, passenger work also featured throughout her career especially following her move to Stratford depot when she was frequently employed heading trains out of London Liverpool Street to destinations in East Anglia and after her Last Classified Repair when she ventured much further afield on both passenger and freight duties.

Her time at Inverness depot in 1993 involved her working the Scottish sections of InterCity trains between London Euston and Aberdeen or Inverness and on returning to England in 1995 more Class 1 and Class 2 passenger work occupied her in the Midlands and the South West. It was at about this time that she became increasingly sought after to head charter special trains. On 4 May 1996 she was drafted in by Past Time Rail to assist steam loco 60009 *Union of South Africa* with 'The Cumbrian Mountain Express' over part of the Settle & Carlisle (S&C) route between Garsdale and Carlisle due to the latter starting lineside fires. On 25 June that year she was on duty again with the special 1Z70/1Z71 from Bristol Temple Meads to Weymouth and return.

Although her freight duties for EWS dominated the final years of the 1990s she did help with Mercia Charters 'The Tiberius Kirk' three-day tour from Northampton to Oban and return to Rugby which ran on 23 to 25 July 1999, taking the leg between Crianlarich and Rugby in combination with 37114. A guest appearance on the Bo'ness & Kinneil Railway followed later that year on 4 and 5 September and on 28 and 29 April 2001 she appeared on the North Yorkshire Moors Railway (NYMR). She arrived at the Chinnor & Princes Risborough Railway on 28 April 2007 where she worked regularly until being reinstated into main line traffic on 9 January 2014 to work for Colas. This employment continues but was interrupted on 12 May 2018 when she was in charge of The Branch Line Society charter between Carnforth and Norwich, the '565 take 2' in which she combined with classmate 37219 for the sections between Crewe and Stowmarket and between Norwich and Crewe on the return.

### 37131 (D6831)
Released by EE Vulcan Foundry as D6831, Works Number EE/VF3276/D805 on 29 March 1963 and allocated to Canton.

Final depot: Doncaster, 12/99.

Name carried: None.

Status: Cut up by C.F. Booth, Rotherham, 4/07.

### 37133 (D6833)
Released by EE Vulcan Foundry as D6833, Works Number EE/VF3278/D807 on 5 April 1963 and allocated to Canton.

**Passing Doncaster** on 19 May 2022 is 37116.

**At Exeter** St David's on 20 October 1991 are 37133 and 37230. (*Jonathan Allen*)

**Stabled at** Exeter St David's on 22 October 1991 is 37133 alongside 33208. (*Jonathan Allen*)

Final depot: Doncaster, 4/99; France, 6/99–9/00.

Name carried: None.

Status: Cut up by HNRC at Carnforth, 11/04.

**37136 (D6836, 37905)** (See also D6836 and 37905 in Class 37s in Colour)
Released by EE Vulcan Foundry as D6836, Works Number EE/VF3281/D810 on 30 April 1963 and briefly allocated to Canton. Final depot: Doncaster, 9/02.

Name carried: *Vulcan Enterprise*, 2/87.

Status: Preserved by BREL, 11/05; Operational for UK Rail Leasing, Leicester (not mainline) from 3/21.

**37137 (D6837, 37137, 37312)**
Released by EE Vulcan Foundry as D6837, Works Number EE/VF3282/D811 on 24 April 1963 and allocated to Landore.

Final depot: Toton, 3/94.

Name carried: *Clyde Iron*, 7/86–6/96.

Status: Was one of several Class 37s which was adorned with a silver roof courtesy of Motherwell depot during 1979, a very short-lived livery variation. Cut up at T.J. Thomson's scrapyard, Stockton, 7/06.

**37138 (D6838)**
Released by EE Vulcan Foundry as D6838, Works Number EE/VF3283/D812 on 26 April 1963 and allocated to Canton.

Final depot: Toton, 3/94.

Name carried: None.

Status: Cut up by HNRC at Toton, 7/04.

**37139 (D6839)**
Released by EE Vulcan Foundry as D6839, Works Number EE/VF3314/D813 on 3 May 1963 and allocated to Canton.

Final depot: Immingham, 5/94.

Name carried: None.

Status: Cut up at T.J. Thomson's scrapyard, Stockton, 2/04.

**37140 (D6840)**
Released by EE Vulcan Foundry as D6840, Works Number EE/VF3315/D814 on 8 May 1963 and allocated to Canton.

Final depot: Doncaster, 4/99.

Name carried: None.

Status: Cut up at Wigan CRDC, 7/01.

**37141 (D6841)**
Released by EE Vulcan Foundry as D6841, Works Number EE/VF3316/D815 on 10 May 1963 and allocated to Canton.

Final depot: Doncaster, 2/00.

Name carried: None.

Status: Cut up by HNRC at Carnforth, 2/05.

**37142 (D6842)**
Released by EE Vulcan Foundry as D6842, Works Number EE/VF3317/D816 on 17 May 1963 and allocated to Canton.

Final depot: Doncaster, 1/02.

Name carried: None.

Status: Transferred to Barrow Hill, 8/02 for HNRC. Preserved by the Bodmin & Wenford Mainline Diesel Group, 5/03. Operational on the Bodmin & Wenford Railway from 6/04 but stopped for overhaul since 2019.

**37144 (D6844)**
Released by EE Vulcan Foundry as D6844, Works Number EE/VF3319/D818 on 8 May 1963 and allocated to Canton.

Final depot: Immingham, 10/92.

Name carried: None.

Status: Cut up at Sims Metal UK Ltd, Newport, 11/03.

## 37146 (D6846)

Released by EE Vulcan Foundry as D6846, Works Number EE/VF3321/D820 on 10 June 1963 and allocated to Canton. Final depot: Doncaster, 10/00.

Name carried: None.

Status: Preserved at the Stainmore Railway, 2/07; Reinstated into traffic, 8/19; Allocated to EuroPhoenix Locomotives UK, 10/19; Cut up at Leicester LIP, 4/21.

Notable movements:
While based in South Wales her work was mainly with freight traffic and this would continue when she moved north and into Scotland in the 1970s, though by the latter years of the decade she was increasingly in demand to head passenger services north of the border and was in charge of the Scottish Railway Preservation Society's (SRPS) 'Lothian Coast Express' charter from Edinburgh to Fort William and return on 5 August 1978. After repairs at Swindon Works in mid-1984 she was soon back in Scotland working passenger services and this type of duty would continue throughout that decade, interspersed with freight turns and occasional charter appearances such as on 6 June 1987 between Perth and York, again for the SRPS.

Equally at home with passenger and freight traffic, this pattern would continue into the mid-1990s when having been transferred south again she continued to be sought after to head 'specials' including on 23 October 1994 Pathfinder Railtours' 'The Pixie Returns', Bristol Temple Meads to Plymouth and return. The final years of the decade saw her employed on freight work before being put into store by EWS on her return from France, and when bought for preservation in 2007 her future seemed to be assured, but that turned out not to be the case. She was reinstated into traffic as a PODL in August 2019 and though allocated to EuroPhoenix UK she was soon to be deposited at Leicester depot prior to scrapping.

## 37152 (D6852, 37152, 37310, 37152)

Released by EE Vulcan Foundry as D6852, Works Number EE/VF3327/D826 on 8 July 1963 and allocated to Landore. Final depot: Doncaster, 12/99.

Name carried: *British Steel Ravenscraig*, 3/86–5/90.

Status: Preserved and operational at Peak Rail from 3/06; Renumbered again to 37310 and painted in BR Large Logo blue livery from 8/19.

Notable movements:
Having spent a greater proportion of her early years than was usual under repair she made up for her lack of route miles during the 1980s first with involvement in the marathon D.A.A. Tours' 'The Anglo-Scottish Freighter' railtour which originated at London Marylebone on 4 June 1984 and ran to Newcastle via Toton and Worksop and the ECML and on to Edinburgh Waverley, Stirling (where she and 37152 took charge) to Grangemouth and Mossend. Then a tour of freight lines (headed by two Class 20s) before returning

**With a** train of ARC empties on 4 November 1992, 37146 passes Hungerford Common near Newbury, Berkshire.

southwards to Glasgow Central, Carlisle, Crewe, Birmingham New Street and finally London Euston on the morning of 6 June. After this she was involved with regular passenger duty in the Glasgow and Edinburgh area before another charter, 1Z10 from Perth to London King's Cross on 4 July 1989 had her in charge from Morpeth to Newcastle. From May 1990 her work for Scotrail saw her heading services to such destinations as Dundee, Montrose, Perth, Aberdeen and Inverness. This work continued throughout her time based at Eastfield and at Inverness, where she extended her influence to Kyle of Lochalsh and also was involved with the sections of Anglo-Scottish expresses from London Euston to Aberdeen and Inverness, taking charge from Edinburgh in the company of a classmate.

On 5 June 1993 she was in charter action again, this time with 37066 on the tour originating at London Euston and travelling to Kyle of Lochalsh as 1Z36, taking the section between Edinburgh, Inverness, Kyle of Lochalsh and return. Her Scottish duties continued in similar fashion until the end of 1994 when after heading 'The Royal Scotsman' luxury overnight train on 15 September 1997 she worked for EWS out of Motherwell until on 17 April 1999 with classmate 37165 she assisted with Pathfinder Railtours' 'The Settle Excursioner', which ran from Banbury to Carlisle and return. The 37s were in charge from Crewe to Carlisle by way of the WCML and the return via the S&C. After this she was 'retired' into storage, had her Radio Electric Token Block (RETB) equipment, used to control trains on the single line routes in the North of Scotland, removed and seemed destined for the scrap yard following component recovery. However, in June 2005 she was bought for preservation and moved first to West Coast Railway Company headquarters at Carnforth in January 2006 and from there to her new home at the heritage railway Peak Rail in Derbyshire in March of that year.

**37153 (D6853)**
Released by EE Vulcan Foundry as D6853, Works Number EE/VF3328/D827 on 10 July 1963 and allocated to Landore.

Final depot: Doncaster, 12/99.

Name carried: None.

Status: Cut up by C.F. Booth, Rotherham, 1/03.

**37154 (D6854)**
Released by EE Vulcan Foundry as D6854, Works Number EE/VF3329/D828 on 11 July 1963 and allocated to Landore.

Final depot: Doncaster, 12/99.

Name carried: *Sabre*, 9/91–5/92.

Status: Cut up at Wigan CRDC, 7/00.

**37156 (D6856, 37156, 37311)**
Released by EE Vulcan Foundry as D6856, Works Number EE/VF3331/D830 on 25 July 1963 and allocated to Landore.

Final depot: Doncaster, 6/99.

Name carried: *British Steel Hunterston*, 3/86–10/94.

Status: Cut up at Wigan CRDC, 1/00.

**37158 (D6858)** (See also 37158 in Class 37s in Colour)
Released by EE Vulcan Foundry as D6858, Works Number EE/VF3333/D832 on 15 August 1963 and allocated to Landore. Final depot: Doncaster, 8/99.

Name carried: None.

Status: Preserved by the Type 3 Traction Group, Carnforth, 4/00; Cut up by HNRC, Carnforth, 4/08.

Notable movements:
Her early years both in South Wales and Scotland were largely occupied with freight duties but by the mid-1970s she was to be seen at the head of passenger trains and the occasional charter including on 27 August 1978 'The Vulcan Venturer', London Victoria to Bristol Temple Meads and return, working with 37231 between Westbury and Bristol and on 15 June 1980 F+W Railtours' 'The Tinsley Terror', Newton Abbot to Birmingham New Street, then to Sheffield for Tinsley Depot Open Day and then return to Plymouth in the company of classmate 37210. Class 1 passenger duties occupied her throughout the 1980s, with trains from Bristol being regular turns early in the decade until her transfer to March depot saw her occupied with services from London Liverpool Street to Kings Lynn or Cambridge in 1986.

Moving back to South Wales in May 1988 saw her regularly involved with passenger and freight in the Cardiff area and the South West but the early 1990s brought a greater emphasis on Class 1 passenger work and charters including on 20 June 1993 BR (Additional Service) Paddington to Paignton with 37092 and 37197 for the Paignton & Dartmouth Railway Diesel Weekend, then on 24 September 1994, The Branch Line Society tour of freight lines, 'The Port Vale', from Newport to Port Talbot Docks and Margam Yard, top & tail with 37429. By mid-1995 she was occupied with passenger services between Exeter and Plymouth until her transfer to the Midlands in 1996 brought more freight work for EWS until being put into store pending withdrawal from stock and scrapping.

## 37162 (D6862)

Released by EE RSH as D6862, Works Number EE/RSH3340/8393 on 23 July 1963 and allocated to Landore. Final depot: Doncaster, 9/00.

Name carried: None.

Status: Cut up by C.F. Booth, Rotherham, 12/05.

Notable movements:
Though mainly employed with freight movements during the 1960s and early 1970s, she was detailed for passenger work from time to time especially whilst working out of Yorkshire depots and when allocated to Cardiff Canton from 1974 she was used on the Lickey Incline between Bromsgrove and Blackwell to assist passenger services up the hill. These banking duties continued from May 1977 through to May 1981, interspersed amongst more routine freight and passenger work. Class 1 and Class 2 passenger services increasingly occupied her during the 1980s heading trains in the Bristol, Cardiff and Swansea area, including charter work such as 'The Glamorgan Valleys Explorer' for Hertfordshire Railtours, which ran between Milton Keynes and Swansea and Cardiff on 16 January 1988 for which she was in partnership top and tail with classmate 37427 for the sections in South Wales.

This pattern of freight and express passenger workings would continue into the 1990s, interrupted by the occasional charter as pictured above at York station on 5 June 1993 and on 30 June that year for the Worcester Women's Institute between Worcester Shrub Hill and Coventry via Cambridge and Nuneaton, returning by way of Birmingham New Street and Kidderminster. On 14 June 1997 she was coupled with classmate 37254 for Pathfinder Railtours' 'The Lakeland Excursioner' from Cardiff Central to Carlisle and return over the West Coast Main Line between Stafford and Carlisle. Her transfer to Eastleigh in May 1998 to work for EWS, followed by a short time in France signalled the beginning of the end for her career as she was officially withdrawn from stock on 9 August 2005 to be cut up shortly afterwards.

## 37174 (D6874)

Released by EE Vulcan Foundry as D6874, Works Number EE/VF3352/D838 on 16 September 1963 and allocated to Canton.

Final depot: Toton, 5/07.

Name carried: None.

Status: Cut up by EMR, Kingsbury, 4/08.

## 37175 (D6875)

Released by EE Vulcan Foundry as D6875, Works Number EE/RSH3353/D839 on 20 September 1963 and allocated to Canton.

Final depot: Old Oak Common, 9/02.

Name carried: W.S. Sellar, 7/11.

Status: Bought by BREL for preservation, 6/06; Weardale Railway, 8/06; K&WVR, 5/07; Bo'ness & Kinneil Railway, 1/09; Doncaster as a PODL, 1/14 allocated to Colas Rail Freight; Operational with Loram Rail from 6/23. Ran light with 37254 from Derby to Millerhill via Shap on 10 March 2024.

**At a** damp Blackpool North on 15 July 2016 is 37175 in Colas Rail Freight livery working on the rear of 1Q83, the Network Rail Test Train to Derby R.T.C. On the front is 37254, still in InterCity 'Swallow' livery and between them are Plain Line Pattern Recognition (PLPR) and Mentor test coaches including Track Inspection and Overhead Line Inspection vehicles.

Notable movements:
Unlike many of her classmates she spent virtually all of her first twenty years working out of the one depot, Cardiff Canton, where she was employed on local passenger services, longer distance Class 1 trains and freight in South Wales. Her transfer to Scotland in 1982 saw her working trains out of Glasgow Queen Street to Perth, Dundee and beyond into the Highlands until in 1986 she was brought south to briefly work clay trains and passenger services in the south west. This was short-lived however, as from October 1987 she was back in the Scottish Highlands and shortly afterwards returned to work around Glasgow and Edinburgh from Eastfield Depot from May 1989. By the early 1990s, these passenger duties would be extended to Aberdeen or Inverness taking over the Scottish section of the long-distance services from London Euston.

Her move south again in 1998 briefly involved her working trains between Birmingham International and Holyhead as well as some freight duties and while at Old Oak Common in 2002 she spent some time as a guest on the SVR, between 4 and 6 October working trains between Bridgnorth and Kidderminster. Her appearances on heritage railways continued with her featuring on the K&WVR line from May 2007 until mid-June of that year, followed almost immediately by the ELR from July until early September. Next she was heading north again to appear for an extended stay on the Bo'ness & Kinneil Railway from 23 September 2007 until 28 December 2013.

After this she was put to work for Colas Rail Freight, as a PODL but painted in their distinctive orange and yellow livery. She was still in demand for special duties though, and on 2 September 2017 featured on the 565 Railtours/Branch Line Society tour 'The 565 Special' which ran between Carnforth and Carmarthen where she shared the work between Crewe and Carmarthen and between Carmarthen and Chester 'top and tail' with 37257. Classmates 37668 and 37669 were also involved on the tour. Other recent work has seen her in operation for Network Rail with their yellow 'Test Trains' such as that pictured above, which continually monitor the rail network making maintenance more efficient.

**37179 (D6879, 37691, 37612)** (See also 37179 in Class 37s in Colour) Released by EE RSH as D6879, Works Number EE/RSH3357/8400 on 2 October 1963 and allocated to Canton.

Final depot: Kingmoor, 5/00.

Name carried: None.

Status: Operational with HNRC, locomotives for lease, 7/17; Allocated to Colas Rail Freight, 5/18; Operational on the GCR, Loughborough from 9/19.

Notable movements:
Her early duties while at Canton involved a mix of passenger and freight workings including trains to and from London Paddington during 1966 as well as goods trains in South Wales and Freightliners to Tilbury. In the mid-1970s she was frequently employed on Class 1 and Class 2 passenger work out of Cardiff and Swansea as well as being involved with the occasional charter, such as on 20 February 1977 when she was sent to the aid of the Railway Pictorial Publications Railtours' 'The Western Requiem' London Paddington to Merthyr Tydfil tour between Cardiff Central and Pontypridd after number 1010 *Western Campaigner* had failed.

Local passenger work dominated the later years of the 1970s and into the 1980s but she continued to be called upon for charter duty including on 22 March 1980 with Hertfordshire Railtours' 'The Red Dragon', London Paddington to Blaenavon and return between Cardiff Central and Newport coupled with 37182, followed by Oxford Publishing Company's 'The Welsh Collieries Rambler' described above. Her move to Eastfield in April 1982 saw passenger work continue with her heading trains out of Glasgow Queen Street as far as Inverness or Kyle of Lochalsh and moves south in subsequent years involved her with similar duties, though she was also called upon to assist heavy passenger trains up the Lickey Incline for a time in the summer of 1987. By then she had been renumbered to 37691 and as such was involved in Pathfinder Railtours' 'Gloucester Open Day Shuttles' on 1 July 1990 in partnership with 37800.

From the early 1990s her work was to involve mainly freight turns but by the end of the decade she was in demand again for more 'special' duties. Now numbered 37612 on 17 April she headed Eagle Railtours' 'The Esk Valley Explorer', London St Pancras to Whitby with 37610, as far as Battersby and return and a month later on 15 May she was coupled with 37611 for the same promotor's 'The North York Moors Explorer', Worcester Shrub Hill to Whitby, again to and from Battersby. On 24 July she was in charge of John Fishwick & Son's 'The Northern Venturer' charter from Crewe to Carlisle, outward via the S&C and return by the ECML with 37610 through York and on to Carnforth before returning to Crewe. She then appeared as a guest at the K&WVR's 'Autumn Diesel Gala' on 31 July and 1 August before returning to main line duty in September 1999, a period which included more charter work such as on 4 September Mercia Charters 'The Best of Both Worlds' Preston to Brighton and return tour and on 20 May 2000 First North Western/*Railway Magazine*'s 'The Class 37 Farewell' which ran between Crewe and Blaenau Ffestiniog.

Later whilst primarily occupied in the Carlisle area with Nuclear Traffic and local passenger services to Barrow-in-Furness she continued to be sought after for charter work including on 31 August 2012 Pathfinder Railtours' 'The Dartmouth Flyer', Tame Bridge Parkway to Kingswear and return with 37259. On 21 April 2014 'The Heart of Wales Meanderer' which ran from Eastleigh to Llandrindod Wells and return, with 37611, again for Pathfinder Railtours, then on 11 July 2015 for Retro Railtours, 'The Retro Cumbrian Coast Explorer' from Chesterfield to Carlisle and return with 37604. A four-day tour for Pathfinder Railtours from Paignton to Carlisle then on to Fort William, Mallaig and Oban occupied her and classmate 37601 between 30 September and 3 October 2016 before she was transferred south again. Her more recent duties have included working Network Rail Test Trains in 2018 and a period working on the heritage GCR at Loughborough during September 2019.

### 37184 (D6884)

Released by EE RSH as D6884, Works Number EE/RSH3362/8405 on 14 November 1963 and allocated to Landore. Final depot: Doncaster, 3/96.

Name carried: None.

Status: Cut up at T.J. Thomson's scrapyard, Stockton, 10/01.

Notable movements:
While based in South Wales her duties were associated with the heavy industry in the Port Talbot, Ebbw Vale and Llanelli areas though by the mid-1970s she was becoming increasingly employed on passenger trains from Cardiff Central or Swansea stations to Bristol Temple Meads, Birmingham New Street or Crewe. Her transfer to Eastfield in 1982 and to Inverness a short time later led her to be regularly employed on Class 1 services out of Glasgow Queen Street mainly to Fort William or Oban. During this period also she was frequently used on trains to Inverness and featured on the Scottish Railway Preservation Society's tour 'The Highlander' from Edinburgh on 22 September 1987.

With her transfer to Immingham in November 1989 came a shift in emphasis and more freight work was involved for a time until being returned to the Scottish Highlands at Inverness from June 1992 when she was again in charge of Class 1 services, usually to Edinburgh and invariably in the company of a classmate such as 37255, 37261, 37683 or 37685. Her demise began following her transfer back to

**Approaching York** station with a car transporter is 37184 during the 1980s. (*Rick Ward*)

England by EWS in May 1995 when she was initially allocated to their Strategic Reserve, but this amounted to periods spent in storage until she was finally scrapped in 2001.

**37185 (D6885)** (See also 37185 in Class 37s in Colour)
Released by EE RSH as D6885, Works Number EE/RSH3363/8406 on 28 December 1963 and allocated to Landore.

Final depot: Doncaster, 4/99.

Names carried: *Buccaneer*, 11/89–1/91; *Lea & Perrins*, 5/93.

Status: Cut up by C.F. Booth, Rotherham, 1/06.

**37188 (D6888)**
Released by EE RSH as D6890, Works Number EE/RSH3368/8411 on 21 January 1964 and allocated to Landore.

Final depot: Doncaster, 3/96.

Name carried: *Jimmy Shand*, 5/85–5/89.

Status: Cut up at UKRL, Leicester, 7/19.

**37190 (D6890, 37314, 37190, 37314)** (See also 37190 in Class 37s in Colour)
Released by EE RSH as D6890, Works Number EE/RSH3368/8411 on 21 January 1964 and allocated to Landore.

Final depot: Canton, 4/92.

Name carried: *Dalzell*, 7/86–7/93 and in preservation.

Status: Preserved at the Midland Railway Centre, Butterley, 9/01; GCR, 4/08; Midland Railway Centre, Butterley, 9/10; One:One Railway Museum, Margate from 8/21.

**Nameplate of** 37314.

**Nameplate of** 37191.

**37191 (D6891)**
Released by EE RSH as D6891, Works Number EE/RSH3369/8412 on 21 January 1964 and allocated to Landore.

Final depot: Toton, 9/97.

Name carried: *International Youth Year 1985*, 1/85–11/85.

Status: Cut up at Wigan CRDC, 1/01.

**37194 (D6894)**
Released by EE RSH as D6894, Works Number EE/RSH3372/8415 on 16 March 1964 and allocated to Landore.

Final depot: Kingmoor, 2/05.

Names carried: *British International Freight Association*, 9/90; *Neil Webster*, 5/03.

Status: Cut up at C.F. Booth, Rotherham, 2/17.

Notable movements:
Much of her early work involved freight both in the South Wales area

**At Eastleigh** during 1988 is 37188 *Jimmy Shand*. (*Rick Ward*)

and when transferred to Yorkshire and the North East, and this would remain the case through to the early 1980s when passenger duties came more to the fore. From August 1984 until June 1985 she was a regular in charge of Class 1 services out of Glasgow Central and Edinburgh Waverley but by January 1986 she was back in England with both freight and passenger trains. This work took her to such varied locations as Newcastle, York and Liverpool in the north, through Shrewsbury and Wolverhampton down to Banbury and Harwich until in July 1988 she was employed as a banker on the Lickey Incline.

After this she continued to roam the network until her transfer to Inverness in 1992 saw her time occupied with Class 1 services in that area, working in tandem with a classmate. Her move to Motherwell brought her back to freight work for a short time before she became involved in the charter train market when transferred to the south of England. These included Pathfinder Railtours' 'The Southern Mariner' from Bristol Temple Meads to London Victoria and return on 12 December 1993, then on 21 December 1996 with D-Tours' 'The Festive Fiasco' a tour of lines around London Victoria and London Bridge. Shortly after this, while working for EWS her prospects took a downward turn when she was deemed unserviceable and stabled at Old Oak Common for much of 1999 and 2000, but her fortunes improved when transferred to Barrow Hill in August of that year where she was reinstated after working a series of shuttles in connection with Open Weekends in October 2000 and again a year later, being allocated to HNRC, 'Locomotives for Lease'.

From August 2003 through to September 2004 she could be seen working on the heritage ELR and her transfer to Kingmoor and DRS began an involvement with Nuclear Traffic in West Cumbria as well as with charters again, including on 29 December 2006 Pathfinder Railtours' 'The Yo Ho Ho', Swindon to Preston and return with 37229. On 27 July 2009 she was in charter action for Spitfire Tours with 'The Kernow Growler', Birmingham International to Penzance and return, coupled with 37087 throughout. On 7 March 2010 she worked the first service over the new link connecting the heritage North Norfolk Railway with Network Rail before appearing as a guest on the K&WVR during their gala over the weekend of 12 and 13 June that year.

In 2011 she continued to be sought after for 'special' duties including on 30 April with 37688 between Preston and Carmarthen and return, then for Pathfinder Railtours again on 28 May with 37087 for sections of their tour 'The Curnow Irrupter', Tame Bridge Parkway, St Blazey, Plymouth Friary and return. Later on 17 September she was in the company of 37688 again for Spitfire Tours' 'The Cumbrian Crusader V' which ran from Birmingham International to Carlisle and return, taking legs on the outward route including over the S&C line. During early April 2013 she appeared as a guest on the Mid Norfolk Railway before returning to charter duty on 18 May 2013 with Pathfinder Railtours' 'The Northumbrian Explorer', Bristol Temple Meads to Alnmouth and return, coupled with 37604 throughout. Her final charter was again for Pathfinder Railtours when on 11 January 2014 she was involved with 'The Deviationer' tour, Crewe to Ely Papworth Sidings and return. After that she was put into store by DRS until 19 December 2016 when she was moved by road to Rotherham for scrapping.

### 37196 (D6896)

Released by EE RSH as D6896, Works Number EE/RSH3374/8417 on 6 April 1964 and allocated to Landore.

Final depot: Toton, 5/07.

Name carried: *Tre Pol & Pen*, 7/85–5/87.

Status: Cut up by C.F. Booth, Rotherham, 5/09.

### 37197 (D6897)

Released by EE RSH as D6897, Works Number EE/RSH3375/8418 on 15 April 1964 and allocated to Landore.

Final depot: EWS Doncaster, allocated to 'Locomotives for Condemnation & Disposal', 12/99

Name carried: *Loch Laidon* when running for WCRC with 'The Royal Scotsman' in 2005.

Status: Rescued by Riley & Sons (Bury) then operational for WCRC from 2004 and later for DRS. Cut up at EMR, Kingsbury, 5/12.

### 37198 (D6898)

Released by EE RSH as D6898, Works Number EE/RSH3376/8419 on 28 April 1964 and allocated to Landore.

Final depot: Doncaster, 12/99.

Name carried: None

Status: Bought by BREL for preservation, 6/04. Wensleydale Railway, 7/04; Dartmoor Railway, 3/06; EMR Kingsbury, 11/07; GCR, 4/08. Reinstated into traffic at Doncaster, 10/09 as a PODL for the GCR; Moved to Darlington North Road Railway Museum, 8/21.

### 37201 (D6901)

Released by EE Vulcan Foundry as D6901, Works Number EE/VF3379/D845 on 18 October 1963 and allocated to Canton.

Final depot: Barrow Hill, 9/02.

Name carried: *Saint Margaret*, 11/93.

Status: Cut up by C.F. Booth, Rotherham, 3/09.

### 37203 (D6903) See also 37203 in Class 37s in Colour

Released by EE Vulcan Foundry as D6903, Works Number EE/VF3381/D847 on 29 October 1963 and allocated to Canton.

Final depot: Toton, 5/07.

Name carried: None.

Status: Cut up at Hull's scrapyard, Rotherham, 5/10.

### 37207 (D6907)

Released by EE Vulcan Foundry as D6907, Works Number EE/VF3385/D851 on 15 November 1963 and allocated to Landore.

Final depot: Bescot, 2/95.

Name carried: *William Cookworthy*, 5/82–7/87.

Status: Preserved on the Plym Valley Railway, 3/00; Barrow Hill, 6/15; Reinstated into traffic at Doncaster, 12/18 as a PODL; Owned by Meteor Power and operational by the Heavy Tractor Group on the GCR from 4/23 following conversion to run on battery power.

### 37209 (D6909)

Released by EE Vulcan Foundry as D6909, Works Number EE/VF3389/D853 on 24 December 1963 and allocated to Landore.

Final depot: Doncaster, 7/92.

Name carried: *Phantom*, 11/89.

Status: Cut up by HNRC at Doncaster, 7/02.

Notable movements:
Her early career in South Wales was typical in that it involved mainly freight workings associated with the heavy industries of that region and even after her move to Yorkshire freight dominated but with occasional passenger services in the Sheffield area. It was not until the early 1980s that passenger duties became an important part of her workload, appearing on trains between Sheffield and Blackpool, Hull and Doncaster as well as venturing further afield into the Midlands, East Anglia and northwards to Scotland. Her transfer to Stratford in November 1987 resulted in her being used for freightliner as well as Class 1 passenger duties and she continued to roam far and wide.

Not until her move to Scotland, first to Motherwell and then, after a brief time at Immingham and Tinsley, to Inverness did she settle into a regular pattern of passenger work for InterCity. Usually coupled with a classmate she was regularly employed on express passenger trains between Edinburgh, Aberdeen and Inverness during the early summer of 1992 before being retired into store at Tinsley in July of that year. A reprieve seemed possible when in December 1993 she was allocated to Trainload Freight but

**With a** train of fuel tanks at Buxton TMD on 27 August 1996 is 37209.

it wasn't to be and she remained in store until, inevitably she was condemned and scrapped by HNRC.

### 37211 (D6911)

Released by EE Vulcan Foundry as D6911, Works Number EE/VF3389/D855 on 2 December 1963 and allocated to Landore.

Final depot: Toton, 11/98.

Name carried: None.

Status: Preserved on the Churnet Valley Railway, 10/03. Cut up by EMR, Kingsbury, 8/07.

### 37212 (D6912)

Released by EE Vulcan Foundry as D6912, Works Number EE/VF3390/D856 on 6 January 1964 and allocated to Landore.

Final depot: Doncaster, 4/99.

Name carried: None

Status: Cut up by Raxstar at Eastleigh, 2/04.

### 37213 (D6913)

Released by EE Vulcan Foundry as D6913, Works Number EE/VF3391/D857 on 7 January 1964 and allocated to Landore.

Final depot: Doncaster, 5/96.

Name carried: None.

Status: Cut up at T.J. Thomson's scrapyard, Stockton, 5/03.

### 37214 (D6914)

Released by EE Vulcan Foundry as D6914, Works Number EE/VF3392/D858 on 13 January 1964 and allocated to Canton.

Final depot: Doncaster, 3/97.

Name carried: None.

Status: Condemned to Wigan CRDC, 6/00; Moved to Barrow Hill, 9/03. Bought for preservation, 5/04. Reinstated into traffic at Doncaster, 5/05 as a PODL; Moved to WCRC Carnforth, 10/11; Moved to the Bo'ness & Kinneil Railway by road 9/17. Acting as a spares donor for the ongoing restoration there of 37261, 5/24.

### 37215 (D6915)

Released by EE Vulcan Foundry as D6915, Works Number EE/VF3393/D859 on 13 January 1964 and allocated to Landore.

Final depot: Doncaster, 7/92.

Name carried: None.

Status: Preserved by The Growler Group, 4/94; Operational on the Gloucestershire Warwickshire Railway from 9/98.

Notable movements:
Typically her duties from the start involved a mix of freight and passenger work, the latter especially whilst based at Tinsley when she was regularly employed on services between Sheffield and Skegness, Scarborough and even Blackpool. Freight was her main occupation at that time and with this she was kept busy until her move to Stratford in 1973 eventually saw her once more in charge of passenger services, this time out of London Liverpool Street throughout 1981 to Cambridge, Lowestoft, Yarmouth, Norwich or Kings Lynn. By the mid-1980s she was increasingly in demand to head not only Class 1 trains but also charter specials including on 24 April 1985 assisting steam loco number 5690 *Leander* with sections north of Carlisle of 'The Thames-Clyde Express' tour and on 30 June

**Passing Great**
Blakenham, Ipswich in the mid-1970s is 37215.

that year was involved with the F+W charter 'The Severncider TOO' which originated at Cardiff Central and ran to Bristol Temple Meads and Gloucester.

The late 1980s saw her regularly involved with banking duty on the Lickey Incline between Bromsgrove and Blackwell which continued until mid-1990. On 19 January 1992 she was back in charter action again for D.C. Tours/Network SouthEast 'The Solent & Wessex Wanderer (No.3/Train C)' which ran between London Waterloo, Bournemouth and Weymouth via Eastleigh. Between March and July 1992 she was employed hauling oil tanker trains in the south of England before being stored. Her rescue by The Growler Group in April 1994 resulted in her being moved to Toddington for the heritage Gloucestershire Warwickshire Railway where she was started up in preservation for the first time on 5 July 1998. Since then she has worked continuously for the railway and with trains to Cheltenham Racecourse.

### 37216 (D6916)

Released by EE Vulcan Foundry as D6916, Works Number EE/VF3394/D860 on 2 January 1964 and allocated to Landore.

Final depot: Toton, 5/07.

Name carried: *Great Eastern*, 3/92.

Status: Preserved, privately owned on the Pontypool & Blaenavon Railway from 7/07.

### 37218 (D6918) (See also 37218 in Class 37s in Colour)

Released by EE Vulcan Foundry as D6918, Works Number EE/VF3396/D862 on 3 January 1964 and allocated to Landore.

Final depot: Doncaster, 9/02.

Name carried: None.

Status: In store for DRS, Kingmoor, offered for sale, 9/23; Transferred to Leicester for EuroPhoenix Locomotives UK, 10/23.

Notable movements:
Much of her early work centred around South Wales and West Yorkshire involving the freight of those two areas, though as a result of her collision at Britannia Colliery in 1975 she spent over a month stabled at Cardiff Canton before being moved to Doncaster Works for repairs. She remained there until August 1976 after which she went back to Cardiff then into Crewe Works in January 1977 but was back at Doncaster Works by March of that year and appeared on show at the Open Day there on 17 June 1978. Throughout the next few years, she was involved with freight and passenger work mainly in the South Wales area then in April 1982 she was in need of more bodywork repairs and spent some time at Landore depot and then Crewe Works. Bad luck seemed to follow her as in September 1983 she was back in Crewe Works after having suffered more collision damage, but after being outshopped she spent some time in December 1983 to January 1984 on banking duty on the Lickey Incline followed by freight work in the Birmingham area.

For the remainder of the 1980s she was variously employed on passenger and some freight duties first around Bristol and the South West, then following her transfer to Stratford in January 1989 in East Anglia, either with services out of London Liverpool Street or trains between Cambridge and Kings Lynn. Her transfer to Immingham in 1990 and Tinsley a year later added more freight turns to her schedule but passenger work still occupied much of her time until in April 1994 she was put into store for the first time. By July she was up and running again for Rail Freight Distribution but not for long, as from September 1994 to late 1999 she alternated repeatedly between working and storage until in December 1999 it appeared that her time had come to an end when she was condemned for disposal.

However, DRS came to the rescue and by September 2002 she was operational once more based at Carlisle Kingmoor. She spent two days in July 2004 as a guest on the heritage ELR before returning to DRS Nuclear Traffic Pool working again from Kingmoor. From May 2010 she became heavily involved with charter specials such as on 29 May 2010 with Spitfire Railtours' 'The Prisoner', Preston to Pwllheli and return via Crewe and then on 26 June 2010 again for Spitfire Railtours' 'The Kernow Explorer', Gloucester to Penzance and return. From 22 to 25 April 2011 she was busy with Pathfinder Railtours' 'The Easter Highlander' a four-day tour originating from Salisbury, travelling to Inverness by way of Carlisle and including three full days touring the Highlands. On 18 August 2011 she had charge of a special between Crewe and Durham and three days later on 21 August another between Edinburgh and Oban. On 9 February 2013 she was involved with the outward leg of Pathfinder Railtours' 'The Winter Settler' which ran from Bristol Temple Meads to Carlisle via the S&C, returning by way of the WCML, then on the following day she was in action again for Pathfinder Railtours with their Bristol Temple Meads to Liskeard via Looe tour named 'The Hullaba-Looe'. She was on display at the Open Day at Carlisle Kingmoor depot on 17 August 2013 then on 8 March 2014 she was back with Pathfinder Railtours for 'The Mid-Norfolk Navigator', Crewe to Hoe by way of Dereham and return.

Between these tours she spent her time either in store or back on Nuclear Traffic duty. On 18, 19 and 20 July 2014 she was a guest on the heritage Wensleydale Railway in North Yorkshire and then on 29 November 2014 she was heading Pathfinder Railtours' 'The Festive Portsmouth Explorer', Stafford via Portsmouth Harbour to Eastleigh and return. From 3 to 6 April 2015 she worked special trains from Eastleigh to Inverness and then between Inverness and Kyle of Lochalsh before returning to Eastleigh, working with 37607 throughout. In June 2015 she began a two-month period operating passenger services between Carlisle and Barrow-in-Furness, occasionally extending to Preston and then for the remainder of 2015 she was again employed on special trains, mainly centred on Inverness.

More Nuclear Traffic filled her time between these passenger turns and then in June 2017 she worked as a guest on the heritage North Norfolk Railway before being on display at Crewe Gresty Bridge Open Day on 21 July 2018. There then followed yet more 'special' duties in 2019, first with Pathfinder Railtours' 'The Blue Boys Loco Fest' on 9 February, from Newport to Blackburn, Blackpool North then to Crewe and back to Newport. This was followed on 27 April with The Branch Line Society's 'The Gourock Growler' from Crewe to Gourock to Carlisle and return and finally on 29 June 2019 Pathfinder Railtours' 'The Mazey Day Cornishman', from Tame Bridge Parkway to Penzance and return, with 37059 throughout. Then she was back to work for DRS Nuclear Traffic Pool and other freight duties until a final charter on 12 March 2022 for Pathfinder Railtours' 'The Pennine Wayfarer' from Bristol Temple Meads to Bolton via Manchester and return, with 37425 throughout. After this it was back to business as usual for DRS Supply Chain Operations until being offered for sale in November 2023 and transferred to Leicester for EuroPhoenix Locomotives UK in January 2024.

## 37219 (D6919)

Released by EE Vulcan Foundry as D6919, Works Number EE/VF3405/D863 on 16 January 1964 and allocated to Canton.

Final depot: Doncaster, 1/01.

Name carried: *Shirley Ann Smith*, 3/08.

Status: Preserved on the Chasewater Railway, 10/05; Gloucestershire Warwickshire Railway, 3/07; Chinnor & Princes Risborough Railway, 3/08; Reinstated into traffic at Doncaster, 8/10 as a PODL; Mid Norfolk Railway, 9/10; Pontypool & Blaenavon Railway, 10/11; Operated by Colas Rail Freight from 1/14; Operational on main line charters from 7/17; Operational on Network Rail infrastructure inspection trains with 37421, from Mossend Yard, 1/24; Working on the Swanage Railway from 5/24.

## 37220 (D6920)

Released by EE Vulcan Foundry as D6920, Works Number EE/VF3406/D864 on 16 January 1964 and allocated to Canton.

Final depot: Doncaster, 1/00.

Name carried: *Westerleigh*, 6/90–3/93.

Status: Cut up at EMR, Kingsbury, 9/07.

## 37221 (D6921)

Released by EE Vulcan Foundry as D6921, Works Number EE/VF3407/D865 on 17 January 1964 and allocated to Landore.

Final depot: Toton, 5/07.

Name carried: None.

Status: Cut up at C.F. Booth, Rotherham, 5/09.

Notable movements:
Her duties in South Wales were typical and consisted mainly of freight workings associated with steel production and mining for which the area was renowned but with her move to Immingham came the opportunity for more varied assignments including passenger work from the Hull area and with classmate 37252 headed the Railway Pictorial Publication Railtours' charter 'The Hull Hornet' for sections of their tour which ran between London Paddington and Hull on 13 October 1979. Further passenger work was to follow during the 1980s interspersed with parcels and heavy freight

throughout much of the north of England and then East Anglia when working out of Stratford Depot.

Her transfer to Cardiff Canton in October 1988 involved her in similar work including Class 1 services between Cardiff, Manchester and Liverpool. Moving on to Inverness saw the emphasis of her work swing to more full-time passenger duty as through much of 1992 she was regularly involved with the Scottish portions of long-distance services between London Euston and Aberdeen or Inverness, invariably coupled with a classmate. She and 37152 were responsible for the Scottish legs of Pathfinder Railtours' 'The Pathfinder Scot 2' which originated at Swindon and ran to Edinburgh and Glenrothes and return between 14 and 16 August 1992. Following her InterCity work from Inverness depot she was transferred to Motherwell where similar duties occupied her in between freight operations through to the autumn of 1997 when she headed 'The Royal Scotsman' as the luxury train operated by Belmond Management Service toured the Highlands during September. After this she spent time in store for EWS, was put out on contract hire including a time spent in France and was eventually sold for scrap in January 2009.

**37222 (D6922)**
Released by EE Vulcan Foundry as D6922, Works Number EE/VF3408/D866 on 24 January 1964 and allocated to Landore.

Final depot: Toton, 3/94.

Name carried: None.

Status: Cut up at T.J. Thomson's scrapyard, Stockton, 8/08.

**37223 (D6923)**
Released by EE Vulcan Foundry as D6923, Works Number EE/VF3409/D867 on 3 February 1964 and allocated to Landore.

Final depot: Immingham, 12/93.

Name carried: None.

Status: Cut up by Sims Metal UK Ltd, Newport, 3/03.

**37225 (D6925)**
Released by EE Vulcan Foundry as D6925, Works Number EE/VF3411/D869 on 7 February 1964 and allocated to Landore.

Final depot: Doncaster, 4/99.

Name carried: None.

Status: Cut up by C.F. Booth, Rotherham, 6/04.

**37227 (D6927)**
Released by EE Vulcan Foundry as D6927, Works Number EE/VF3413/D871 on 19 February 1964 and allocated to Landore.

Final depot: Doncaster, 11/98.

Name carried: None.

Status: Preserved on the Battlefield Line, owned by HNRC, 4/03; Purchased by Graeme Watkins Railways Ltd, 2/04; moved to Burton-on-Trent, 10/11; Reinstated into traffic at Doncaster, 1/18 as a PODL; Operational on the Chinnor & Princes Risborough Railway from 3/18.

**37229 (D6929)**
Released by EE Vulcan Foundry as D6929, Works Number EE/VF3415/D873 on 28 February 1964 and allocated to Landore.

Final depot: Kingmoor, 7/02.

Names carried: *The Cardiff Rod Mill*, 5/84–10/88; *Jonty Jarvis*, 10/05.

Status: Cut up by C.F. Booth, Rotherham, 9/13.

**37230 (D6930)**
Released by EE Vulcan Foundry as D6930, Works Number EE/VF3416/D874 on 6 March 1964 and allocated to Landore.

Final depot: Doncaster, 1/00.

Name carried: None.

Status: Cut up by C.F. Booth, Rotherham, 1/06.

**37232 (D6932)** (See also 37232 in Class 37s in Colour)
Released by EE Vulcan Foundry as D6932, Works Number EE/VF3418/D876 on 20. March 1964 and allocated to Landore.

Final depot: Motherwell, 3/94.

Name carried: *Institute of Railway Signal Engineers*, 12/90–9/99.

Status: Cut up at Wigan CRDC, 3/00.

**37235 (D6935)**
Released by EE Vulcan Foundry as D6935, Works Number EE/VF3421/D879 on 20 April 1964 and allocated to Landore.

Final depot: Immingham, 12/93.

Name carried: *The Coal Merchants Association of Scotland*, 11/87–3/91.

Status: Bought by I. Riley, Bury, 6/02. Bought by WCRC, Carnforth, 5/04. Cut up at Carnforth, 4/08.

## Locomotive Histories • 49

**37238 (D6938)**
Released by EE Vulcan Foundry as D6938, Works Number EE/VF3424/D882 on 12 June 1964 and allocated to Canton.

Final depot: Toton, 5/07.

Name carried: *Spitfire Mk II*, 1/90–2/91.

Status: Cut up by C.F. Booth, Rotherham, 3/09.

**37240 (D6940)**
Released by EE Vulcan Foundry as D6940, Works Number EE/VF3497/D928 on 25 August 1964 and allocated to Canton.

Final depot: Doncaster, 3/97.

Name carried: *Golden Heart*, 3/03.

Status: Preserved on the Llangollen Railway, 7/02. Bought by HNRC, locos for lease, 8/02: Bought by Boden Rail, Nottingham, 12/18; Doncaster, PODL, 10/23; Moved from Nottingham Eastcroft to Tyseley by road, 12/23.

**37241 (D6941)**
Released by EE Vulcan Foundry as D6941, Works Number EE/VF3498/D929 on 3 September 1964 and allocated to Canton.

Final depot: Doncaster, 3/00.

Name carried: None.

Status: Cut up at T.J. Thomson's scrapyard, Stockton, 9/01.

**37242 (D6942)**
Released by EE Vulcan Foundry as D6942, Works Number EE/VF3499/D930 on 10 September 1964 and allocated to Canton.

Final depot: Doncaster, 12/99.

Name carried: None.

Status: Sent to Wigan CRDC, 12/99; Barrow Hill for preservation, 2/02. Cut up by C.F. Booth, Rotherham, 2/06.

**37244 (D6944)**
Released by EE Vulcan Foundry as D6944, Works Number EE/VF3501/D932 on 24 September 1964 and allocated to Canton.

Final depot: Toton, 11/98.

Name carried: None.

Status: Cut up at Wigan CRDC, 11/01.

**37245 (D6945)**
Released by EE Vulcan Foundry as D6945, Works Number EE/VF3502/D933 on 1 October 1964 and allocated to Canton.

**At the** head of a line of classmates near Healey Mills during 1988 is 37235 *The Coal Merchants Association of Scotland*. (*Rick Ward*)

**Passing Ryecroft** Junction, Walsall on 4 July 1989 is 37240. (*Steve Jones*)

**At Toton** on 25 April 1988 is 37250 (*Rick Ward*)

**At Toton** on 25 April 1988 are classmates 37250 and 37244 (*Rick Ward*)

Final depot: Doncaster, 12/98.

Name carried: None.

Status: Cut up at Wigan CRDC, 9/00.

**37248 (D6948)** (See also 37248 in 37s in Colour)
Released by EE Vulcan Foundry as D6948, Works Number EE/VF3505/D936 on 30 October 1964 and allocated to Canton.

Final depot: Doncaster, 12/03.

Name carried: *Midland Railway Centre*, 10/95.

Status: Preserved at Doncaster, as PODL, 10/05 and moved to GCR (N); Gloucestershire Warwickshire Railway, 10/09; West Somerset Railway, 4/19; Gloucestershire Warwickshire Railway from 7/19.

**37250 (D6950)**
Released by EE Vulcan Foundry as D6950, Works Number EE/VF3507/D938 on 10 December 1964 and allocated to Canton.

Final depot: Toton, 5/07.

Name carried: None.

Status: Preserved. Stored at Warcop, 1/08; Operational and based on the Wensleydale Railway from 11/11. Appeared as a guest loco for the K&WVR Diesel Gala, 20–23 June 2024, in EWS livery, now re-registered for Special Trains Charter as a PODL.

**37251 (D6951)**
Released by EE Vulcan Foundry as D6951, Works Number EE/VF3508/D939 on 30 December 1964 and allocated to Canton.

Final depot: Doncaster, 3/96.

Name carried: *Gladiator*, 11/89–1/90.

Status: Sent to Wigan CRDC, 7/99. Cut up by Type 3 Traction at C.F. Booth, Rotherham, 9/01.

**37252 (D6952)**
Released by EE Vulcan Foundry as D6952, Works Number EE/VF3509/D940 on 7 January 1965 and allocated to Canton. Final depot: Immingham, 3/94.

Name carried: None.

Status: Cut up by HNRC, Doncaster, 8/02.

Notable movements:
Her early years mainly as a freight loco working from a whole string of depots in the north and east of England took a turn towards more varied duties in the years after her transfer to Immingham in 1974 when she began to be called upon to head passenger services.

# Locomotive Histories • 51

On 4 November 1978 she joined classmate 37024 to head Railway Pictorial Publication Railtours' 'The Lincolnshire Coaster', a charter from London Paddington to Cleethorpes by way of Doncaster and return. On 13 October 1979 she was on charter duty again for the same operator, this time with 37221 for 'The Hull Hornet', described earlier. Passenger work then dominated through the 1980s, though in March 1982 she was required to act as banker on the Lickey Incline and on 5 June 1983 she was on display at Coalville Open Day in Leicestershire.

Her transfer to Thornaby in 1986 saw her occupied with services between Edinburgh and Dundee for a short while that year before her move to Tinsley resulted in more passenger turns amongst her freight workings, which continued after her subsequent transfers to Immingham, Stratford and back to Tinsley in 1989. For a time in 1991 she was occupied with services in East Anglia and on Freightliner trains on the ECML, but her transfer to Inverness to join InterCity in May 1992 saw her in full-time work with services between London Euston and Aberdeen or Inverness, being responsible for the Scottish sections north from Edinburgh. This continued until September of that year when she was transferred south again to be reacquainted with freight movements for Trainload Freight North between periods in store pending withdrawal and scrapping at Doncaster.

### 37253 (D6953, 37699)

Released by EE Vulcan Foundry as D6953, Works Number EE/VF3510/D941 on 5 January 1965 and allocated to Canton.

Final depot: Immingham, 4/94.

Name carried: None.

Status: Cut up by M.R.J. Phillips, Crewe Adtranz, 8/97.

### 37254 (D6954)

Released by EE Vulcan Foundry as D6954, Works Number EE/VF3511/D942 on 5 January 1965 and allocated to Canton.

Final depot: Canton, 11/73.

Names carried: *Driver Robin Prince MBE*, 2/09; *Cardiff Canton*, 4/17.

Status: Preserved at Sellindge Railway Works, 5/03; Spa Valley Railway, 3/08; Barrow Hill, 11/15. Reinstated into traffic at Doncaster, 3/16 and allocated to Colas Rail Freight. Operational on main line charters from 4/17.

**At Barnetby** on 24 August 1982 37252 and 37221 are heading eastwards.

**Nameplate of** 37254.

**At Taunton** with a NR 'ultrasonic' train on 20 February 2019 is 37254. (*Geoff Sheppard*)

**37255 (D6955)** (See also 37255 in Class 37s in Colour)
Released by EE Vulcan Foundry as D6955, Works Number EE/VF3512/D943 on 6 January 1965 and allocated to Canton.

Final depot: Doncaster, 12/99.

Name carried: None.

Status: Sent to Wigan CRDC, 12/99. Preserved by Fragonset Railways on the GCR, Loughborough, 10/02; Nemesis Rail, 3/07; Barrow Hill, 7/07 then back to GCR, Loughborough; Moved to Nemesis Rail, Burton Wagon Shops, 1/16.

**37259 (D6959, 37380, 37259)**
Released by EE Vulcan Foundry as D6959, Works Number EE/VF3519/D948 on 13 January 1965 and allocated to Darnall.

Final depot: Kingmoor, 9/02.

Name carried: None.

Status: In store for HNRC, Barrow Hill from 8/22.

Notable movements:
Workings during her early years mainly involved movements of oil and other freight from the traction maintenance depot at Ripple Lane. This work continued into the early 1980s alongside passenger services out of London Liverpool Street. Her transfer to Healey Mills in 1983 saw her become more involved with Class 1 duties in the north of England and on 11 May 1985 she was one of several locos involved in the three-day railtour by F+W Railtours, 'The Skirl o' the Pipes 6', which originated at Plymouth the day before and ran by way of Bristol and Derby to Newcastle and Millerhill, Edinburgh. She and classmate 37121 had charge between Newcastle and Millerhill. On 8 November 1986 she assisted the Hertfordshire Railtours charter 'The Eden Serpent' in the Carlisle area, the tour having started at Clapham Junction and run to Carlisle via Birmingham, Blackburn and the S&C, returning by way of the WCML. Passenger work continued to play a major part in her schedule throughout the remaining years of the 1980s whilst working in the Midlands and in Scotland though freight duties also kept her busy into the 1990s. In June 2004 she was a guest on the K&WVR together with 37670 and during September 2006 appeared on the Mid-Norfolk Railway.

Her transfer to DRS Nuclear Traffic from January 2007 saw her involved with such trains on the Cumbrian Coast Line as well as being called upon again for charter work. On 28 November 2009 she and 37609 headed Spitfire Railtours' 'The Yuletide York/The Geordie Growler' tour which ran from Birmingham International to Huddersfield, York and Newcastle, returning by way of Sheffield and Guide Bridge after York. This was followed on 26 June 2010 by another for Spitfire Railtours' 'The Kernow Explorer', Gloucester to Penzance and return with 37218 throughout and later that year on 31 July Spitfire Railtours again with 'The Cumbrian Crusader III', from Birmingham International to Sheffield then over the S&C to Carlisle, the Tyne Valley Line to Newcastle and the ECML to York and Doncaster before the return to Birmingham.

Now becoming increasingly sought after for such work, on 13 May 2012 she took an Eastleigh to Edinburgh 'special', 1Z77 with 37602, then on 31 August that year had charge of Pathfinder Railtours'

*Near Dalston on 21 January 2017 37259 with 37612 take a nuclear flask train, 6K73 Sellafield to Crewe Coal Sidings, on the Cumbrian Coast Line. 37259 would later be renumbered to 37380 and then back to 37259 as not modified. (Jonathan Allen)*

'The Dartmouth Flyer', Tame Bridge Parkway to Kingswear and return, with 37612 throughout. On 12 January 2013 she was in action again for Pathfinder Railtours, this one from Crewe to Acton Canal Wharfe, Wolverton and return, 'The Enigmatic Logistician', accompanied by 37425 and 37611. Another 'special' on 21 June 2013 saw her helping with 37608 on sections of 1Z53 and 1Z55, Bangor to Barrow-in-Furness via Carlisle and then Barrow to Fort William. Later that year on 17 August she was on show at the DRS Open Day at Carlisle Kingmoor depot and her charter duty continued into 2014 when on 11 April she and classmates 37409 and 37425 were entrusted with The Settle-Carlisle Railway Development Company's 'The S&C 25th Anniversary Express', Leeds to Carlisle and return celebrating twenty-five years since the famous line was saved from closure. On 25 April 2014 she featured with 37423 on 1Z50/1Z51 Crewe to Kyle of Lochalsh and return and then followed a period when 'normal service' was resumed, as she worked local passenger services between Carlisle, Barrow-in-Furness and Preston over the Cumbrian Coast Line.

In 2017 she was recalled to charter duty for Pathfinder Railtours, with the four-day 'The Spring Highlander' which departed Eastleigh on 14 April and visited Inverness, Aberdeen and Kyle of Lochalsh, the work being shared with 37605 and 37609 throughout. On 22 July 2017 she was on show again at Carlisle Kingmoor Open Day then working for Pathfinder Railtours again in 2018, first with 'The Pennine Pathfinder' on 17 February in the company of 37069 for the charter which originated at Gloucester and ran to Carlisle. A four-day trip for Pathfinder Railtours followed from 30 March with 'The Easter Chieftain', Cardiff to Birmingham, York, Edinburgh and on to Inverness, Elgin and Inverurie then Kyle of Lochalsh and return which she took throughout with 37605. Finally on 26 May 2018 for Retro Railtours' 'The Retro Bath Centurion and Retro Salisbury Cathedral Belle' when she was paired with 37069 again for the tour from Huddersfield to Crewe, Salisbury and return. Another Open Day appearance followed on 21 July 2018 when she was on show at Crewe Gresty Bridge before being committed into store by DRS in March 2022, only to be saved as operational by LSL for use on Rail Head Treatment Trains and then transferred to HNRC and stored at Barrow Hill.

### 37260 (D6960)

Released by EE Vulcan Foundry as D6960, Works Number EE/VF3520/D949 on 15 January 1965 and allocated to Darnall.

Final depot: Inverness, 5/82.

Name carried: *Radio Highland*, 7/84–8/89.

Status: Cut up at MC Metals, Glasgow, 8/91.

### 37261 (D6961)

See also 6961 in Class 37s in Colour
Released by EE Vulcan Foundry as D6961, Works Number EE/VF3521/D950 on 20 January 1965 and allocated to Darnall.

Final depot: Kingmoor, 11/05.

Name carried: *Caithness*, 6/85–8/99.

Status: Bought by WCRC, Carnforth, 5/04; Transferred to DRS Kingmoor, 11/05; Transferred to Bo'ness & Kinneil Railway, operational from 2/17. Undergoing restoration, 5/24, receiving parts from 'spares donor' 37214.

**At Crewe** Works on 12 March 1988 is 37261 *Caithness*. (*Rick Ward*)

**Nameplate of** 37260.

**Nameplate of** 37261.

**37262 (D6962)**
Released by EE Vulcan Foundry as D6962, Works Number EE/VF3522/D951 on 22 January 1965 and allocated to Darnall.

Final depot: Doncaster, 12/99.

Name carried: *Dounreay*, 6/85.

Status: Cut up by Sims Metal UK Ltd. Newport, 2/04.

**Nameplate of** 37262.

**37263 (D6963)**
Released by EE Vulcan Foundry as D6963, Works Number EE/VF3523/D952 on 27 January 1965 and allocated to Darnall.

Final depot: Doncaster, 12/89.

Name carried: None.

Status: Preserved by the Class 37 Preservation Group, 12/03; Operational on the SVR from 5/23.

**37264 (D6964)** (See also 37264 in Class 37s in Colour)
Released by EE Vulcan Foundry as D6964, Works Number EE/VF3524/D953 on 29 January 1965 and allocated to Darnall.

Final depot: Toton, 11/98.

Name carried: None.

Status: Sold to a private buyer, 12/01 and moved to Tyseley to join the Deltic 9000 Locomotive Ltd. fleet; Operational on the NYMR from 9/10, repainted into BR Standard Blue livery (from BR Large Logo) while undergoing an overhaul at Grosmont in March 2024. Operational for their Diesel Gala held from 14 to 16 June 2024 along with 'guest' locos including 37418 *An Comunn Gaidhealach*.

**37271 (D6603, 37303, 37271, 37333)**
Released by EE Vulcan Foundry as D6603, Works Number EE/VF2563/D992 on 16 September 1965 and allocated to Landore.

Final depot: Immingham, 6/93.

Name carried: None.

**At Doncaster** on 25 April 1988 is 37264 (*Rick Ward*)

Locomotive Histories • 55

Status: Cut up at Crewe Adtranz, 8/97. Even though finally carrying a sub-class 37/3 number she remained unmodified and therefore stayed in sub-class 37/0.

### 37272 (D6604, 37304, 37272, 37334)
(See also 37272 in Class 37s in Colour)
Released by EE Vulcan Foundry as D6604, Works Number EE/VF3564/D993 on 22 September 1965 and allocated to Landore.

Final depot: Barrow Hill, 2/05.

Name carried: None.

Status: Cut up by C.F. Booth, Rotherham, 8/05.

### 37273 (D6606, 37306, 37273)
Released by EE Vulcan Foundry as D6606, Works Number EE/VF3566/D995 on 11 October 1965 and allocated to Canton.

Final depot: Canton, 2/86.

Name carried: None

Status: Cut up by Gwent Demolition at Canton, 5/93.

### 37275 (D6975)
Released by EE Vulcan Foundry as D6975, Works Number EE/VF3535/D964 on 9 April 1965 and allocated to Canton.

Final depot: Doncaster, 8/99.

Names carried: *Stainless Pioneer*, 12/88–5/92; *Oor Wullie*, 10/93.

Status: Bought by BREL for preservation, 6/04; Wensleydale Railway, 7/04; Weardale Railway, 8/06; Barrow Hill, 9/07; Moved to Doncaster as a PODL, 5/08; Swanage Railway, 5/08; Mid Norfolk Railway, 9/10; NVR, 10/10; GCR, 5/11; ELR, 7/12; Bo'ness & Kinneil Railway, 7/12; ELR, 8/12; NYMR, 9/12; South Devon Railway, 8/14; Dartmouth Steam Railway from 10/18.

**Above left**: **At Grosmont** on the NYMR, 37264 prepares to depart for Pickering on 9 May 2015. (*Rick Ward*)

**Above right**: **Passing Moorgates** near Goathland on the NYMR with a short freight on 10 October 2022 is 37264.

**At Doncaster** during 1989 is 37275 *Stainless Pioneer* with 37351 behind. (*Rick Ward*)

**37278 (D6978)** (See also 37278 in Class 37s in Colour)
Released by EE Vulcan Foundry as D6978, Works Number EE/VF3538/D967 on 23 April 1965 and allocated to Canton.

Final depot: Toton, 1/94.

Name carried: None.

Status: Cut up at T.J. Thomson's scrapyard, Stockton, 5/03.

**37280 (D6980)**
Released by EE Vulcan Foundry as D6980, Works Number EE/VF3540/D969 on 6 May 1965 and allocated to Canton.

Final depot: Stratford, 1/94.

Name carried: None.

Status: Cut up by M.R.J. Phillips, Old Oak Common, 4/97.

**37293 (D6993)** (See also D6993 in Pre-TOPS Days)

**37294 (D6994)**
Released by EE Vulcan Foundry as D6994, Works Number EE/VF3554/D983 on 8 July 1965 and allocated to Canton.

Final depot: Toton, 5/07.

Name carried: None.

Status: Preserved and operational on the Embsay & Bolton Abbey Railway from 3/09.

**37298 (D6998)**
Released by EE Vulcan Foundry as D6998, Works Number EE/VF3558/D987 on 12 August 1965 and allocated to Canton.

Final depot: Doncaster, 10/00.

Name carried: *Victor*, 12/89–5/91.

Status: Sent to Wigan CRDC, 10/00. Cut up by C.F. Booth, Rotherham, 2/06.

**37308 (D6608, 37274)** (See also 37308 in Class 37s in Colour)
Released by EE Vulcan Foundry as D6608, Works Number EE/VF3568/D997 on 9 November 1965 and allocated to Landore.

Final depot: Toton, 5/07.

Name carried: None.

Status: Preserved at Kidderminster as a PODL, 11/07; Old Oak Common ('The Factory'), 11/07; Knight's Rail, Eastleigh, 4/09; Canton (Pullman Workshops), 6/09; RVEL, Derby, 3/12; Dean Forest Railway, 5/12; Operational on the SVR from 7/20.

**Sub-class 37/3**
After giving stalwart service for well over twenty years, a decision was necessary on their future. Rather than replacement, the fleet was chosen for the kind of major refurbishment which would prolong the life of the locomotives perhaps beyond the turn of the century. From 1988, Crewe Works and others would be busy with the major upgrades which would create a series of sub-classes intended to equip them for the increasing demands about to be placed upon them. The plan as envisaged would see all locos enhanced with strengthened couplings and increased braking capability in preparation for working heavy freight trains with many also being re-bogied and re-geared to permit faster working speeds to be achieved with the heavier loads.
Redundant train heating equipment was removed to allow fuel capacity to be doubled. Some would also receive new engines and traction motors. Although it had been intended to refurbish the entire class, in 1988 it was decided to curtail the programme after 135 locos had been dealt with. A number of re-geared bogies were thus left un-used which were fitted to the next tranche of locos, creating sub-class 37/3. They were numbered from 37330 to 37384, though a number of intended sub-class 37/3 locomotives were not modified and subsequently renumbered back again to 37/0 between October 1988 and June 1992 (apart from 37380 which had to wait until September 2002).
These included:

37310 (D6852) back to 37152
37311 (D6856) back to 37156
37312 (D6837) back to 37137
37314 (D6890) back to 37190
37320 (D6726) back to 37026
37321 (D6737) back to 37037
37323 (D6788) back to 37088
37324 (D6799) back to 37099
37325 (D6808) back to 37108
37326 (D6811) back to 37111
37352 (D6708) back to 37008
37353 (D6732) back to 37032
37354 (D6743) back to 37043
37355 (D6745) back to 37045
37356 (D6768) back to 37068
37357 (D6779) back to 37079
37374 (D6865) back to 37165
37380 (D6959) back to 37259.

**37330 (D6828, 37128)**
Released by EE RSH as D6828, Works Number EE/RSH3273/8388 on 7 March 1963 and allocated to Canton.

Final depot: Doncaster, 3/97.

Name carried: None.

### Table 2. Locos numbered as sub-class 37/3.

**37/3**

| | | | |
|---|---|---|---|
| D6828: 37330 | D6715: 37341 | D6818: 37359 | D6899: 37376 |
| D6902: 37331 | D6749: 37343 | D6703: 37360 | D6900: 37377 |
| D6939: 37332 | D6753: 37344 | D6827: 37370 | D6904: 37378 |
| D6603: 37333 | D6801: 37345 | D6847: 37371 | D6926: 37379 |
| D6604: 37334 | D6700: 37350 | D6859: 37372 | D6984: 37381 |
| D6985: 37335 | D6702: 37351 | D6860: 37373 | D6845: 37382 |
| D6709: 37340 | D6791: 37358 | D6893: 37375 | D6867: 37383 |
| | | | D6958: 37384 |

NB. 37333 (previously 37303) and 37334 (37304) remained in sub-class 37/0 as never modified, even though renumbered.

Status: Cut up at T.J. Thomson's scrapyard, Stockton, 11/01.

**37331 (D6902, 37202)** (See also 37331 in Class 37s in Colour) Released by EE Vulcan Foundry as D6902, Works Number EE/VF3380/D846 on 23 October 1963 and allocated to Canton.

Final depot: Immingham, 8/94.

Name carried: None.

Status: Cut up by HNRC, Barrow Hill, 8/03.

Notable movements:
Very much in the mantle of a mixed traffic loco she spent her first years both in South Wales and in the North East hauling freight and the occasional passenger service. Her move to Immingham resulted in a change of emphasis, with passenger work becoming gradually more frequent and by the early 1980s she was heading Class 1 services to Newcastle and King's Cross as well as local passenger trains in Lincolnshire, Nottinghamshire and East Anglia. On 20 August 1985 she was in charge of 1Z97, a York to Derby Relief and on 26 October 1991 was in charter action for Pathfinder Railtours with 'The Brush Refiner'. Starting at Swindon it ran to Birmingham then north to Barnetby, on to Immingham, Cleethorpes and return. She and classmate 37285 had the section from after Barnetby to Cleethorpes. On 5 September 1993 she was involved along with 37504 and other locos in the Worksop Open Day Committee 'Trainload Coal Motive Power Day', Worksop Open Day Shuttles, a series of six return 'specials' from Sheffield to Cottam and West Burton Power Stations by way of Worksop, immediately after which she took their train from Sheffield to Liverpool Lime Street, again with 37504. Her usual freight duties were then resumed out of Thornaby and then Immingham depots until being put into store in March 1995 and eventually scrapped at Barrow Hill after component recovery.

**37332 (D6939, 37239)**
Released by EE Vulcan Foundry as D 6939, Works Number EE/VF3496/D927 on 21 August 1964 and allocated to Canton.

Final depot: Doncaster, 12/98.

Names carried: *The Coal Merchants Association of Scotland*, 3/91–9/94; renamed *The Coal Merchants Association of Scotland*, 2/96–1/00.

Status: Cut up by HNRC at Old Oak Common, 6/00.

**37335 (D6985, 37285)**
Released by EE Vulcan Foundry as D6985, Works Number EE/VF3545/D974 on 31 May 1965 and allocated to Canton.

Final depot: Immingham, 8/94.

Name carried: None.

Status: Cut up by Raxstar at Immingham, 5/00.

**37340 (D6709, 37009)**
Released by EE Vulcan Foundry as D6709, Works Number EE/VF2872/D588 on 17 February 1961 and allocated to Stratford.

Final depot: Doncaster, 11/01.

Name carried: None.

Status: Preserved on the Churnet Valley Railway, 5/03; Moved to the Nottingham Transport Heritage Centre, 6/07.

**37341 (D6715, 37015)**
Released by EE Vulcan Foundry as D6715, Works Number EE/VF2878/D594 on 19 May 1961 and allocated to Stratford.

Final depot: Thornaby, 3/94.

Name carried: None.

Status: Cut up by C.F. Booth, Rotherham, 2/03.

**37343 (D6749, 37049, 37222, 37049)**
Released by EE Vulcan Foundry as D6749, Works Number EE/VF3041/D703 on 17 August 1962 and allocated to Darnall.

Final depot: Immingham, 7/91.

Name carried: *Imperial*, 7/86.

Status: Cut up by HNRC at Toton, 12/03.

**37344 (D6753, 37053)**
Released by EE Vulcan Foundry as D6753, Works Number EE/VF3045/D707 on 14 September 1962 and allocated to Darnall.

Final depot: Barrow Hill, 2/05.

Name carried: None.

Status: Cut up by C.F. Booth, Rotherham, 3/06.

**37345 (D6801, 37101)** (See 37101 in sub-class 37/0)
Released by EE Vulcan Foundry as D6801, Works Number EE/VF3230/D755 on 28 December 1962 and allocated to Darnall.

Final depot: Immingham, 12/93.

Name carried: None.

Status: Cut up by HNRC at Immingham, 8/03.

**37350 (D6700, 37119)** (See also D6700 and 37350 in Class 37s in Colour)
Released from EE Vulcan Foundry as D6700, Works Number EE/VF2863/D579 on 2 December 1960 and allocated to Stratford.

Final depot: Doncaster, 12/99.

Name carried: *NRM National Railway Museum*, 11/98.

Status: Preserved as part of the National Collection.

Notable movements:
Her celebrity status as Class Leader has ensured an impressive and varied career, from her early days in the 1960s working passenger services out of Liverpool Street station, surviving in green (without the yellow end panels) only until June 1969 when she was painted into Standard Blue livery, then transferring to Thornaby in 1971 to be seen regularly in the Darlington and York areas. She was renumbered to 37119 in February 1974 and later to 37350 in March 1988 during her Last Classified Repair at Crewe after which she transferred back to her original home of Stratford where she was later rebuilt and repainted into original green livery as D6700.

Though passenger duties were to continue she was to be increasingly sought after to attend events such as The Newport Rail-Fair in June 1988, Open Days at Gloucester, Coalville and Hereford and to haul rail-tours such as 'The Coalville Cobbler' (Euston to Coalville, 5 June 1988), 'The Tynesider' railtour (Reading to Newcastle, 10 September 1988) and 'The Power to the Tower' (Sheffield to Blackpool, 1 May 1989). Transferring to Cardiff Canton in November 1988 and then to Immingham in March 1993 freight work for EWS occupied the 1990s but after being named *National Railway Museum* at the NRM on 11 November 1998 she was increasingly in demand as a guest on heritage railways.

An appearance at the ELR in July 2002 was followed by an unfortunate collision with 37515

**At Crewe** during 1988 Is 37101, which was later modified and renumbered to 37345 in September 1994. (*Rick Ward*)

whilst at Barrow Hill on 5 October 2003, which required a visit to Derby for repairs. She was then registered by Network Rail as a PODL. She spent time on the NYMR between April 2007 and September 2009, then after an appearance at the NRM during October 2010 she went on to the K&WVR in May 2011, the NVR in September 2012, the Wensleydale Railway in June 2013, the Mid Norfolk Railway in September 2013, the SVR in October 2013, the Swanage Railway in May 2014, then back to the NRM during September and October 2014 before the Mid Hants Railway in October 2017 and finally to the GCR at Loughborough from March 2022 where she is on long term loan following an agreement between the NRM and the Heavy Tractor Group, a small group of volunteers who also look after sister loco number 37714 on the GCR.

### 37351 (D6702, 37002)

Released by EE Vulcan Foundry as D6702, Works Number EE/VF2865/D581 on 19 December 1960 and allocated to Stratford. Final depot: Doncaster, 12/99.

Name carried: None.

Status: Cut up at T.J. Thomson's scrapyard, Stockton, 11/07.

Notable movements:
While at Stratford Depot she was employed on passenger services out of London Liverpool Street to Cambridge and East Anglia, and when moved to Yorkshire from 1967 this type of work continued both around York and south through the Midlands to Cardiff and as far as St Pancras. From the mid-1970s heavy freight duties became more regular, often taken in tandem with a classmate, a pattern which would continue interspersed with passenger services until her move to Scotland in the early 1990s when passenger work dominated again for a time, working between Edinburgh and Aberdeen or Inverness with trains originating at London Euston. This lasted until 1996. On 28 June 1997 she was involved with Pathfinder Railtours' 'The Minehead Mariner', a tour from York to Minehead of which she had charge between York and Derby and return and on 13 September that year she featured at the head of 'The Royal Scotsman' from Gartshore near Glasgow to Edinburgh.

Her move back to England in 1998 saw her responsible for passenger trains between Manchester and Birmingham as well as services in the South West to Bristol, Exeter and Plymouth. During September 1999 she was a guest on the heritage ELR and completed that year with Rail Head Treatment Train workings in the Selby area of North Yorkshire, 'top and tail' with 37216 followed by a transfer into store at EWS Headquarters, Doncaster in December. She was later moved back to Toton in May 2007 and withdrawn from stock, being cut up during November of that year.

### 37358 (D6791, 37091)

Released by EE RSH as D6791, Works Number EE/RSH3218/8337 on 31 January 1963 and allocated to Gateshead,

Final depot: Doncaster, 3/97.

Name carried: *P&O Containers*, 4/88–1/94.

Status: Cut up at T.J. Thomson's scrapyard, Stockton, 5/07.

### 37359 (D6818, 37118)

Released by EE Vulcan Foundry as D6818, Works Number EE/

**At Crewe** Works during 1988 Is 37002, later to be modified and renumbered to 37351 in May 1989. (*Rick Ward*)

VF3247/D772 on 15 March 1963 and allocated to Darnall.

Final depot: Thornaby, 5/94.

Name carried: None.

Status: Cut up by HNRC, Carnforth, 1/05.

**37360 (D6703, 37003)** (See 37003 in sub-class 37/0 and in Class 37s in Colour)

**37370 (D6827, 37127)**
Released by EE RSH as D6827, Works Number EE/RSH3272/8387 on 28 May 1963 and allocated to Canton.

Final depot: Toton, 11/98.

Name carried: None.

Status: Cut up by C.F. Booth, Rotherham, 9/05.

**37371 (D6847, 37147)**
Released by EE Vulcan Foundry as D6847, Works Number EE/VF3322/D821 on 13 June 1963 and allocated to Canton.

Final depot: Doncaster, 11/99.

Name carried: None.

Status: Cut up at Wigan CRDC, 6/01.

**37372 (D6859, 37159)** (See also 37372 in Class 37s in Colour)
Released by EE RSH as D6859, Works Number EE/RSH3337/8390 on 26 June 1963 and allocated to Canton.

Final depot: Toton, 5/07.

Name carried: None.

Status: Bought by HNRC for spare parts, 12/07; Bought by the Baby Deltic Project (BDP), Barrow Hill, 2/09 for conversion into a 'new build' 'Baby Deltic' to be numbered 5910.

Notable movements:
True to her design brief she was a typical 'mixed traffic' loco from the beginning. She worked freights in South Wales and around southern Scotland in the 1960s and early 1970s, took passenger services in the Bristol and in the Birmingham area and also between Crewe and Cardiff and was a regular sight banking with a classmate on the Lickey Incline into the early 1980s. On 19 June 1983 she had charge of the BR Day Excursion 1Z15 between Taunton and Skegness and return, then on 5 August 1984 she and classmate 37224 took 1Z38, the charter from Gloucester to Skegness and return. Similarly on 11 August that year she headed 1Z83, a charter from Bristol Temple Meads to Gloucester between Bristol and Wolverhampton. Throughout the remainder of the 1980s she was occupied with passenger services in the south west and from there and South Wales to the Midlands, though by 1990 she was being called upon once more to help expresses up the Lickey Incline.

During the early years of the 1990s she had regular charge of Class 1 services in the south and south west of England and to Birmingham New Street. On 27 April 1996 she was in charter action again with Hertfordshire Rail Tours' 'The Tinsley Humper & The Pennine Perambulator', a tour from King's Cross to Sheffield and return, including a 'mini-tour' around Manchester. A charter for VSOE occurred on 2 May 1997

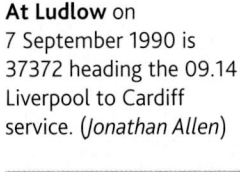

**At Ludlow** on 7 September 1990 is 37372 heading the 09.14 Liverpool to Cardiff service. (*Jonathan Allen*)

from London Victoria to Margate and return followed by further passenger services between the Midlands and Manchester in August of that year after which she was allocated to EWS at Eastleigh. Her next charter outing was on 11 September 1999 for Pathfinder Railtours' 'The Rotating Cleric' which ran from Birmingham International to Preston, before going on to York, Newcastle then back to York and Birmingham.

She then continued with routine workings until 8 June 2002 when she was part of an 'all-37' charter from Crewe to Portbury Docks in Somerset and return, 'The (Post) Festive Freighter), again for Pathfinder Railtours. The other locos involved were 37042, 37670 and 37798. On 27 July 2002 she found herself in the company of steam loco 6024 *King Edward I* for Daylight Railtours' '6024 to Minehead' from Alton to Minehead, including the West Somerset Railway, and return. She then worked Class 1 services out of London Victoria to Southampton and Folkestone until September 2003 when she was transferred to Crewe Diesel depot. Before that though she had charge of sections of the Past Time Rail charter 'The Cambrian Growler', Milton Keynes to Aberystwyth and return. Another 'all-37' tour, this time in the company of 37042 (again), 37114 and 37248. She and 37248 took the opening and closing legs, between Milton Keynes and Bescot Goods Loops.

Her transfer to Crewe led to her involvement in Hertfordshire Rail Tours' 'The Lounge Lizard', a tour which originated at London King's Cross and ran to Deepcar in South Yorkshire by way of Derby outwards and Tinsley and Doncaster on the return to King's Cross. Her allocation to EWS Strategic Reserve in August 2004 led to a busy time taking trains between Knaresborough, Leeds and over the S&C to Carlisle, always in the company of classmate 37408. By the end of September 2004 though she was in the 'Sandite Reserve' pool and by February 2006 was in store at Toton. By mid-May 2007 she had been sold by EWS and officially withdrawn from stock.

Bought by HNRC in December 2007 and then by the BDP, her reincarnation was to begin as the starting point for recreating a Class 23 'Baby Deltic' to be numbered 5910. Work began in 2011 and involved shortening the underframe at the centre and at both ends, replacing the roof and superstructure above the frame and marrying this with Class 20 bogies, traction motors and all the associated auxiliary components. The work is ongoing and at March 2024 no date for its completion was available from the BDP, though the *Railway Magazine* of April 2024 stated that the team at Barrow Hill is preparing for the final stages of the project.

**37373 (D6860, 37160)**
Released by EE RSH as D6860, Works Number EE/RSH3338/8391 on 5 July 1963 and allocated to Canton.

Final depot: Stratford, 6/93.

Name carried: *Lightning*, 12/92–12/93.

Status: Cut up by M.R.J. Phillips, Old Oak Common, 7/97.

**37374 (D6865, 37165)**
Released by EE RSH as D6865, Works Number EE/RSH3343/8396 on 29 August 1963 and allocated to Landore.

Final depot: Doncaster, 12/99.

Name carried: None.

Status: Cut up at WCRC, Carnforth, 5/22.

**37375 (D6893, 37193)**
Released by EE RSH as D6893, Works Number EE/RSH3371/8414 on 20 February 1964 and allocated to Landore.

Final depot: Toton, 5/07.

Name carried: None.

Status: Cut up at EMR Kingsbury, 1/08.

Notable movements:
Her duties during her early years both in South Wales and in Yorkshire consisted of freight workings of coal, oil and general goods but by the mid-1970s passenger work was becoming a more major part of her schedule. Whilst based at Thornaby from 1970 her first ten years saw her largely confined to Yorkshire and the North East but by the end of the decade she was being employed further afield including cross-country passenger services to Cardiff, to the south coast or trains to East Anglia. Though freight still played a major role in her duties into the 1980s she was entrusted with more Class 1 and Class 2 workings including services out of Peterborough and even as far south as London Liverpool Street and Bristol Temple Meads or north to Edinburgh.

**Leaving York** and passing Holgate in 1988 is 37193, later to be modified and renumbered to 37375 in September of that year. (*Rick Ward*)

Her move north to Eastfield in 1989, now renumbered to 37375, involved her in power station coal traffic as well as passenger work such as a golf 'extra' from Glasgow to Ayr followed by a service to Carlisle and back to Ayr, all on 4 August 1990. Her short stay at Motherwell depot between May 1992 and January 1993 saw her once more allocated to coal distribution duty but with her move to Eastleigh later that month came more prestigious workings. The first on 19 June 1993 for The Branch Line Society, 'The Hampshire & Sussex Explorer' involved her in several stages of a tour from London Euston to Southampton and eventually back to London Victoria. On 5 March 1994 she was employed on charter duty in the Southampton area again with Pathfinder Railtours' 'The Hampshire Hog', originating at Manchester Piccadilly then to Southampton Docks by way of Crewe and Eastleigh before returning to Manchester. On 9 October she had been a guest at Yeovil Junction Open Day but when that concluded she was called upon to assist with Pathfinder Railtours' 'The Dorset Docker', a tour from Wolverhampton to Newport, Yeovil, Westbury, Bristol Parkway and return to Wolverhampton, a tour loco having failed.

In 1997, now based at Stewarts Lane but having been stabled at Bescot she was again in charter action for the start of a three-day tour by A1A Charters/Pathfinder Railtours, 'The Pirates of Penzance', when with 31450 she headed the initial section from Preston to Swindon on 16 May. The tour continued to Bristol, Penzance, St Ives and Par before returning to Preston. The following day, 17 May 1997 she had charge of a 'footex' service, 1Z46 from Wembley to Middlesbrough between Rugby and Crewe, again with 31450. Brief moves to Eastleigh again and then to Toton followed, then on 5 May 1999 she was one of four of her class involved with Pathfinder Railtours' 'The Syphon Symphony' the others being 37071, 37154 and 37178. It ran from Finsbury Park to London Victoria then on to Brighton and Hastings and return.

Following this she was again stabled at Bescot from where she had charge of Class 1 services out of the Midlands during the remainder of 1999. Following her transfers with EWS to Crewe and to Old Oak Common in 2000 and 2001 respectively she then headed Pathfinder Railtours' 'Lincoln Excursion', Swindon to Lincoln and return on 7 December 2002 with classmate 37248 throughout. Her transfer back to Crewe Diesel depot in September 2003 was followed by her involvement with Pathfinder Railtours' 'The Metallic Maiden', a charter from Newport to Peterborough and return. In January 2004 she was placed on Tactical Reserve for EWS and transferred to Toton in May 2007 with a view to disposal. She was withdrawn from stock in December of that year and scrapped soon afterwards.

**37376 (D6899, 37199)**
Released by EE Vulcan Foundry as D6899, Works Number EE/VF3377/D843 on 10 October 1963 and allocated to Canton.

Final depot: Doncaster, 6/99; France, 8/99–10/00.

Name carried: None.

Status: Wigan CRDC, 10/00; Cut up by C.F. Booth, Rotherham, 2/06.

## Locomotive Histories • 63

**37377 (D6900, 37200)**
Released by EE Vulcan Foundry as D6900, Works Number EE/VF3378/D844 on 15 October 1963 and allocated to Canton.

Final depot: Toton, 5/07.

Name carried: None.

Status: Cut up by C.F. Booth, Rotherham, 10/09; Cab preserved and restored as 37200, Poulton-le-Fylde, 10/09.

**37378 (D6904, 37204)**
Released by EE Vulcan Foundry as D6904 Works Number EE/VF3382/D848 on 5 November 1963 and allocated to Canton.

Final depot: Immingham, 1/95.

Name carried: None.

Status: Cut up by C.F. Booth, Rotherham, 6/96.

**37379 (D6926, 37226)**
Released by EE Vulcan Foundry as D6926, Works Number EE/VF3412/D870 on 14 February 1964 and allocated to Landore.

Final depot: Toton, 5/07.

Name carried: *Ipswich WRD Quality Approved*, 2/94.

Status: Cut up by C.F. Booth, Rotherham, 1/08.

**37381 (D6984, 37284)**
Released by EE Vulcan Foundry as D6984, Works Number EE/VF3544/D973 on 21 May 1965 and allocated to Canton.

Final depot: Immingham, 10/93.

Name carried: None.

Status: Cut up by Raxstar at Frodingham mpd, 5/00.

**37382 (D6845, 37145, 37313)**
Released by EE Vulcan Foundry as D6845, Works Number EE/VF3320/D819 on 29 May 1963 and allocated to Canton.

Final depot: Immingham, 6/92.

Name carried: None.

Status: Cut up by Raxstar at Immingham, 4/00.

**37383 (D6867, 37167)**
Released by EE RSH as D6867, Works Number EE/RSH3345/8398 on 16 September 1963 and allocated to Canton.

Final depot: Toton, 11/98.

Name carried: None.

Status: Cut up at Crewe LNWR, 1/08.

**37384 (D6958, 37258)**
Released by EE Vulcan Foundry as D6958, Works Number EE/VF3515/D946 on 15 January 1965 and allocated to Canton.

Final depot: Doncaster, 12/99.

Name carried: None.

Status: Cut up at EMR, Kingsbury, 11/05.

Notable movements:
After several years working freight trains, mainly coal, in South Wales until the late 1970s she began to be allocated passenger duties, an early one being a charter for F+W Railtours, 'The Sussex Downsman', which ran on 14 May 1978 from Worcester to Gloucester, Bristol, Brighton and return, where she and classmate 37247 had charge from Worcester to Bristol and return, the middle section, Bristol to Brighton and return being taken by 37234 and 37294. From that time passenger and freight occupied her schedule in equal measure until a period as Lickey Banker with 37279 in 1981 was followed by a charter from Bristol to Gloucester via Cardiff on 2 June 1982.

**Stabled at** York mpd on 13 July 1985 is 37258, later to be modified and renumbered to 37384 during October 1998. (*Rick Ward*)

**Entering Glasgow** Queen Street station during 1988 is 37401 *Mary Queen of Scots*. (*Rick Ward*)

This heralded a period when passenger services dominated as she headed mainly Class 1 trains originating in South Wales and visiting the South West or the Midlands, which continued into the early 1990s, though she was called upon to assist on the Lickey on occasions during this time. On 23 April 1994 she was in charter action again, 'top and tail' with classmate 37402 for the Monmouthshire Railway Society tour 'The Gwaun-cae-Gurwen Growler' which ran from Newport to Gwaun-cae-Gurwen, Jersey Marine near Swansea, Cardiff Docks then back to Newport. After this she was in demand for passenger duty virtually full-time, working regularly out of Bristol Temple Meads mainly to Weymouth until being transferred to Bescot in September 1996 when once again freight duties became interspersed amongst her passenger turns. Periods spent mainly in store were to follow from 1999 until her final demise in November 2005.

### Sub-class 37/4

These were converted from the original fleet in 1985 and 1986. They were fitted with electric train heating, having had their steam heating removed. Tractive effort was increased to 57,440lb (256kN). They weighed 107 tonnes.

**37401 (D6968, 37268)** (See also 37401 in Class 37s in Colour)
Released by EE Vulcan Foundry as D6968, Works Number EE/VF3528/D957 on 17 February 1965 and allocated to Darnall.

Final depot: Kingmoor, 10/11.

Name carried: *Mary Queen of Scots*, 11/85–12/23.

Status: Withdrawn from DBS stock, 3/13 and moved to Bo'ness & Kinneil Railway by road; Reinstated into traffic for DRS at Kingmoor, 7/15; Allocated to DRS Supply Chain Operations, 3/22; Allocated to DRS Locomotives stored/for disposal, 11/23; Moved to Crewe Diesel depot for LSL Operational Locomotives, 10/23 and due to be renamed *Mary Queen of Scots* and repainted into BR ScotRail livery.

Notable movements:
Her career has been dominated by passenger working from her earliest days as her transfer to Stratford involved her heading trains out of London Liverpool Street, then when moved to Cardiff Canton she was busy with services between Newport and Swansea as well as to Bristol Temple Meads, Paddington or into The Midlands. In October 1979 she was briefly employed as Lickey Banker with classmate 37234 and around this time was used on freights associated with the heavy industries of South Wales as well as on parcels trains in that area. Her transfer to Eastfield in 1984, now as a Class 37/4 saw her primarily occupied with Class 1 services out of Glasgow Queen Street. She appeared on display at Haymarket Open Day on 25 August 1985 and on 29 August 1987 was in charge of the SRPS Railtour from Gourock to Fort William and Mallaig and return. This pattern of passenger train work continued with only

### Table 3. Locos numbered as sub-class 37/4

**37/4**

| | | | |
|---|---|---|---|
| D6968: 37401 | D6970: 37409 | D6969: 37417 | D6992: 37425 |
| D6974: 37402 | D6973: 37410 | D6971: 37418 | D6999: 37426 |
| D6607: 37403 | D6990: 37411 | D6991: 37419 | D6988: 37427 |
| D6986: 37404 | D6601: 37412 | D6997: 37420 | D6981: 37428 |
| D6982: 37405 | D6976: 37413 | D6967: 37421 | D6600: 37429 |
| D6995: 37406 | D6987: 37414 | D6966: 37422 | D6965: 37430 |
| D6605: 37407 | D6977: 37415 | D6996: 37423 | D6972: 37431 |
| D6989: 37408 | D6602: 37416 | D6979: 37424 | |

NB. 37403 (previously 37307), 37407 (37305), 37412 (37301), 37416 (37302) and 37429 (37300) remained in sub-class 37/0 as not modified, even though renumbered.

occasional freight duties into the 1990s. On 3 March 1990 she headed a Leeds to Perth charter then on 17 July that year had charge of 'The Royal Scotsman' between Edinburgh and Fort William. On 11 May 1991 she took 'The West Highland Railtour' for the SRPS and on 4 January 1992 she was again in action for the same promoter with 'The Border Riever' railtour, taking the sections between Edinburgh and Stirling then Carlisle to Linlithgow.

As the 1990s progressed she became increasingly in demand to head charters including on 15 June 1996 again for the SRPS, this time with 37404 for 1Z64 Paisley Gilmour Street to Kyle of Lochalsh and return. On 6 July 1996 she led Pathfinder Railtours' 'The Caley Sou'wester', a tour from Birmingham New Street to Carlisle and Glasgow Central and return and on 25 October 1997 she was employed by Hertfordshire Railtours on their tour 'The Sally Forth' which ran from London King's Cross to Rosyth Royal Dockyard. In between times, on 16 September 1996 she again had charge of 'The Royal Scotsman', on this occasion between Spean Bridge in the Great Glen and Mallaig. Her transfer to Cardiff Canton in 1998 and soon after to Crewe Diesel saw her used extensively on passenger services including between Birmingham International and Holyhead, between Birmingham New Street and Holyhead or Chester and from Crewe to Bangor.

This continued until her transfer to Motherwell in 2001 when Class 1 services north of Edinburgh occupied her full time throughout the year, interrupted only by occasional '1Zxx specials' such as 1Z36 Edinburgh to Dundee on 20 April 2001, 1Z98 Preston to York on 22 July 2001 and a Regional Railways 'Rugby Additional' between Crewe and Cardiff on 25 November 2001 when although still officially a Motherwell loco she then worked extensively in The Midlands, the North West and in South Wales. She was still sought after for 'special' duties though, including trains to and from Cardiff in early 2002, then a move to Scotland again from 29 March 2002 with Hertfordshire Railtours' 'The Easter Highlander', with which she was involved with classmate 37415 north from Carlisle. Following this four-day tour of The Highlands she was engaged on a further series of 'specials' in the Inverness area and down to Edinburgh, often accompanied by 37415 until from May 2002 resuming 'normal' Class 1 services from the Scottish Capital, most often to the Fort William and Kyle of Lochalsh area interspersed with charter appearances including for Pathfinder Railtours' 'The Lord of the Isles' on 10 April 2004 between Inverness and Kyle of Lochalsh, for the SRPS on 1 May 2004 'The Fort William and Mallaig', again for the SRPS on 12 June 'The Plockton and Kyle of Lochalsh', for Hertfordshire Railtours' 'The Orcadian' between 25 and 28 June and on 7 August 2004 'The West Highlander', again for the SRPS.

This pattern would continue until on 13 May 2005 she appeared as a guest on the heritage railway The Watercress Line in Hampshire where she stayed until returning to her work in Scotland from 18 May until the end of July 2005. On 30 July that year she was back in the south of the UK again to take Pathfinder Railtours' 'The Snowdonian II', Bristol Temple Meads to Machynlleth, Pwllheli and return with 37427 before heading back to her regular haunts in the Highlands of Scotland where she worked until June 2006.

Transferring south again in 2007 saw her highly sought after for numerous special train duties including on 5 April 2008 with 37405 for Compass Tours' 'The Pennine Fellsman', which ran from Wolverhampton to York and return, until August 2009 when, now owned by EWS/DB Schenker she took on a more varied role including freight and sandite duties. Between March 2013 and July 2014 she worked on the Bo'ness and Kinneil railway northwest of Edinburgh then moved to Carlisle Kingmoor to work Class 2 passenger services to Barrow-in-Furness, Lancaster and Preston for DRS. This would be her regular work until December 2018, interrupted only by 'The Nosey Peaker', a charter on 14 June 2018 from Stafford to Buxton and return for the Branch Line Society and a brief spell as a guest on the K&WVR from 30 June to 1 July that year.

She was then back to Carlisle to work the Barrow trains once more until in December 2018 she was taken off passenger work and allocated to freight turns in the Stowmarket area, work interrupted by a time hauling passengers again on the North Norfolk Railway during June 2022 and again on the Keighley and Worth Valley Railway in June 2023. She was involved with 'The Garsdale Growler' for The Branch Line Society on 27 August along 37425, from Derby to Carlisle over the testing S&C route. On 8 December 2023 she was noted

**Nameplate of** 37401.

**At Eastfield** in 1988 is 37402 *Oor Wullie*. (Rick Ward)

**Running light** engine towards York at Copmanthorpe on 3 July 2013 is 37402 resplendent in her DRS livery. (Rick Ward)

working a Rail Head Treatment Train running into Carlisle before being put into store for LSL Operational Locomotives at Crewe Diesel depot in January 2024. In July 2024 she was stabled at Barrow Hill depot in the company of 37424, 37425 and 37602.

On 16 December 2023 Network Rail organised a night photoshoot at their Engineering Works at Holgate, York which raised £3,000 for the Yorkshire-based charity Martin House Children's Hospice. The one-off photoshoot involved the five DRS Class 37s which had been used regularly to haul the season's RHTTs around Yorkshire. The locos were 37407 *Blackpool Tower*, 37419 *Driver Tom Kay*, 37422, 37425 *Sir Robert McAlpine/Concrete Bob* and 37716. This was expected to be the last year that DRS Class 37s would be used on RHTTs and before the event some of the participants volunteered to clean the filthy locos, after which they returned to DRS for an expected sale as part of the company's modernisation programme.

**37402 (D6974, 37274)** (See also 37402 in Class 37s in Colour)
Released by EE Vulcan Foundry as D6974, Works Number EE/VF3534/D963 on 6 April 1965 and allocated to Canton.

Final depot: Kingmoor, 5/12.

Names carried: *Oor Wullie*, 12/85–9/93; *Bont Y Bermo*, 2/94; *Stephen Middlemore 23.12.1994–8.6.2013*, 10/13–6/23.

Status: Stored by DRS at Kingmoor, 5/23, offered for sale, 9/23; In store at Kingmoor for Special Trains Charters, PODLs; sold to Sheaf Engineering, 10/23.

Notable movements:
Her early days in South Wales saw her involved with freight workings in the Newport and Port Talbot industrial area with movements of coal and steel products from mines and foundries in the Valleys but by the 1980s she was being used increasingly on passenger services in the south west and to destinations in the Midlands and as

Locomotive Histories • 67

far as York. Her transfer to Eastfield in 1984 saw this pattern of working continue with her schedule now dominated by Class 1 trains from Glasgow to Edinburgh or further north including taking the Scottish sections of expresses originating at London Euston destined for Fort William.

Highland passenger services occupied her until her transfer south to Crewe Diesel in 1993 when she was engaged on similar duties between the Midlands and Holyhead, Liverpool or Manchester which continued until her move to Toton in late 1998. During this time she began to be called upon to head charter 'specials', including on 23 April 1994 the Monmouthshire Railway Society's 'Gwaun-cae-Gurwen Growler II' from Newport to Jersey Marine (Neath) and return, top and tail with classmate 37258. Then on 12 July 1997 for Hertfordshire Rail Tours' 'The Dungeness Pebbledasher', Finsbury Park to Dungeness and return followed on 24 April 1998 by a two-day tour for Regency Railcruises 'The Lord of the Isles' which ran from Bristol to Kyle of Lochalsh and return and also involved 37406, 37410 and 37431. Shortly afterwards on 25 May 1998 she was paired with 37429 to head 'The Settle-Carlisle Scotsman', from Hull to Edinburgh and return.

Following her transfer to Toton later that year she became involved with passenger services out of Bristol Temple Meads. Transferring to Cardiff Canton in 2001 saw her heavily occupied with services to Rhymney and Fishguard until in 2004 she was moved back to Toton and put into store by EWS and eventually sold to DRS in 2011.

After spending some further time in store, her active life resumed in 2013 with passenger services out of St Pancras as far as Chesterfield and to York. She appeared on display for the DRS Weekend at Crewe Heritage Centre on 22 March 2014 and before that charter duties had also resumed including on 8 March 2014 'The Mid Norfolk Navigator' for Pathfinder Railtours. It ran from Crewe to Wymondham, Hoe and return in the company of 37218 and 37409. On 28 May 2014 she was in action again, this time for Compass Tours with their charter 'The Canterbury Tales Explorer', Crewe to Canterbury and return with 37405. Then on 13 June 2014, again for Pathfinder Railtours, 'The Purbeck Explorer', Stafford to Southampton and Swanage and return with classmates 37423 and 37604.

During 2015 she was engaged on passenger duty along the Cumbrian Coast Line from Carlisle to Barrow-in-Furness, Lancaster and Preston, daily services which would continue until September 2018 when a short period in store was followed by a series of 'special' engagements which occupied her for much of 2019. These included for Pathfinder Railtours first 'The Surrey Currier/Thames Valley Flyer/Kent & Sussex Roundabout' on 15 and 16 February, starting and finishing at Eastleigh with 37409, then their 'Easter Highlander', a four-day charter which began at Eastleigh on 19 April then ran to Aviemore for a tour of The Highlands, again with 37409 throughout. On 27 May she was paired with 37025 for North East Railtours' 'The Oban', Newcastle to Oban and return followed from

**Taking her** Rail Head Treatment Train through York station on 6 October 2021 is 37402 with 37401 on the rear. Operated by DRS as train 315R, York Thrall Europa to York Thrall Europa by way of Scarborough, Bridlington, Beverley, Hull, Selby, Goole and Brough.

13 to 15 June by 'The Railway Children–Three Peaks Challenge by Rail', Crewe to Fort William and return via the Cumbrian Coast Line both ways. On 21 December 2019 she headed UK Railtours' 'Beverley at Christmas', King's Cross to Beverley and return, and finally on 18 August 2021 she was paired with 37069 for Pathfinder Railtours' 'The Cambridge & Norfolk Explorer', Eastleigh to Norwich and return by way of Cambridge. After this she was allocated to DRS Stored Locomotives at Kingmoor and in May 2023 was listed as 'Stored/For Disposal' then bought by Sheaf Engineering. She is being overhauled for spot hire contracts.

### 37403 (D6607, 37307)

Released by EE Vulcan Foundry as D6607, Works Number EE/VF3567/D996 on 22 October 1965 and allocated to Landore.

Final depot: Kingmoor, 4/16.

Names carried: *Isle of Mull*, 1/86–10/88; *Glen Darroch*, 11/88–1/94; *Ben Cruachan*, 2/94; Later renamed to *Isle of Mull*.

Status: Sold by EWS, 11/07; Reinstated as a PODL, 11/08 and transferred to Kingmoor for DRS from Bo'ness depot, 4/16; After working on several heritage railways she returned to Bo'ness in 8/20; Moved to the NYMR, 5/22; From 2/23 has been engaged with charter trains including in the Scottish Highlands from 3/24, though based on the Bo'ness & Kinneil Railway and owned by the SRPS.

### 37404 (D6986, 37286)

Released by EE Vulcan Foundry as D6986, Works Number EE/VF3546/D975 on 1 June 1965 and allocated to Canton.

Final depot: Doncaster, 12/01.

Names carried: *Ben Cruachan*, 1/86–9/93; *Loch Long*, 2/95–11/99.

Status: Cut up by HNRC, C.F. Booth, Rotherham, 1/02.

Notable movements: Based in South Wales until 1984, her early years involved the heavy freight associated with that area. It was not until being fitted with twin tanks in 1979 that passenger work featured more prominently in her schedule, initially assisting as a banker on the Lickey Incline between Bromsgrove and Blackwell and later taking services from Bristol Temple Meads to Cardiff and further afield. Her rebuilding to 37/4 and move to Eastfield in 1984 saw her given charge of Class 1 passenger duties north from Glasgow to destinations including Perth, Inverness and Oban as well as between Fort William and Mallaig. She also handled the Scottish sections of trains for the Highlands which originated at London Euston and continued with this type of work until September 1992, now repainted into InterCity Mainline Livery.

She was then transferred to Inverness depot and was busy with services mainly to Aberdeen or to Kyle of Lochalsh until being allocated to Motherwell in 1993 when she was often involved with trains between Edinburgh and Fort William. At around this time she was called upon to assist

Nameplate of 37403.

**Light engine** at Glasgow Queen Street in 1988 is 37404 *Ben Cruachan*. (*Rick Ward*)

with charter trains for the SRPS including on 16 October 1993 from Edinburgh Waverley to Fort William, on 3 June 1995 between Dunbar and Kyle of Lochalsh and return with 37428 and on 15 June 1996 between Glasgow and Kyle of Lochalsh and return, this time with 37401. Her Class 1 duties from Edinburgh continued until January 1999 after which she was sent south into storage and eventual disposal.

**37405 (D6982, 37282)**
Released by EE Vulcan Foundry as D6982, Works Number EE/VF3542/D971 on 13 May 1965 and allocated to Canton.

Final depot: Kingmoor, 5/12.

Name carried: *Strathclyde Region*, 4/86.

Status: Stored by DRS, Kingmoor, 1/21. Sold to Colas, 11/22.

Notable movements:
General duties in South Wales involving local freight and passenger workings occupied her until her move to Eastfield in 1984, though she had been used on charter trains before her move to Scotland including on 14 October 1978 (still as 37282) she and classmate 37204 headed the opening leg of the D1041 Preservation Society's tour 'The Pennine Explorer'. This ran from Cardiff via Gloucester to Birmingham New Street, then on to Manchester Piccadilly and return. Her conversion to sub-class 37/4 and move to Eastfield saw her taking charge of regular Class 1 services north from Glasgow as far as Fort William or Oban, or to Mallaig from Fort William. Although allocated to freight pools, her dominant occupation was with passenger services in the Highlands and this continued largely uninterrupted until her move south, initially to Tinsley in 1992 and even then it was to largely similar duties wherever she was transferred. Occasional charter work was also forthcoming for Pathfinder Railtours including on 6 November 1993 'The Itchen-Piddle', when she and 37377 worked top and tail from Manchester Piccadilly to Eastleigh, Poole, Weymouth and return. Then on 5 March 1994 she was involved with their tour 'The Hampshire Hog', again starting from Manchester Piccadilly then on to Crewe, Eastleigh, Southampton Eastern Docks and return, though unfortunately on this occasion she was replaced by 37425 at Crewe after ETH failure.

Passenger duties out of Crewe occupied her until her transfer to Toton in 1997 when the Bristol to Cardiff route dominated. Then her move to Motherwell saw her heading services north from Edinburgh once more, again with a sprinkling of charters amongst her regular workings. Notable amongst these were on 29 August 1998 for the SRPS 'The Fort William and Mallaig' from Edinburgh Waverley, then on 22 and 23 April 2000 she was involved with Hertfordshire Rail Tours' 'The Saint Columba' which originated at King's Cross and ran to Glasgow Central then on to Oban and return. On 20 August 2000 she and 37415 had charge

**At Glasgow** Queen Street in 1988 is 37405 *Strathclyde Region*. (*Rick Ward*)

of Grampian Railtours' 'The 21st Century Limited', Aberdeen to Kyle of Lochalsh and return. From then on charter work became more frequent particularly for the SRPS, including 'Oban' with 37427 from Berwick-upon-Tweed on 23 September 2000, 'Fife to Mallaig' between Fort William and Mallaig on 5 May 2001, 'Dunbar to Mallaig' with 37415 on 4 May 2002 and 'Kyle of Lochalsh' with 37427 from Dunbar on 25 May 2002.

These were followed on 1 June 2002 by 'The Lochalsh Special' from Paisley with 37426, then on 25 August, this time for Grampian Railtours, Aberdeen to Kyle of Lochalsh and return with 37401 and finally with the SRPS again on 6 September 2003 for 'The Oban & Lorn Explorer', Carlisle to Oban and return with 37406. This demanding schedule on top of her regular 'day to day' duties kept her busy until her transfer to Crewe Diesel depot in late September 2003. Even from there she was in demand on a daily basis to take services from Leeds, often over the testing S&C route, work which continued until late 2004 when she was transferred further south to work mainly with Class 2 services out of Cardiff.

Her transfer back to Motherwell in 2006 briefly reunited her with the Edinburgh to Fort William route but she was soon moved back to England and resumed charter duty in July of that year for Kingfisher Tours with first 'The Heart of Wales Rambler' with 37401 on 22 July from Ealing Broadway to Cardiff then on to Shrewsbury and return. Next came 'The Sunny Seaside Spitfire' on 17 August from Bristol Temple Meads to Eastbourne and return, followed on 9 September by 'The Eden & Penzance Explorer' between Bournemouth, Exeter and Penzance. She was then allocated to EWS Fleet Management Unit based at Toton until February 2008 when charter work soon called again in the shape of Pathfinder Railtours' 'The Buffer Puffer 6.1' when she worked top and tail with 37401 from London Cannon Street to Uckfield, East Grinstead, London Victoria, Finsbury Park and King's Cross on 8 March 2008. She was paired with 37401 again on 5 April for Compass Tours' 'The Pennine Fellsman' from Wolverhampton to Huddersfield, Leeds, York, Sheffield and return.

She was then returned to the EWS Fleet Management Unit followed by several years in store at Toton, Barrow Hill and Kingmoor before returning to active service in June 2013. More charter work was to follow including on 30 November 2013 with 37261, for Pathfinder Railtours' 'The Festive Festival Express' from Whitchurch to Salisbury, Portsmouth Harbour, Eastleigh and return. This was followed on 25 January 2014 with 37610 again for Pathfinder Railtours' 'The Buffer Puffer 11.0', Crewe to London Blackfriars, London Cannon Street, Stewarts Lane, Epsom Downs, Tattenham Corner, Clapham Junction and return to Crewe. On 28 May 2014 she was coupled with 37402 for Compass Tours' 'The Canterbury Tales Explorer' which ran from Crewe to Canterbury and return.

From June 2015 she worked between Lowestoft, Norwich and Great Yarmouth. This continued until March 2018 with only occasional interruptions such as a charter for Virgin Trains/DRS/*Railway Magazine* with 37401, Chester to Bournemouth and return on 22 August 2015 when she was called in to replace an unavailable classmate. A very brief move to Carlisle followed from where she worked the Cumbrian Coast Line to Barrow-in-Furness for a few days only before returning to resume her duties in East Anglia, now often in the company of 37716. This work lasted until June 2019 after which she worked test trains for Network Rail from Derby RTC until being put into store by DRS in January 2021 and then acquired on hire by Colas Rail from November 2022 from new owners HNRC. Ran light with 37610 from Crewe to Millerhill on 20 March 2024 and similarly from Derby to Grosmont (NYMR) on 13 June 2024.

**37406 (D6995, 37295)** (See also 37406 in Class 37s in Colour)
Released by EE Vulcan Foundry as D6995, Works Number EE/VF3555/D984 on 13 July 1965 and allocated to Canton.

Final depot: Kingmoor, 10/11.

Name carried: *The Saltire Society*, 6/86.

Status: Cut up by C.F. Booth, Rotherham, 5/13.

Notable movements:
Early days in South Wales were occupied with colliery and quarry traffic typical of her class, but she

**Nameplate of** 37405.

was also involved with excursions such as F+W Tours' 'The Anglian Adventurer' on 14 June 1981 from Plymouth via Bristol to Gloucester, Stratford, Harwich Town, Ely and return and on 2 June 1982 from Cardiff to Barry Island and return. During the late 1970s and early 1980s she was also a regular banker on the Lickey Incline as well as taking services herself in the south and south west. Her transfer to Eastfield in 1984 saw her heading trains north from Glasgow and between Fort William and Mallaig, plus the Scottish sections of 'Sleepers' from London Euston, taking them on to Mossend or Fort William.

Only interrupted by the occasional 'FootEx' service her Highland duties continued into the early 1990s, though from 1991 usually from Edinburgh. On 4 and 5 December 1993 she was involved between Fort William and Mallaig on 'The Mallaig Weekender' charter from Wolverhampton. By February 1999 she was back working in the Cardiff area with services to such destinations as Bristol or Weymouth but only briefly, as from July 1999 to March 2000 she was once more operating between Edinburgh and Fort William. A transfer to Toton then saw her reunited with South Wales again until May of that year when she was put into store until a Light Overhaul at Canton in March 2003 allowed her to be returned to traffic from Motherwell Depot.

Now RETB fitted she was equipped to take services over the single-track lines in the Highlands as well as regular trains north from Edinburgh to Fort William. Charter duties still featured such as on 31 August 2003 for Grampian Railtours' 'The 20th Anniversary Rail Tour to Kyle of Lochalsh' from Aberdeen and back with 37421 throughout, then on 6 September that year for the SRPS tour from Carlisle to Oban and return, 'The Oban & Lorn Explorer' with classmate 37405. More work in the Cardiff area followed from January 2004 with Class 2 trains mainly to Rhymney occupying her on a daily basis until she was drafted north once more to operate beyond Edinburgh again mainly to Fort William until September 2006.

Also during this time she was regularly involved with charters including on 12 April 2004 the final day of a four-day tour by Hertfordshire Rail Tours, 'The Easter West Highlander' which originated at King's Cross and ran to Dumbarton and Mallaig, outward via Carlisle. On 19 February 2005 she was top and tail with 37416 for Pathfinder Railtours' 'The Buffer Puffer Volume 3', which roamed between London Blackfriars, Shoeburyness, London Fenchurch Street, Bethnal Green, London Liverpool Street, Enfield Town, Kensington Olympia and London Bridge. Then on 26 March 2005 she was paired with 37427 again for another Hertfordshire Rail Tours four-day tour, 'The Easter Highlander (Pride of the Nation Excursion)', taking day two from Dumbarton to Oban and return, the train originating at King's Cross and running to Oban, Aviemore and Mossend

**At Spean** Bridge near Fort William on 23 August 2003, 37406 *The Saltire Society* and 37428 *Royal Scotsman* head the SRPS Railtour 'The Fort William & Mallaig', Edinburgh to Mallaig and return excursion. *(Jonathan Allen)*

before returning to London. On 9 April 2005 she and 37401 had charge of sections of Pathfinder Railtours' 'The Solent Syphons' which ran from Derby to Salisbury, Southampton, Weymouth then Bristol and back to Derby.

Her busy schedule continued with Pathfinder Railtours on 18 June 2005 when the booked charter from Sheffield 'The Snowdonian I' had to be redirected instead to Blackpool North due to operational problems which continued throughout the day. Then on 9 July that year she had a less problematic tour for Worksop Open Day Committee's 'The Worksop Cambrian Coast Express' when with 37416 she ran between Worksop and Aberystwyth and return. A week later on 16 July she was in action again, this time for Past Time Rail's 'The Cambrian Coast Flyer' from Bristol Temple Meads to Pwllheli and return, ostensibly in partnership with 37416, but that loco's failure at Machynlleth left her to return the train on her own. Normal duties then until another four-day charter for Hertfordshire Rail Tours between 7 and 10 October 2005 when she and 37417 top and tail took 'The Autumn Highlander' north from Carlisle to tour the Scottish Highlands. At the end of the month she was in action for Kingfisher Tours with 37416 taking 'The Snowdonian Explorer'

Nameplate of 37406.

from High Wycombe to Pwllheli and return.

Into 2006 and the charters continued with Pathfinder Railtours' 'The Pennine Syphons' when top and tail with 37417 they ran from Liverpool Lime Street to York via Huddersfield then by way of Leeds to Settle and on to Carlisle, returning via the Tyne Valley line to York and back to Liverpool via Leeds. Finally on 16 September 2006 she was involved in various legs of The Branch Line Society's tour of north east goods lines 'The Tees Rail Again Railtour', originating at Birmingham New Street and running to Tyne Yard via York. A demanding schedule accompanying as it did her regular passenger and occasional freight duties throughout this period, which then came to a temporary pause with her transfer back to South Wales in October 2006 working Class 2 trains mainly between Cardiff and Rhymney.

When moved to Toton in November that year she took special trains from Cardiff to Gloucester on 25 November 2006 before returning to Edinburgh for services to Fort William and to Aberdeen until January 2007. Then began another series of charters beginning on 20 January that year with a ramble for Pathfinder Railtours, 'The Buffer Puffer 4.0' top and tail with 37410 from London Paddington to Haywards Heath, finishing at London St Pancras. Another Pathfinder Railtours ramble with 37410 followed on 10 February 2007, 'The McBuffer Puffer', as the name suggests over Scottish lines from Glasgow Central to Helensburgh, Glasgow Queen Street, Eastfield, Gourock, Lanark, Wemyss Bay and back to Glasgow Central. On 28 and 29 March 2007 she and 37410 were involved in sections of Past Time Rail's five-day charter 'The Devon & Cornwall Branch Week' and on 12 May that year she was engaged by the Mid-Cheshire Rail Users Association for their tour 'The Heart of Wales Express' which ran from Altrincham to Cardiff Central and return by way of Chester.

A week later on 19 May she was back with Pathfinder Railtours for their Cardiff Central to Machynlleth, Pwllheli and return charter 'The Snowdonian' working with 37410 and for Pathfinder Railtours again from 8 June 2007 with 'The Orcadian', a four-day tour which began at Swindon and ran to Preston, then Inverness, Kyle of Lochalsh, Thurso, Wick and return to Swindon via Preston. She and 37410 had charge from Preston to Preston. After this series of charters she was allocated to EWS Fleet Management Unit at Toton or stored there or at Eastleigh until her 'final fling', Pathfinder Railtours' 'The West Highlander', a four-day charter from Salisbury to Preston, Carlisle, Fort William, Mallaig, Oban and return between 10 and 13 April 2009, during which she had charge of several sections, mainly in the Highlands with classmate 37670. Back into the Fleet Management Unit for the last time in late April of that year she was sold by EWS in January 2011 and eventually cut up in May 2013.

### 37407 (D6605, 37305)
Released by EE Vulcan Foundry as D6605, Works Number EE/VF3565/D994 on 6 October 1965 and allocated to Cardiff Canton depot.

Final depot: Kingmoor, 6/16.

Names carried: *Loch Long*, 8/86–1/95; *Blackpool Tower*, 2/95, renamed *Blackpool Tower*, 5/19; renamed *Blackpool Tower* again, 5/24.

Status: Bought for preservation 12/07 and moved to the Churnet Valley Railway; Reinstated into traffic, 7/08; Moved from the Churnet Valley Railway to Derby by road, 4/15; Operational with DRS in East Anglia until 8/19; Occasional charter train haulage including for Rail Charter Services until joining DRS Stored Fleet, 2/22; Reassigned as 'stored/for disposal', 2/24; Sold to EuroPhoenix Locomotives UK and transferred to Leicester, 5/24.

### 37408 (D6989, 37289)

Released by EE Vulcan Foundry as D6989, Works Number EE/VF3549/D978 on 17 June 1965 and allocated to Canton.

Final depot: Toton, 5/07.

Name carried: *Loch Rannoch*, 9/86.

Status: Cut up at EMR, Kingsbury, 1/08.

Notable movements:
Her early duties in South Wales were typical in that they involved a mix of passenger services and freight associated with the heavy industry of the area. She was also used on charter 'specials' whilst based in 'the Valleys', first on 18 September 1977 'The Ebbw Vale Wander' for the Oxford Publishing Company, when she and Class 45 number 45055 headed the train between Newport, Ebbw Vale and return. On 17 June 1978 she was called upon for DAA/DEG with 'The Chopper Railtour' as she and classmate 37229 banked the train up the Lickey Incline.

The tour originated at London St Pancras and ran to Toton via Worcester and return hauled by Class 20 locomotives. The same tour operators were involved on 27 August 1978 with 'The Vulcan Venturer', London Victoria to Bristol Temple Meads then Birmingham New Street and return. She and 37270 had charge between Bristol and Birmingham. On 25 July 1980 she was on display at 'The Age of the Train' exhibition at Newton Abbot Goods Yard and charter duty called again after her transfer to Eastfield when on 21 August

**Stabled at** Eastfield during 1988, 37407 *Loch Long* awaits her next duty. (*Rick Ward*)

**Passing through** Twyford with a freight on 10 November 1980 is 37289. She was modified and renumbered to 37408 in August 1985.

expresses from London Euston. This continued until her transfer back to Canton in 1989 when she was employed mainly on Class 1 services between Cardiff and Manchester or Liverpool interspersed with the occasional freight or football or rugby 'specials'. Transferring back to Eastfield in January 1991 she often found herself heading Class 2 services between Inverness and Kyle of Lochalsh or Class 1s to Aberdeen until her move to Crewe Diesel in May 1993. On 8 May 1993 she was back in charter action again for a tour by the NYMR (NYMR) and *Rail Magazine*, 'The Rail 200', celebrating issue number 200 of that publication. She hauled the train from Birmingham New Street to the NYMR via Battersby. Now allocated to Regional Railways North West she was kept busy with services in that area and south to the Midlands, South Wales or as far as the south coast.

Though she was involved in several depot moves throughout the 1990s this pattern of work continued until her transfer to Motherwell in April 2000 and involved further charters including 'The Worksop Wanderer' on 19 March 1994 for the Worksop Open Day Committee, then on 22 April 1995 for Pathfinder

**At Eastfield** during 1988 is 37408 *Loch Rannoch*. (*Rick Ward*)

**On 11** September 2002, 37408 *Loch Rannoch* is at Cardiff heading a Regional Railways 'Rugby Additional' from Cardiff Central to Rhymney.

1983 she was busy with F+W Tours 'The Scots Streaker', a three-day charter from Plymouth to Ayr via Bristol and Gloucester, then on to Kilmarnock, Glasgow and Carstairs before returning to Plymouth.

Following her Heavy Overhaul and now reclassified to 37/4 as 37408 she worked extensively north from Glasgow to Oban, Fort William and Mallaig including taking over for these sections of Anglo-Scottish

**Nameplate of** 37408.

Railtours' 'The Scrummager 3.1' between Cardiff and Swansea and on 24 January 1998, again for Pathfinder Railtours' 'The Thames Valley Freighter. Working out of Motherwell depot saw her taking services north from Edinburgh until after moving back to Cardiff in late 2001 she was detailed mainly to Class 2 work between there and Rhymney until her move to Crewe Diesel in September 2003. During this period she was again in demand for charters which included on 17 June 2000 the Scottish Railway Preservation Society (SRPS) tour to York from Kirkaldy working with classmate 37416. This was followed on 2 September by their tour to Fort William and Mallaig from Ayr, then between 6 and 9 October for Hertfordshire Railtours on 'The Autumn Highlander' from King's Cross. On 16 April 2001 she was in action for Pathfinder Railtours with 'The Lake District/The Citadel Crusader', Cardiff to Carlisle and return top and tail with 37421. Finally in 2001 involvement in a three-day charter for Pathfinder Railtours, 'The Monarch of the Glen' from Cardiff to Fort William and return with 37416 from 5 to 7 October.

Her transfer to Crewe Diesel saw her put in charge of Class 2 services between Leeds and Knaresborough and the more demanding Class 1 trains to Carlisle over the S&C route, often in the company of 37405 or 37411. By late 2004 she was back in South Wales again working between Cardiff and Rhymney until her accident on 1 August 2005 when she ran into parked stock at Rhymney suffering extensive damage which effectively ended her career.

**37409 (D6970, 37270)** (See also 37409 in Class 37s in Colour)
Released by EE Vulcan Foundry as D6970, Works Number EE/VF3530/D959 on 4 March 1965 and allocated to Canton.

Final depot: Kingmoor, 6/17.

Names carried: *Loch Awe*, 8/86; *Lord Hinton*, 7/10–12/23, renamed *Loch Awe*, 1/24.

Status: Operational for Locomotive Services Ltd at Crewe Diesel, 7/22; Leased to ScotRail and painted into their Retro InterCity livery from 12/23.

Notable movements:
Whilst in South Wales her duties involved working the heavy freight trains associated with the coal and steel industries of that area together with occasional local and longer distance passenger services usually to the Midlands. She did feature though on charters from a fairly early stage in her career including on 27 August 1978 for DAA/DEG 'The Vulcan Venturer', London Victoria to Weymouth then Bristol Temple Meads to Birmingham New Street and return, working with 37289 between Bristol and Birmingham. On 15 July 1979 she was involved with the Gloucester to Sharpness charter 'The Severnsider' for F+W Railtours, then for the same tour operator on 3 July 1983 with 'The Menai Marauder' which ran from Plymouth to Gloucester then on to Crewe and Llandudno Junction, working with 37272 between Plymouth and Crewe. Also during the early months of 1983 she was used as a Lickey Banker, paired with classmate 37180. She continued to be employed mainly on passenger services between South Wales and the South West until her move to Eastfield in January 1985.

Following her conversion to 37/4 and her overhaul at Crewe Works her work in Scotland consisted largely of Class 1 services north from Glasgow to Oban, Fort William and Mallaig plus taking over the Scottish sections of services from London Euston destined for The Highlands. On 5 May 1985 she had charge of 1Z36, the 'special' from Cowlairs 'The Land of the Lochs', the last train to Balloch Pier on Loch Lomond. The rail service had been provided to connect with the Loch Lomond steamer which ceased sailing in 1981. On 23 April 1988 she was involved with the BR Merrymaker Excursion which ran from Lancaster to Fort William, Mallaig and return, taking the Highland sections north from Mossend near Motherwell.

After her Light Overhaul at Glasgow Works in 1989 she was used more often on services to Aberdeen and Inverness and on 2 September that year she featured on the LCGB (North West Branch) charter 'The West Highlander No.7' which originated at Leeds and ran to Wigan then on to Fort William, Mallaig and return, heading the return section from Fort William to Mossend. Then on 31 August 1991 she was in charter action again for the SRPS rail-tour from Edinburgh to Inverness, Kyle of Lochalsh and return. This pattern of Class 1 passenger services (with the occasional freight turn) continued until April 1999 when she was moved south to work once more in South Wales and south west of England. These services, based around Cardiff and Bristol occupied her only until 19 June of that year when she was allocated to the SRPS rail-tour from Perth to York via Edinburgh when she and classmate 37430 had charge between Perth and Edinburgh, after which she resumed her role heading services between Edinburgh and Fort William.

From March 2000 until March 2008 she was in and out of storage for EWS until being bought by DRS, eventually moved to Carlisle Kingmoor and reinstated into traffic. There then followed charter appearances for Spitfire Railtours which included on 19 February 2011 'The Cumbrian Crusader IV', Birmingham International to Sheffield then on to Carlisle via the S&C, returning by way of Newcastle, York and Sheffield to Birmingham. Then on 25 June that year, again for Spitfire Railtours she and classmate 37229 had charge of 'The Kernow Explorer III' from Birmingham International to Bristol, Penzance and return.

Around this time she also featured on several 1Zxx 'specials' in Scotland, the Midlands and the south of England interrupted by a period on the Cumbrian Coast Line during January 2012 and resumed from April that year. On 17 August 2013 she was a guest at the DRS Open Day at Kingmoor depot and then followed tours including the multiple charter for Pathfinder Railtours' 'The Curried Goyt/ The Red Rose Kipper/ The Clay Box', three tours in one which ran from Crewe to Rose Hill Marple and return, Crewe to Windermere, Preston, Blackpool South then Manchester Airport and return and Crewe to Daventry, Warrington, Birmingham International and return. All this occupying 21 and 22 February 2014 and handled throughout by Class 37s, featuring also 37402, 37609 and 37703. On 8 March 2014 she was in charter action again for Pathfinder Railtours with 'The Mid-Norfolk Navigator', Crewe to Ely, Wymondham, Hoe and return.

Then she was back on the Cumbrian Coast Line again taking Class 2 services between Carlisle, Barrow, Lancaster or Preston, work which kept her busy until May 2017 when she spent a weekend as a guest on the Wensleydale Railway in North Yorkshire before transferring to East Anglia to work with classmates 37407, 37419 or 37423 on passenger services in the Norwich and Great Yarmouth area. This continued until October 2018 after which she was returned to Kingmoor to be reunited with the Cumbrian Coast Line once more until December that year, after which she was recalled to charter duties. On 9 February 2019 she worked with classmate 37218 on Pathfinder Railtours' 'The Blue Boys Loco Fest' from Newport to Bristol, Derby, Blackpool North, Crewe, Birmingham and back to Newport. She was back with Pathfinder Railtours a week later when on 15 and 16 February she and 37402 worked top and tail throughout with 'The Surrey Currier/Thames Valley Flyer/ Kent & Sussex Roundabout', a trip which wandered from Eastleigh to Reading, Maidenhead, Slough, back to Paddington then to Sheerness, Ashford International, Horsham, Reading and on to Eastleigh. A weekend on the Chinnor & Princes Risborough Railway followed on 5 to 7 April then from 19 to 22 April 2019 another demanding charter, Pathfinder Railtours' 'The Easter Highlander', four days beginning at Eastleigh and running to Carlisle then on to Aviemore, Kyle of Lochalsh, back to Aviemore then to Thurso, Wick, then back to Carlisle and Eastleigh. She and 37402 worked the sections north from Carlisle and back.

After this she was transferred to the less demanding terrain of East Anglia once more to work top and tail with 37424 over familiar territory in the Norwich area until in September 2019 she returned to Carlisle to take over Pathfinder Railtours' 'The Autumn Highlander' which had been brought from Paignton via Bristol, Shrewsbury and Warrington on 27 September. This time she was paired with 37419 for the four-day charter which then ran to Aviemore, Kyle of Lochalsh, Thurso, Wick, Aviemore again then back to Carlisle where the 37s left the train to return to Bristol then Exeter St Davids. After this she was de-registered by DRS and in March 2022 put into store. In July that year she was transferred to Crewe Diesel depot where she was allocated to Locomotive Services and by January 2023 had been transferred to Barrow Hill. On 8 and 9 April 2024 she combined 'top & tail' with 37667

Nameplate of 37409.

*Flopsie* to haul LSL/Inter-City's Fort William to Mallaig and return 'The West Highlander', repeated on 19 April, running in place of WCRC's 'The Jacobite' daily steam trips which had been suspended due to an on-going dispute with The Office of Rail and Road (ORR) concerning central door locking on that company's Mk1 coaches. During May 2024 she was stabled at Crewe, briefly visiting the SVR for their Spring Diesel Festival beginning on 16 May, which also featured classmate 37263.

## 37410 (D6973, 37273)

Released by EE Vulcan Foundry as D6973, Works Number EE/VF3533/D962 on 5 April 1965 and allocated to Canton.

Final depot: Kingmoor, 10/11.

Name carried: *Aluminium 100*, 9/86.

Status: Cut up by C.F. Booth, Rotherham, 3/13.

Notable movements:
During her years based in South Wales she was occupied with passenger services in the Cardiff area and to the Midlands as well as the freight traffic associated with the area. She also spent time as a Lickey Banker and was used on 'specials' such as Rugby 'extras'. Following her transfer to Eastfield and rebuilding as a 37/4 she became greatly involved with Class 1 services north from Glasgow to Fort William, Oban and Mallaig as well as taking over the Scottish sections of expresses from London Euston destined for the Highlands. In addition to the occasional freight working she was involved from time to time with charters such as on 30 May 1992 when she was called upon by the SRPS to rescue their tour from Inverkeithing to Oban following the failure of 37405. Then on 12 June 1993 she was in action on the middle day of three for Pathfinder Railtours' 'The Skirl Revisited' which began at Minehead (West Somerset Railway) then to Bristol, Crewe and Carlisle followed by Fort William to Mallaig and return where she and 37196 took over as far as Glasgow Central, after which the tour ran to Ayr then Carlisle and back to Bristol. On 24 June 1995 she and 37423 had charge of a charter from Edinburgh to Fort William and return, then on 8 May 1999 she was paired with 37413 for a SRPS tour to Kyle of Lochalsh and Inverness from Kilmarnock.

Later that year she was back in action for the SRPS, this time coupled with 37405 for 'The Total Eclipse', a three-day tour beginning at Linlithgow on 10 August and running via Edinburgh to Birmingham then Penzance and return. After her transfer south and period in store she featured on Hertfordshire Rail Tours' 'The Cambrian Explorer' on 8 February 2003 which originated at Finsbury Park and ran to Bescot where she and 37042 took over to Aberystwyth and return, which included a visit to the Talyllyn Railway before returning to Finsbury Park. On 31 May 2003 she appeared at Crewe Works Open Day and after her transfer to Cardiff Canton in June her attention turned to heading Class 2 services between Cardiff and Rhymney before a return to Motherwell in September 2003 saw her taking Class 1 trains to the Highlands again. Amongst timetabled services were charter duties including on 1 May 2004

**On 11** March 1986 37410 and classmate wait at Crianlarich.

a charter for the SRPS 'The Fort William & Mallaig' from Dunbar, top and tail with 37427.

This signalled the beginning of a period involving regular charter work beginning on 22 May with SRPS 'The Fort William & Mallaig' railtour from Ayr, with 37667 followed on 12 June again for the SRPS 'The Plockton & Kyle of Lochalsh' from Dunbar, with 37401. Then on 15 August she and 37427 took the VSOE (Northern Belle) 'Fort William from Edinburgh/Dumbarton'. On 18 September she was busy with sections of Pathfinder Railtours' 'The Industrial Invader' which had originated at Crewe, then went on to Gloucester and tours of industrial lines to Bath Spa, Cheltenham Spa, Wolverhampton and back to Crewe. Next she featured on the middle two days of four for Pathfinder Railtours' 'The Highland Venturer', which had begun at Cardiff Central on 24 September and ran to Dumbarton where she and 37418 took over to Oban, Aviemore and back to Dumbarton for the train to return to Cardiff. Finally she was back in action with the VSOE (Northern Belle) on 16 and 17 October 2004 taking 'The Isle of Skye from Aberdeen' to Kyle of Lochalsh and return with 37406.

She was then transferred south again and after a period in store at Doncaster followed by a move to Margam she resumed Class 2 passenger duties between Cardiff and Rhymney from October to December 2006. January 2007 heralded another busy time with charter duties occupying a substantial amount of her schedule, beginning on 20 January with Pathfinder Railtours' 'The Buffer Puffer 4.0' from London Paddington with 37406 followed on 10 February by their 'The McBuffer Puffer' from Glasgow Central again with 37406. A five-day tour for Past Time Rail 'The Devon & Cornwall Branch Week' began on 25 March followed on 31 March by Pathfinder Railtours' 'The Buffer Puffer 4.1' with 37401 from London Paddington. On 14 April again for Pathfinder Railtours she and 37422 took 'The Principality Freighter' from Birmingham International to Llanelli, Jersey Marine Junction South (Neath Port Talbot) and return followed on 19 May for the same operator 'The Snowdonian' from Cardiff Central to Machynlleth, Pwllheli and return with 37406. Between 8 and 11 June she was involved with Pathfinder Railtours' 'The Orcadian', Swindon to Inverness and return with 37406 followed on 12 August with another Northern Belle for VSOE, 'The Aberdeen to Dunrobin Castle' with 37422. On 16 August she was working for Kingfisher Tours with their 'Eastbourne Flyer I' from Derby to Eastbourne and return.

This was followed by two tours for Past Time Rail, both in the company of 37417. First on 31 August 'The Dartmouth Arrow' from Bristol Temple Meads to Kingswear then on 2 September 'The Torbay Express' over the same route. Her close relationship with 37417 continued throughout the following months of 2007. On 29 September they headed Pathfinder Railtours' 'The Lakeland Coast Express' from Worcester Shrub Hill to Carlisle and return by way of Carnforth and Barrow-in-Furness. From 13 to 15 October they had charge of Hertfordshire Rail Tours' 'The Autumn West Highlander' which had begun the day before from London Euston to Dumbarton where the 37s took over to Oban, Stranraer, Kilmarnock and Carstairs where they left the train for it to return to Euston. Further work for Pathfinder Railtours followed in November with 'Silverlink Swansong No.1 and No.2' both departing London Euston for Bletchley and return on 3 and 10 November respectively. Finally on 1 December 2007 she and 37417 had charge of Pathfinder Railtours' 'The Festive Yorkshiremen' which ran from Swindon to Crewe, Leeds then Manchester Victoria and return. After this intense activity she went into store for EWS, was then sold by DB Schenker and was scrapped by them not long after.

### 37411 (D6990, 37290)

Released by EE Vulcan Foundry as D6990, Works Number EE/VF3550/D979 on 18 June 1965 and allocated to Canton.

Final depot: Kingmoor, 9/11.

Names carried: *The Institute of Railway Signal Engineers*, 5/87–10/90; *Ty Hafan*, 5/97; *The Scottish Railway*

Nameplate of 37410.

*Preservation Society*, 4/01; *Castell Caerffili/Caerphilly Castle*, 11/05.

Status: Cut up by C.F. Booth, Rotherham, 5/13. A cab has been placed on display in the Alexandra Hotel car park near the station in Derby.

Notable movements:
Movements of the heavy freight associated with industrial South Wales occupied her throughout her early years whilst working from Canton and Landore Depots, with coal, oil and steel being the regular materials transported. She was called upon for Lickey Banking duties and to head the occasional Class 1 service to and from Birmingham in the summer of 1979, but her main work centred on freight until her transfer to Eastfield in February 1985 when passenger duties took over in the form of services north from Glasgow to Oban, Fort William or Perth and between Fort William and Mallaig. She was also regularly involved with Anglo-Scottish expresses from London Euston, taking them on from Glasgow to the Highlands.

Her move south in 1989, first back to Canton and then to Tinsley saw her used on banking duty from Peak Forest during February and March of that year followed by involvement in charters for Pathfinder Railtours including 'The Pennine Voyager' on 4 November. This tour originated at Swindon then went on to Bristol, Birmingham, Blackburn and Carlisle via the S&C before returning by way of the WCML to Crewe, then back to Birmingham and Bristol. On 10 March 1990 she was in action again with their tour 'The Pennine Wanderer', again from Swindon to Bristol, then to Carlisle via the WCML returning by the S&C to Derby, Bristol and Swindon.

She was displayed at Coalville Open Day on 3 June 1990 before being transferred to Laira the following September after which she headed passenger services in the south west. During 1993 she had charge of what was known as Britain's longest distance freight train, the 'Silver Bullets' which ran between Burngullow in Cornwall and Irvine in North Ayrshire, Scotland carrying China Clay slurry in the distinctive 'silver' bogie tanks which gave the train its nickname, usually 'double-headed' by Class 37s. The slurry was used in the manufacture of paper by the Caledonian Paper Company and the train ran up to thrice weekly by way of Bristol, the North & West route and the WCML. Her transfer back again to Cardiff in January 1994 led to her regular use on passenger services to the south coast, to Liverpool and to Manchester Oxford Road, duties which kept her busy until February 1996 when she moved briefly to Motherwell only to be returned to Cardiff less than a month later to resume her work there.

Allocated to Transrail she regularly had charge of Class 1 trains between Crewe and Bangor or Holyhead, between Cardiff and Birmingham or to Manchester, or south with Class 2 services from Bristol to Weymouth. This pattern continued throughout 1996, augmented with occasional freight workings, rugby 'extras' or charters such as Pathfinder Railtours' 'The Dyfed Docker' on 16 November, which ran from Birmingham to Cardiff by way of Carmarthen and return during which she shared the work with 37412 and 37902. In May 1997 she appeared at Open Days at Aberthaw Power Station and Newport before resuming her regular passenger duties in the Cardiff area.

Her transfer to Toton in November 1998 for EWS Systemwide saw her continue with similar work and the same involvement followed her move to Motherwell in March 1999. On 1 May 1999 she and sister loco 37419 had charge of the SRPS charter 'The Fort William & Mallaig' from Glenrothes with Thornton north of Edinburgh, and return. On 5 July that year she featured on the 'Royal Scotsman' between Kyle of Lochalsh and Perth via Aberdeen and for the following two years was mainly occupied with Class 1 services north from Edinburgh, though she was increasingly in demand now to head charter 'specials', notably for the SRPS including on 28 August 1999 'The Kyle of Lochalsh' from Dunbar to Inverness, Kyle and return with 37413. This was followed on 6 May 2000 by 'The West Highlander', Dunbar to Fort William and Mallaig, taking the return section with 37674. Then on 10 June that year, 'The Heartbeat Special', from Edinburgh to Tees Yard, Battersby, Whitby and return, sharing the work with 37425. This was followed on 8 July by 'The Skirling Postie' a two-day tour beginning at Sheffield and running to Crewe, Edinburgh Waverley, Tyneside Royal Mail Platform, Low Fell Junction, York, then to Sheffield, Birmingham New Street and Crewe. A total of eight locos were involved including classmate 37419. A month later on 5 August she was back with 'The West Highlander', Edinburgh Waverley to Fort William, Mallaig and return, sharing the work with 37415 while 37503 handled the Fort William to Mallaig and return legs.

Passenger work in the Highlands continued throughout 2000 and into the spring of 2001 when charter duty returned. On 5 May 2001 she was engaged by the SRPS again for 'The Fife to Mallaig', working between Glenrothes with Thornton and Fort William with 37416 while 37405 took the Fort William to Mallaig and return section. On 26 May she and 37416 were heading the North East Railtours charter from Dunbar to Kyle of Lochalsh and return. Then on 9 June 2001 she was again working for the SRPS with their 'Ayr to Kyle of Lochalsh' tour in the company of 37426. Grampian Railtours were her next employers when on 19 August she and 37405 headed 'The Dunrobin Castle' from Aberdeen and return. On 1 September she and 37415 had responsibility for the Scottish sections of Pathfinder Railtours' 'The Poly Granite', a two-day charter from Birmingham New Street to Edinburgh Waverley by way of York and Newcastle, then on to Aberdeen and return via Carlisle and the WCML. Her final charter for 2001 was her involvement in a four-day tour for Hertfordshire Rail Tours, beginning at King's Cross on 12 October and running to Edinburgh, Kyle of Lochalsh, Inverness and Thurso before returning to London. She featured on the Scottish sections with classmates 37415 and 37428.

A brief period spent working Class 2 services between Cardiff and Rhymney occupied November before in December she returned to working Edinburgh to Fort William trains until April 2003 when charter duties resumed once more. From 18 to 21 April she was involved with Pathfinder Railtours' 'The Orcadian' which ran from Swindon to Crewe then Carlisle, Edinburgh, Inverness, Wick and return, she and 37418 having responsibility for the sections from Carlisle and back. May began with the SRPS 'Fort William and Mallaig' tour on the third from Glenrothes with Thornton with 37426 throughout. Two days later the pair were in action for North Eastern Railtours between Newcastle and Oban and return and again on 17 May for the SRPS with their 'Keighley (for Worth Valley), Leeds and York' charter from Ayr.

She then returned to regular passenger duties north from Edinburgh until being transferred to Crewe Diesel depot in September 2003. From then until November 2004 she was fully occupied with passenger services between Leeds, York, Knaresborough and occasionally as far as Carlisle, often coupled with 37408. On 6 November 2004 she took a rugby special between Carmarthen and Cardiff before transferring to Margam on 12 December and becoming involved with services between Cardiff and Rhymney once more including her participation in Arriva Trains Wales 'Rhymney Valley Diesel Extravaganza' on 4 December, when numerous special trains ran between Rhymney and Cardiff Central. She continued with this busy schedule until on 20 May 2006 when she was in charge of Pathfinder Railtours' 'The Snowdonian' between Sheffield and Pwllheli by way of Birmingham and Machynlleth North, now in green livery and carrying the number D6990.

There then followed a series of day tours for Past Time Travel top and tail with steam loco 76079 beginning with 'The Fowey Pony', Plymouth to Fowey, Carne Point and return on 29 May. On 30 May 'The China Clay Pony' ran between Plymouth and Parkandillack, then the next day 'The South Hams Pony' operated between Plymouth, Buckfastleigh, Totnes and Newton Abbot followed on 1 June by 'The Tarka Pony' between Exeter St Davids and Barnstable. Her final charter was on 17 February 2007 when she and 37425 had charge of Pathfinder Railtours' 'The Bard & Birch' from Bristol Temple Meads to Birmingham, Stratford-upon-Avon, Oxford, Princes Risborough, Banbury and return. After this she was put in store at Margam before being transferred to Toton in May 2007 into the EWS Fleet Management Unit. She appeared at the 'Eastleigh 100' Open Day on 24 May 2009 but was returned to store until in January 2011 she was sold, awaiting collection, then moved first to Carlisle Kingmoor, then on to Derby and finally by road to CF Booth's at Rotherham where she was cut up in May 2013.

Nameplate of 37411.

**37412 (D6601, 37301)**

Released by EE Vulcan Foundry as D6601, Works Number EE/VF3561/D990 on 6 September 1965 and allocated to Landore.

Final depot: Kingmoor, 10/10.

Names carried: *Loch Lomond*, 3/87–5/89; *Driver John Elliot*, 1/95.

Status: Cut up at EMR Kingsbury, 8/12.

Notable movements:
Her duties in South Wales centred around the heavy industry of that area and included iron ore trains from Llanwern, coal from Rose Hayworth and oil through Port Talbot. From the 1980s she became more involved with passenger work including a time as Lickey Banker in mid-1981 and a period heading passenger services in East Anglia whilst stabled at March depot during the spring of 1983. On 2 July 1983 she featured on a BR Day Excursion from Llanelli to Llandudno via Crewe and return, being in charge between Llanelli and Crewe, then on the following day she was involved for the Monmouthshire Railway Society's 'The Red Dragon' charter which ran from Swansea to Shrewsbury by way of Newport, taking the Swansea to Newport and return legs. During 1984 she was again on Lickey banking duty but on 25 August that year she was given charge of 1Z12 the Bristol Temple Meads to Paddington Relief and 1Z33 the Paddington to Swansea Relief, followed the following day by 1Z44, an Aberdare to Clacton and return charter.

After her transfer to Eastfield in February 1985 she was employed on Class 1 passenger services north from Glasgow mainly to Oban or Fort William and taking over the Highland sections of Anglo-Scottish expresses from London Euston, as well as local trains between Fort William and Mallaig. This work occupied her until her transfer to Inverness in January 1989, interrupted by the occasional charter such as on 3 September 1988 for the SRPS from Edinburgh Waverley to Mallaig and return where she had charge between Waverley and Fort William and return. Whist based at Inverness she worked Class 1 services between there and Glasgow Queen Street but her transfer to Laira in February 1989 led to her being used on China Clay workings in Cornwall for a time. In 1994 she was based at Crewe Diesel depot and then at Cardiff Canton, from where on 23 October she was involved with classmate 37146 on Pathfinder Railtours' 'The Pixie Returns', a charter from Bristol Temple Meads to Plymouth by way of Exeter St Davids, then to Liskeard, Coombe and return.

Following this she was occupied mainly with Class 2 services between Bristol and Weymouth or Class 1 trains between Cardiff and Birmingham, Crewe or Manchester Oxford Road. During this time she was involved with charters including on 2 March 1996 'The Glamorgan Freighter' with 37895 for Pathfinder Railtours, which ran from Birmingham New Street to Newport, Cardiff Docks, Ninian Park, Bridgend, Pontycymmer and on to Gloucester via Newport. Then on 16 November that year, again for Pathfinder Railtours' 'The Dyfed Docker' in the company of 37411. Her transfer to Toton in November 1998 saw a gradual change in her schedule with more regular appearances on Class 2 trains from Cardiff to Rhymney or Bristol, though on 24 April 1999 she was called upon to take the Railtours North West charter 'The Southport–Settle Scotsman' which ran from Southport to Wigan Springs Branch, Blackburn, Settle, Carlisle and on to Edinburgh. The return to Springs Branch was by way of the WCML then back to Southport. Her move to Crewe Diesel depot in July 1999 led to greater involvement with Class 1 services between Birmingham or Crewe to Chester, Bangor or Holyhead.

As she was transferred between Crewe Diesel, Toton and Cardiff Canton over the following years her schedule followed the pattern established earlier, again with occasional charter appearances adding variety. On 7 October 2000 she and 37419 had charge of 'The Cumbrian Coast Special' a tour for the SRPS/North East Railtours which ran from Edinburgh Waverley to Newcastle then to Carlisle, Carnforth, Barrow-in-Furness and Ravenglass (for the R&ER) and return. On 12 May 2001 she had a different kind of 'special' experience when she and 37428 worked a Regional Railways 'Football Additional' between Gloucester and Cardiff Central for the FA Cup Final at the Millenium Stadium, Cardiff. After a period working mainly Class 2 services out of Cardiff, usually to Rhymney, which occupied her until September 2002 she was put into store by EWS in October that year and that signalled the beginning of the end of her active life. A series of transfers between storage locations followed until she was finally scrapped in August 2012.

Nameplate of 37413.

**37413 (D6976, 37276)**
Released by EE Vulcan Foundry as D6976, Works Number EE/3536/D965 on 15 April 1965 and allocated to Canton.

Final depot: Kingmoor, 9/15.

Names carried: *Loch Eil Outward Bound*, 3/87; *The Scottish Railway Preservation Society*, 9/97–5/00.

Status: Cut up by C.F. Booth at Rotherham, 4/17.

**37414 (D6987, 37287)** (See also D6987 and 37414 in Class 37s in Colour).

Released by EE Vulcan Foundry as D6987, Works Number EE/VF3547/D976 on 6 June 1965 and allocated to Canton.

Final depot: Doncaster, 3/00.

Name carried: *Cathays C&W Works 1846–1993*, 1/94.

Status: Bought by BREL for preservation, 8/05; Cut up at T.J. Thomson's scrapyard, Stockton, 3/09.

Notable movements:
Her early years in South Wales were typical of her class as she was involved with heavy freight workings related to the steel and coal industries which dominated that area at the time but by the early 1980s, following her modifications, she was increasingly employed on passenger services and as a banker on the Lickey Incline. She worked Class 1 and Class 2 trains from Cardiff and in the south west and her move to Scotland saw her involved more frequently with this kind of work, initially north from Glasgow to Oban or Fort William then from Inverness to Wick, Aberdeen or Kyle of Lochalsh. This continued until May 1989 after which she transferred to the south of England where her workload was more varied. After an appearance at Tinsley Open Day on 29 September 1990 and her move to Immingham she was given sole charge of the Wirral Model Railway Society charter from Hooton to Chester, Manchester Victoria, York, Scarborough and return by way of Edge Hill.

A mix of passenger and freight duties followed until her transfer to Crewe Diesel involved her being sent north of the border again to work passenger services between Inverness, Aberdeen and Edinburgh until January 1993 when she moved back to work from Crewe taking trains to Shrewsbury or more regularly between Liverpool Lime Street and Cardiff and from Manchester Victoria to the Lancashire coastal resorts of Southport and Blackpool. The spring of 1993 also saw her become involved with charter 'specials' again including for the Class 37 Group on 17 April 'The Felixstowe Phoenix' which ran from Derby to Ipswich and Norwich then travelled over various lines in the Felixstowe area before returning to Derby by way of Grantham and Nottingham. Also taking part were classmates 37154, 37271 and 37370.

She then featured on charters between Nottingham and Whitby on 1 May, Chester and Scarborough on 8 May and Shrewsbury and Carmarthen on 16 May before resuming her regular duties between the Midlands, the North West or South Wales which occupied her schedule until late 1998. After taking Railtours North West's

Passing Rhyl No.1 signal box on 23 June 1993 is 37414 with the 09.50 Manchester Victoria to Holyhead service. (*Jonathan Allen*)

## Locomotive Histories • 83

'The Southport–Settle Scotsman' with 37428 and 37716 on 5 December 1998, which ran from Southport to Wigan Springs Branch, Blackburn, Settle, Carlisle and on to Edinburgh, returning via the WCML to Lancaster, Wigan and back to Southport she was returned to Class 2 passenger services in South Wales and the south west until July 1999 when she was briefly reinstated onto Class 1 turns between Crewe or Birmingham and North Wales. By September 1999 she was being called upon to head a variety of Class 1 and Class 2 services between Crewe, South Wales and beyond through Bristol to the south coast but by February 2000 she was confined to the Cardiff to Rhymney 'locals'. Going into store for EWS in March 2000 signalled the end of her active life and though there were hopes of preservation, with a time spent on the heritage Weardale Railway in County Durham from October 2005 she was removed from there in March 2009 and subsequently scrapped.

**37415 (D6977, 37277)**
Released by EE Vulcan Foundry as D6977, Works Number EE/VF3537/D966 on 22 April 1965 and allocated to Canton.

Final depot: Toton, 5/07.

Name carried: *Mt. Etna*, 5/93.

Status: Cut up by C.F. Booth, Rotherham, 11/13.

**37416 (D6602, 37302)** (See also 37416 in Class 37s in Colour) Released by EE Vulcan Foundry as D6602, Works Number EE/VF3562/D991 on 9 September 1965 and allocated to Canton.

Final depot: Kingmoor, 9/11.

Names carried: *Mt. Fuji*, 5/93; *Sir Robert McAlpine/Concrete Bob*, 5/01–12/04.

Status: Cut up at C.F. Booth, Rotherham, 3/13.

Notable movements:
Her early years in South Wales were spent working heavy freight trains for the steel and coal industries of that area and it was not until the late 1970s that passenger duties featured regularly in her schedule in the Cardiff and Swansea area. On 2 June 1982 she had charge of a 1Zxx 'special' from Bristol Temple Meads to Cardiff, Barry Island and return. Following her move to

**Waiting at** Colwyn Bay on 23 June 1993 is 37414 *Cathays C&W Works 1846–1993* with the 14.30 Holyhead to Crewe service. (*Jonathan Allen*)

**Passing near** Swindon on 13 January 2001 is 37415. (*Steve Jones*)

Scotland and then her overhaul at Crewe Works in October 1985, she was occupied fully with Class 1 and Class 2 services north from Glasgow and then in the Highlands from Inverness to Thurso, Wick and Kyle of Lochalsh until her transfer to Yorkshire in January 1991.

Whilst at Tinsley she worked regularly from Manchester Victoria to Southport and Blackpool, with occasional services to Liverpool and after moving back to Inverness in August 1991 was frequently employed on passenger trains to Aberdeen or less often to Kyle of Lochalsh. Back at Tinsley in April 1992 she resumed her previous passenger schedule but now working more often out of Liverpool Lime Street than Manchester Victoria. Further transfers to Laira and then Cardiff Canton brought a change in operating region though not in workload, but her move to Springs Branch in July 1995 saw her employed on Class 1 services between Crewe and North Wales while her subsequent transfer back to Canton in September 1996 led to her employment on services to Birmingham New Street or south to Bristol Temple Meads.

Whilst not a regular performer on charters at this time she was involved with Pathfinder Railtours' 'The Hardy Devonian' which ran on 18 January 1997 from Gloucester via Worcester to Bristol Temple meads, then to Weymouth, Exeter St Davids and return. Otherwise until her transfer to Motherwell in February 1999 she mainly ran Class 2 services between Cardiff and Bristol or on to Weymouth. Once back in Scotland she was reunited with Class 1 services out of Edinburgh to the Highlands and was more frequently called upon for charter train duty including for the SRPS on 11 September 1999 'The Keighley & York' from Ayr to Carlisle then via the S&C to Keighley, York and return paired with 37413. On 17 June 2000, again for the SRPS, 'The York', Edinburgh Waverley to York and return with 37408 and for the same operator on 23 & 24 June 2000 'The Far North Explorer' with 37419 and 37521 from Edinburgh Waverley to Wick, Thurso, back to Wick then to Inverness and return.

In 2001 a four-day tour for Hertfordshire Rail Tours originated at King's Cross on 13 April and ran to Edinburgh, Inverness, Kyle of Lochalsh and return, then to Thurso and return and finally back to King's Cross via Edinburgh and Newcastle. She and classmate 37427 had charge of all the Scottish sections and as far south as Newcastle. On 5 May 2001 she was again with the SRPS for 'The Fife & Mallaig' charter from Glenrothes with Thornton to Fort William, Mallaig and return with 37411 throughout. Later that month on 26 May she was again paired with 37411, this time for the North East Railtours charter from Dunbar to Kyle of Lochalsh and return and two days later they were paired yet again for a football special between Preston and Cardiff. On 5 and 7 October 2001 she was reunited with 37408 for Pathfinder Railtours' 'The Monarch of the Glen' which originated at Cardiff and ran to Carlisle, Fort William then to Glasgow and return to Cardiff. The two 37s were in charge from Carlisle northwards and return.

Her busy schedule with Class 1 services north from Edinburgh continued until mid-2005, a time which also saw her regularly in demand to head charters and 1Zxx 'specials' including on 25 April 2002 1Zxx Edinburgh to Oban with 37426, then on 17 May 2003 with 37428 she headed 1Z50, Birmingham International to Inverness between Edinburgh and Inverness. This was followed on 14 June 2003 by a charter for the SRPS 'The Plockton & Kyle of Lochalsh' with 37406 between Dunbar and Kyle of Lochalsh and return. On 4 July that year she and 37418 had charge of 1Z62 from Edinburgh Waverley to Thurso and the following day they took 1Z66 from Wick to Edinburgh. Then over 12 and 13 July she and 37421 were responsible for 1Z58 which originated at Birmingham International destined for Inverness, taking over at Edinburgh. The second day included the Inverness to Kyle of Lochalsh 'Northern Belle'. On 9 May 2004 she was back in action again with 1Zxx, Aberdeen to Kyle of Lochalsh and return in the company of 37421 once more. From 25 to 28 June 2004 she worked Hertfordshire Rail Tours 'The Orcadian', a charter from King's Cross to Edinburgh then to Inverness, Kyle of Lochalsh for a Highlands tour then back to Inverness for the return to King's Cross.

More 'specials' were to follow including on 16 July 2004 1Z71 Inverness to Kyle of Lochalsh, on 18 July 1Z75 Sterling to Ayr and on 31 August 1Z20 Edinburgh to Dalmally. She was called upon to head 'The Royal Scotsman' on 1 September 2004 between Taynuilt and Perth and on 7 September took 1Z92 from Tain north of

Inverness to Kyle of Lochalsh. This was followed on 19 September by 1Z95 from Edinburgh to Taynuilt. She was employed by Pathfinder Railtours on 19 February 2005 to take 'The Buffer Puffer Volume 3' from London Blackfriars in the company of 37406, then on 2 May 2005 she was working with 37417 for North East Railtours heading 'The Oban Excursion' from Newcastle to Oban and return via Edinburgh Waverley. This was followed on 7 May that year by the SRPS 'West Highlander' charter from Glenrothes with Thornton to Fort William, Mallaig and return with 37410 and 37417.

Between 28 May and 11 June 2005 she was busy with a series of 1Zxx 'specials' based on Inverness but by early July she had transferred back to the south of the UK and on 9 July worked the Worksop Open Day Committee's 'The Worksop Cambrian Coast Express' from Worksop to Aberystwyth and return by way of Birmingham New Street and Welshpool with 37406. A week later she was paired with 37406 again to head 1Z37, the Birmingham New Street to Pwllheli 'special' between Birmingham and Machynlleth. On 29 October 2005, again working with 37406 they had charge of Kingfisher Railtours' 'The Snowdonian Explorer' which ran from High Wycombe to Machynlleth, Pwllheli and return. Reunited with 37417 again on 5 November 2005 they took The Branch Line Society's 'Tees Rail Tour' from Birmingham New Street via York to Tyne Yard for a tour of local lines in the Middlesborough and Hartlepool areas. Finally on 19 November she led 'The Guild 'n' Docker' for Pathfinder Railtours which ran from Newport by way of Birmingham to Crewe then on to Preston Docks. By 2006 she was back on regular duty with Class 1 services between Edinburgh and Fort William which occupied her until her transfer to Toton in May 2007, soon after which she was placed into store, eventually to be sold for scrap.

**37417 (D6969, 37269)**
Released by EE Vulcan Foundry as D6969, Works Number EE/VF3529/D958 on 26 February 1965 and allocated to Canton.

Final depot: Kingmoor, 9/11.

Names carried: *Highland Region*, 12/85; *Rail Magazine*, 8/98; *Richard Trevithick*, 2/04.

Status: Cut up by C.F. Booth, Rotherham, 2/13.

**37418 (D6971, 37271)** (See also 37418 in Class 37s in Colour)
Released by EE Vulcan Foundry as D6971, Works Number EE/VF3531/D960 on 18 March 1965 and allocated to Canton.

Final depot: Toton, 5/07.

Names carried: *An Comunn Gaidhealach*, 10/86–2/91; *Pectinidae*, 3/91–3/92; *Gordon Grigg*, 3/92–4/92; *Pectinidae*, 4/92–3/94; *ELR*, 4/94; *An Comunn Gaidhealach*, 2/24.

**Nameplate of** 37417.

**Approaching Llandudno** Junction on 23 June 1993 is 37418 *Pectinidae* with the 13.30 Holyhead to Manchester Victoria service. (*Jonathan Allen*)

Status: Bought for preservation, 12/07; ELR, 3/09; Reinstated to traffic as a PODL, 7/17; Allocated to Colas Rail Freight, 1/19; Allocated to Rail Express Systems Special Charter Trains as a PODL, 9/22; Operational with Loram Rail from 6/23 and painted into their red & white livery, 1/24.

Notable movements:
During her early years in South Wales, she was occupied with freight associated with the heavy industry of that area notably coal and steel but also had involvement in passenger services from Cardiff Central. By the early 1980s passenger work was becoming her more regular employment, including a time spent as Lickey Banker in 1984 before her transfer to Eastfield. This move led to her use on passenger trains north from Glasgow and later with services centred on Inverness which would keep her busy until her transfer to Immingham in September 1990 when her duties became more varied. During this time she was given charge of passenger trains from the Midlands to the Welsh holiday destinations of Pwllheli or Aberystwyth, to the major cities of South Wales or to the North West of England including to Liverpool, Manchester or Blackpool. By 1992 she was becoming sought after to head charters including on 9 August with classmate 37502 from Wolverhampton to Carlisle and return by way of the S&C, followed on 14 November that year by a tour from London St Pancras to Matlock and return with 37425.

Her move to Crewe Diesel saw her busy with Class 1 services between the Midlands and the North West, especially trains from Crewe, Birmingham or Stafford to Llandudno and Holyhead and in the Liverpool and Manchester areas and this heavy schedule continued throughout the 1990s until in July 1999 she was transferred to Toton for EWS and in October that year to Motherwell. This move saw her reunited with the Scottish Highlands once more as she was kept busy with services between Edinburgh and Fort William including the occasional charter such as that for NER/GER with 37427 from Alnmouth to Carlisle on 8 July 2000 then by way of the S&C to Leeds and York, retracing their route the following day back to Alnmouth.

After a brief return to the Cardiff area from November 2000 to January 2001 she was returned to the Scottish Highlands for the summer before transferring back to Canton in September 2001 where she was occupied with services mainly between Cardiff and Rhymney until March 2002 when her routine was interrupted by a series of 1Zxx Regional Railways' 'Rugby Additionals' between Crewe and Cardiff Central. Normal service was resumed in April with Fishguard being added to her regular destinations from Cardiff until her transfer to Motherwell in March 2003, after which she worked again between Edinburgh and Fort William. Another short transfer to South Wales in November 2003 saw her working Class 2 services again between Cardiff Central and Rhymney before she returned to her Scottish Class 1 duties in February 2004. This lasted until September but was interrupted by more prestigious work including the VSOE 'Northern Belle' from Edinburgh to Oban on 11 April with 37421, 'The West Highlander' from Edinburgh to Mallaig top and tail with 37401 for the SRPS on 7 August and sections of Pathfinder Railtours' 'The Industrial Invader' which originated at Crewe on 18 September 2004.

She was in action again for Pathfinder Railtours' 'The Highland Venturer' which ran from Cardiff on 24 September to Dumbarton where she was in the company of 37410. Between 2 and 8 October 2004 she was paired with 37406 for the Scottish sections of a Hertfordshire Rail Tours charter, 'The English, Welsh & Scottish Rail Tour' which began at London Paddington then toured lines in the Bristol area before heading to Cardiff, then to Motherwell, Inverness, Kyle of Lochalsh, on to Wick and Thurso before returning to Inverness, Edinburgh and terminating at King's Cross. Finally, a less glamourous duty was hers on 6 November 2004 when she had charge of rugby specials between Cardiff and Gloucester.

After this she was put into store by EWS before being bought for preservation in December 2007 and moved to the ELR where she began work in May 2009 until March 2016. After that she was reinstated into traffic initially as a PODL (PODL) then in January 2019 for Colas Rail Freight. Again she was allocated the Class 2 Cardiff Central to Rhymney rostas from June that year until March 2020 after which she was returned to PODL status and was involved with a series of 1Zxx 'specials' including on 19 October 2022 that between Derby and Shildon, on 14 January 2023 for the Branch Line Society 'The Shooter's Swansong' which ran between Derby, Birmingham New Street, London Marylebone, Stratford-upon-Avon then to London Paddington and back to Derby. On 24 and 25 June she was busy again with trips from Derby. First 'The Jolly Vacman' to Skegness, then 'The Eyre Valley Explorer' to Keighley for the Worth Valley Railway, both organised by The Branch Line Society. On 26 October 2023 she and EuroPhoenix 37901 *Mirrlees Pioneer* worked with Inspection Saloon number 975025 *Caroline* from York to Boulby (Redcar & Cleveland), having previously propelled her between Derby and Mossend on 22 August. On 11 November 2023 she replaced the unavailable 37240 on Vintage Trains 'The Blackpool Illuminations Explorer' from Birmingham New Street to Blackpool and return. On 10 April 2024 ran with Inspection Saloon 975025 *Caroline* from Tonbridge to London Victoria and on 11 May 2024 ran with 37057 as 3Q66, a NR Survey Train between Norwich and Derby RTC. She replaced the unavailable 55009 *Alycidon* for the NYMR Diesel Gala, 14–16 June 2024.

**37419 (D6991, 37291)** (See also 37419 in Class 37s in Colour) Released by EE Vulcan Foundry as D6991, Works Number EE/VF3551/D980 on 24 June 1965 and allocated to Canton.

Final depot: Kingmoor, 8/11.

Names carried: *Mt. Pinatubo*, 7/93–7/93; *Driver Tony Kay 1974–2019*, 7/23 following removal of *Carl Haviland 1954–2012*. Name *Driver Tony Kay 1974–2019* removed 3/24.

Status: Operational with DRS Supply Chain Locomotives from 3/22. Allocated to DRS Locomotives stored/for disposal from 2/24. Sold to HNRC, locomotives for lease, and transferred to Barrow Hill, 3/24.

**37420 (D6997, 37297)** Released by EE Vulcan Foundry as D6997, Works Number EE/VF3557/D986 on 21 July 1965 and allocated to Canton.

Final depot: Toton, 5/07.

Name carried: *The Scottish Hosteller*, 6/86.

Status: Cut up at Hull's scrapyard, Rotherham, 2/08.

**37421 (D6967, 37267)** Released by EE Vulcan Foundry as D6967, Works Number EE/VF3527/D956 on 13 February 1965 and allocated to Darnall.

Final depot: Doncaster, as a PODL, 1/14.

Names carried: *Strombidae*, 3/91–3/93; *Star of the East*, 3/93–4/93; *The Kingsman*, 11/93.

Status: Operational with EWS, 12/98; Bought for preservation by L&S Locomotives, for the Pontypool & Blaenavon Railway, 12/08; Reinstated into traffic as a PODL, 1/14; Operational with Colas Rail Freight from 6/15; Operational on Network Rail infrastructure inspection trains with 37219, from Mossend Yard, 1/24.

**Passing Great** Rocks Junction, Derbyshire on 4 June 1997 are EWS liveried 37419 and 'Civil Engineers' liveried 37146 with their train of empties. (*Jonathan Allen*)

**At Crewe** Works in ex-works condition on 23 November 1985 is 37421.

**37422 (D6966, 37266, 37558)** (See also 37422 in Class 37s in Colour) Released by EE Vulcan Foundry as D6966, Works Number EE/VF3526/D955 on 13 February 1965 and allocated to Darnall.

Final depot: Toton, 2/07.

Names carried: *Robert F. Fairlie Locomotive Engineer 1831–1885*, 5/93; *Cardiff Canton*, 1/03; *Victorious*, 1/21–3/24.

Status: Operational with DRS Supply Chain Locomotives from 3/22; Reassigned to 'DRS locomotives, stored/for disposal', 2/24. Sold to HNRC and transferred to Barrow Hill, 3/24.

Notable movements:
Before her rebuilding to sub-class 37/4 freight haulage was an important feature of her workload and included regular oil tank trains in the south east and East Anglia regions. Passenger services were always important in her schedules and she was frequently employed on Class 1 trains out of London Liverpool Street. By the early 1980s she was to be seen more regularly heading services in the Bristol, south east and South Wales areas and on 11 September 1983 she was employed by F+W Railtours on 'The Pembroke Haven Harbourer'. On 3 March 1984 she was in charter action again for F+W Railtours with 'The Welsh Central Liner' which originated at Plymouth and ran to Taunton, Bristol Temple Meads then on to Gloucester, Port Talbot, Llandrindod Wells, Craven Arms, Severn Tunnel Junction and return. Two weeks later on 17 March she was involved with Severnside Railtours' 'The Tyne Tees Explorer' which ran from Swansea to Bristol Temple Meads then to Gloucester, Toton, Doncaster, York, Stockton, Durham and Middlesborough before returning via Sheffield, Derby and Bristol. From April 1984 she was employed on Class 2 services in the Bristol and Cardiff area until her transfer to Eastfield in March 1985 when she was busy with trains north from Glasgow to Oban or Fort William.

After her Heavy General Overhaul and renumbering to 37422 in January 1986, she was frequently used on Fort William to Mallaig services as well as taking over for the Scottish sections of Class 1 trains from London Euston. In January 1989 her transfer to Canton saw her heading trains to Liverpool and Manchester until her move to Tinsley in May 1989 and then to Immingham in September 1990 involved her in more varied duties including heavy freight. Charters still featured in her schedule including on 6 September 1992 for Pathfinder Railtours' 'The Leicester Looper' between Manchester Piccadilly and Leicester, for the Branch Line Society 'The Tyne-Tees Wanderer IV' on 31 October 1992 from Derby to Billingham via Sheffield, then on to Newcastle, Jarrow and return with 37514 throughout. On 28 November that year she headed a 'Shoppers Special' from Butterley to London St Pancras via Nottingham and return and on 6 March 1993 she was back with Pathfinder Railtours for 'The Coker Coaler' which ran from Manchester Piccadilly to Derby for a collieries tour which included Bolsover Colliery (Derbyshire), Harworth Colliery (Nottinghamshire) then on to the South Yorkshire pits at Rossington, Bentley and Grimethorpe before returning by way of Wakefield,

**Stabled at** York Station Parcels Sidings on 7 July 2022 is 37422 *Victorious*, carrying 'cockney sparrow' decals on her DRS Plain Blue livery, received on 12 November 2020 to honour her previous links to the Stratford depot.

Sheffield and Birmingham New Street, again with 37514 throughout.

She was then transferred to Crewe Diesel depot and was used regularly on services to North Wales and the north west of England including the occasional charter such as Pathfinder Railtours' 'The Anglesey Odyssey II' from York to Llandudno and return on 9 October 1993. In June 1999 she moved to Toton and was employed on services between Bristol Temple Meads and Weymouth or Cardiff to Rhymney until being put into store for EWS in October 1999.

She was back in regular service after her Light Overhaul at Canton in February 2003 and again was employed on services between Cardiff and Rhymney or Fishguard until November 2004. After spending some time in the EWS Tactical Reserve there began a period of regular charter commitments which would keep her busy for the next four years. These included for Pathfinder Railtours on 2 May 2005 'The Cumbrian Warrior' with 37427 which ran from Cardiff Central to Preston, Workington, Maryport and return. Unfortunately, she failed near Wigan and was removed at Preston leaving 37427 to complete the tour. Working for Pathfinder Railtours again on 14 April 2007 heading 'The Principality Freighter' with 37410 they began at Birmingham International and travelled to Bristol Parkway, Newport and Llanelli for a tour of South Wales lines before returning to Birmingham. On 12 May 2007 she was in charge of 'The Heart of Wales Express' for The Mid-Cheshire Rail Users Association running from Altrincham to Chester, Cardiff Central and return in the company of 37406. A charter for Kingfisher Tours was next on 30 June 2007, 'The Welsh Mountain Explorer' from Ealing Broadway to Craven Arms, Aberystwyth and return with 37405 throughout. Next came two outings with VSOE 'Northern Belle'. First on 12 August from Aberdeen to Dunrobin Castle and return and then on 19 August from Edinburgh Park to Oban and return, both with 37410 throughout. Finally for 2007 she was back with Pathfinder Railtours for 'The Heart of Wales Explorer' on 25 August, from Eastleigh to Cardiff Central then Bridgend, Port Talbot, Craven Arms and Birmingham New Street to Bristol Parkway and return, this time paired with 37417 throughout.

Charter workings in 2008 began with Pathfinder Railtours' 'The Buffer Puffer 6.0' on 2 February. This meandering tour began at London Bridge and ran to Uckfield including investigating lines in the Clapham Junction area, then going on to London Victoria and further minor lines before finishing at King's Cross. On 14 June 2008 she was involved with Compass Tours 'The Edinburgh Merryman' which ran from Runcorn to Liverpool Lime Street then to Leeds, Carlisle by the S&C and on to Edinburgh and return. She featured only on the return leg from Liverpool Lime Street to Runcorn. A week later on 21 June she headed the SRPS 'The Edinburgh to Dunrobin Castle & Brora' followed by three 'specials' accompanied by 37417. On 12 July 1Z26/27 Edinburgh to Oban and return, then 1Z37/38 on 10 August, Aberdeen to Dunrobin and return and finally on 17 August 1Z26/27 again between Edinburgh and Oban. On 25 August 2008 she was involved with sections of the three-day tour 'Alloa Alloer' for Pathfinder Railtours which ran from Bristol Temple Meads to Crewe, York, Newcastle, Edinburgh Waverley then on to Glasgow Central, Carlisle, Wigan North Western, Crewe and back to Bristol Temple Meads. Finally on 7 September 2008 she had charge of 1Z26/27 again between Edinburgh and Oban, this time with 37401. That concluded a busy period of 'special' duties, though on 24 May 2009 she was on display at 'Eastleigh 100' Open Day after being in store for EWS.

She was back in store after that until August 2015 when she was restored to active service to work East Anglian trains between Norwich, Great Yarmouth and Lowestoft often with 37425, work which continued until September 2015 when she was transferred north to Carlisle to head trains to Barrow-in-Furness and Preston, which she did only until November that year when she returned to services in East Anglia. Here she stayed until August 2016 when she was sent back to resume working the Cumbrian Coast line until early September. This pattern of transfers between Cumbria and East Anglia continued until August 2019 when she was put into store by DRS at Kingmoor, interrupted only by an

**Nameplate of** 37422.

appearance at Crewe Gresty Bridge Open Day on 21 July 2018.

Various minor duties including some freight movements occupied her until on 9 April 2022 when she and 37425 had charge of Day Two of Four for UK Railtours' 'The West Highland & Royal Deeside', between Dumbarton, Oban and return. From 15 to 18 April 2022 she was busy with Pathfinder Railtours' 'The Easter Highlander' which originated at Eastleigh and ran to Skipton Class 68 hauled, there she and 37425 took over for a tour of Scotland by way of Paisley, Dumbarton, Oban, Dalmuir and Aberdeen before heading back south to York, after which the tour was returned to Eastleigh by Class 68. In the November 2022 edition of *The Railway Magazine*, it was reported that she and other classmates including 37218, 37401, 37419 and 37425 have been operating Rail Head Treatment Trains throughout Yorkshire while based at York Thrall Europa. In February 2024 she was sold to HNRC (locomotives for lease) and transferred to Barrow Hill.

**37423 (D6996, 37296)**
Released by EE Vulcan Foundry as D6996, Works Number EE/VF3556/D985 on 16 July 1965 and allocated to Canton.

Final depot: Doncaster, 11/99.

Names carried: *Sir Murray Morrison 1873–1948 Pioneer of the British Aluminium Industry*, 5/88; *Spirit of the Lakes*, 7/09–12/23

Status: Bought by WCRC, Carnforth, 5/04; Re-registered by NR as a PODL, 8/07; Stored at Kingmoor for DRS, 5/23, offered for sale, 9/23; Transferred to Leicester for EuroPhoenix Locomotives UK, 10/23.

Notable movements:
Although some freight haulage was undertaken in her early years in South Wales, passenger work was an important part of her schedule even then, with services in the Swansea and Cardiff areas as well as banking duties on the Lickey Incline and Class 1 trains to Birmingham and Crewe occupying her time into the 1980s. A first 'special' was taken on 5 May 1984 for the Marlow & Maidenhead Passenger Association in the form of 1Z44, originating at Ealing Broadway, Class 47 hauled to Gloucester where she and 37299 took over to Birmingham New Street, then on to Wolverhampton and Shrewsbury. From there they proceeded to Craven Arms, Llandrindod Wells, Bridgend, Cardiff Central, Chepstow and finally back to Gloucester from where the Class 47 returned the

**Standing in** York station Parcels Sidings on 23 May 2013 are 37423 *Spirit of the Lakes* and NR Inspection Saloon 975025 *Caroline*, with York's Rail Operating Centre under construction in the background.

tour to Ealing Broadway. Her move to Scotland in the mid-1980s led to her featuring regularly on services north from Glasgow to Fort William and Mallaig as well as taking over Anglo-Scottish trains from London Euston for their continued journey from Glasgow.

This pattern continued until the mid-1990s, with occasional freight duties and charters interspersed, including for the SRPS on 10 November 1990 'The Lochaber' from Edinburgh Waverley to Fort William and return, working with steam loco 'Black 5' 5305. On 26 September 1992 again for the SRPS she was in charge of their tour from Dunblane to Whitby and return, then on 2 October 1993 she was involved with 'special' 1Z12, Cleethorpes to Edinburgh Waverley and on to Fort William, having the train between Edinburgh and Fort William. Similarly on 24 June 1995, with 1Z53 Edinburgh Waverley to Fort William and return, on this occasion working with classmate 37410.

From then until her purchase and move to Bury in 2003 she was occupied with passenger services in South Wales and the south west of England, though this period did include a charter for the SRPS to Inverness from Kirkaldy on 26 June 1999 in the company of 37419. While allocated to DRS Nuclear Traffic Pool from December 2007 she was again in demand to head charters including day two of four for Stobart Rail Tours 'The Easter West Highlander' which began at King's Cross and ran to Edinburgh Waverley, then to Dumbarton, Oban, Kilmarnock and Ayr, when she and 37069 were in charge between Dumbarton and Oban. She was also involved with 1Zxx 'specials' between such locations as Crewe and Paignton on 21 June 2008, Glasgow Central and Fort William on 13 July and Wolverhampton and Cleethorpes on 16 August that same year. On 7 February 2009 she was in action again with 1Z21 between Carlisle and Birmingham International.

From late November 2009 until March 2010 she worked the Cumbrian Coast Line regularly with Class 2 trains between Maryport and Workington but after that she was involved almost totally with charters and specials beginning with day two of four for UK Railtours' 'The Easter West Highlander on 3 April 2010. This tour, like its namesake mentioned earlier ran from King's Cross but then to Wakefield, Settle, Carlisle, Dumbarton, Oban, Stranraer and Paisley, returning to King's Cross by the ECML. She and 37607 had charge between Dumbarton and Paisley. On 24 April 2010 she was working for Spitfire Railtours' 'The Broadsman', a tour from Crewe to Ely, Norwich, Cromer and Holt and return, followed on 5 June 2010 for Pathfinder Railtours' 'The Powys Chugger' which originated at Bristol Temple Meads and ran to Birmingham International, Crewe, Welshpool, Newtown then Wolverhampton and Bescot for a tour of goods lines before going on to Coventry and returning to Bristol.

Another series of 1Zxx 'specials' followed beginning on 19 June 2010 between Chester and Liverpool Lime Street, then on 22 August between Gourock and Edinburgh, followed on 2 September between Darlington and Wemyss Bay and finally with 37409 for three days beginning on 3 September 2010 from Edinburgh to Oban and return, then Dundee to Dunrobin and from Aberdeen to Perth and return. A guest appearance on the heritage Mid Norfolk Railway followed on 24 to 26 September before in combination with 37610 she took the Scottish sections of UK Railtours' 'The Cock of the North' charter which ran from King's Cross to Edinburgh Waverley, then to Inverness and Kyle of Lochalsh for a tour of the Highlands. After a brief visit to the Bo'ness and Kinneil Railway on 2 January 2011 and further specials in the Highlands during August and September 2011 she returned to the Cumbrian Coast Line to work Class 2 services between Carlisle and Barrow-in-Furness until February 2012. More 'specials' and charters followed including 1Z39 between Edinburgh and Oban on 19 August, 1Z72/73 Aberdeen to Dunrobin Castle and return on 20 July 2013 and 1Z12 Carlisle to Newcastle on 17 August 2013. For Retro Railtours on 31 August she and 37605 had charge of 'The Retro Fenland Explorer' from Crewe to Ely, Norwich, Great Yarmouth and return, then on 30 and 31 May 2014 'The Forth & Tay Highlander' with 37419 for Compass Tours, followed on 13 June that year for Pathfinder Railtours' 'The Purbeck Explorer'

**Nameplate of** 37423.

with 37402 and 37604 from Stafford to Southampton, Swanage and return.

Then she was back on the Cumbrian Coast services until July 2016 when she was transferred to work Class 2 trains out of Norwich to Lowestoft and Great Yarmouth often top and tail with 37403, 37405, 37419 37424 or 37425. This she did until May 2017 when she was moved back to Carlisle to resume workings to Barrow-in-Furness or on to Preston. By November that year she was returned to East Anglia to work usually with 37419 again from Norwich then in March 2018 she moved back to Cumbria but this time for only one month before returning to work with her classmates out of Norwich once more. This was interrupted only by another visit to the Mid Norfolk Railway on 6 and 7 April 2019, otherwise she was fully occupied with East Anglian services until May 2019 when after working a freight to Bridlington with 37419 in October 2020 she was next involved with a series of charters for The Branch Line Society, 'The Summer Syphons', the first of which, 'The Europort Explorer' ran from Edinburgh and Glasgow to Carlisle, Wakefield Europort and on to York on 2 July 2021. Next day 'The Sinfin Syphon' ran from York to Retford, Castle Donnington, Sinfin Rolls Royce, Derby, Toton and back to York. Finally on 4 July 2021 'The Primary Colours' from York to Sheffield, Rose Hill, Glossop, Crewe Basford Hall, Manchester Piccadilly then back to Sheffield and York. She was accompanied on this three-day marathon by classmates 37419 and 37422 plus locos from classes 60, 66, 70 and 90. More freight work followed then in February 2022 she was put into store by DRS and as of May 2023 was listed at 'For Disposal'. In January 2024 she was transferred to Leicester for EuroPhoenix Locomotives UK.

**Waiting at** Glasgow Queen Street during 1988 is 37424 Glendarroch. (Rick Ward)

### 37424 (D6979, 37279)

Released by EE Vulcan Foundry as D6979, Works Number EE/VF3539/D968 on 3 March 1965 and allocated to Canton.

Final depot: Toton, 5/07.

Names carried: *Glendarroch*, 12/87–10/88; *Isle of Mull*, 4/90–10/94; *Avro Vulcan XH558*, 7/16.

Status: Stored at Kingmoor for DRS from 11/23, listed as 'For Disposal'; Sold to Meteor Power, 3/24; Sold to HNRC at Barrow Hill, 5/24.

Notable movements:
Her early years in South Wales involved her working the heavy freight trains of the area and it was not until her modification in the late 1970s that passenger duties began to appear on her roster including on 14 April 1979 a charter for F+W Railtours' 'The Pixieland Express'. This originated at Cheltenham Spa and ran to Gloucester, Bristol Temple Meads, then to Penzance, Par, Newquay and return. It was hauled by Class 37s throughout and reputed to be the first time this class of loco had hauled a passenger train in Cornwall. She was based at St Blazey for driver and staff familiarisation at the time and had charge from Par to Newquay and return. Other '37s' involved were 37011, 37084, 37178 and 37276. In the early 1980s a mix of freight and passenger workings occupied her time, including a period spent as banker on the Lickey Incline, but as time went on it was passenger duties which were to occupy her more fully and her transfer to Scotland in 1985 saw her in charge of Class 1 services out of Glasgow to such destinations as Edinburgh and Perth or to Oban, Fort William and Mallaig.

She was also used on Anglo Scottish services from London Euston for the sections north of the border. This work continued until in July 1999 a move south meant she was involved with trains in the Cardiff and South Wales area once more as well as those from Bristol Temple Meads. This was short-lived however, as by September 1999 she was back in Scotland again. On 16 October 1999 she and classmate 37419 had charge of The Branch Line Society's 'The Aberdeen Requiem' from Linlithgow to Aberdeen, Elgin, Inverness, Aviemore, Kingussie, then to Pitlochry, Perth and back to Linlithgow, after which she resumed her duties with services between Edinburgh and Fort William until going into store for EWS in March 2000.

From June 2008 until April 2015 she was based on the Churnet Valley heritage railway in the Staffordshire Moorlands area of Staffordshire. From December 2016 to March 2017 she was employed heading Class 2 services from Norwich to Great Yarmouth and Lowestoft then was transferred north to Carlisle to work trains along the Cumbrian Coast line to Barrow-in-Furness or Preston. By April 2017 she was back in East Anglia but by May had returned to Cumbria where she stayed until June 2018. She was reunited with The Branch Line Society on 14 June 2018 for their tour 'The Nosey Peaker' from Stafford to Crewe, then to Buxton by way of Manchester Victoria, returning via Chinley, Northwich and Sandbach, mostly top and tail with 37407. On 21 July that year she was displayed at Crewe Gresty Bridge Open Day then from August 2018 was back working in the Norwich area, mainly with classmate 37405. In November she was transferred again to Carlisle but only briefly as by December she was back in East Anglia where she remained until September 2019. On 21 December 2019 she worked UK Railtours' 'Beverley at Christmas' charter which ran from King's Cross (by Class 90) to Doncaster Royal Mail Terminal where she and 37402 took the train on to Cottingham, West Parade North Junction (Hull) and Beverley, returning to Doncaster where the Class 90 resumed the journey back to King's Cross. Occasional freight workings followed during 2020 and 2021 before she was allocated to DRS Supply Chain Operations from March 2022, other than a period in store between September 2022 and May 2023. Allocated to HNRC at Crewe Gresty Bridge, May 2024.

**37425 (D6992, 37292)** (See also 37425 in Class 37s in Colour)

Released by EE Vulcan Foundry as D6992, Works Number EE/VF3552/D981 on 5 July 1965 and allocated to Canton.

Final depot: Toton, 5/07.

Names carried: *Sir Robert McAlpine/Concrete Bob*, 10/86; *Balchder y Cymoedd/Pride of the Valleys*, 11/05; Re-named *Sir Robert McAlpine/Concrete Bob*, 8/13–3/24.

Status: Operational at Kingmoor for DRS Supply Chain Locomotives from 3/22; Charter train haulage from 4/22; In store/For Disposal by DRS at Kingmoor from 2/24. Sold to Meteor Power, 3/24: Sold to HNRC at Barrow Hill, 5/24.

Notable movements:
In her early years her duties revolved around the heavy industry of the South Wales valleys, notably

**Stabled in** York station Parcels Sidings on 31 March 2022 is 37425 *Sir Robert McAlpine/Concrete Bob*, in Regional Railways livery.

**Nameplate of** 37425.

**Opposite side** nameplate of 37425.

**Nameplate of** 37425, named at Caerphilly on 28 November 2005. The opposite side carried the name *Pride of the Valleys* until 17 August 2013 when the names *Sir Robert McAlpine/Concrete Bob* were reinstated at DRS Kingmoor depot.

in the movement of coal from collieries such as Rose Heyworth, Margam, Oakdale or Taff Merthyr to steelworks at Llanwern or to power stations such as Aberthaw. Passenger work at this time was restricted to services out of Cardiff or Swansea, or banking duty on the Lickey Incline. It was not until the early 1980s and her transfer to Scotland that she was more regularly used on Class 1 and Class 2 trains, these in the Glasgow and Edinburgh regions. By the time she had been rebuilt to sub-class 37/4 in 1985 she was a frequent feature on the route to Oban, Fort William and Mallaig as well as taking over services originating at London Euston for their final leg into the Highlands. Her transfer south, first back to Cardiff Canton and then to Tinsley and Immingham saw her continue with similar duties in these areas and by the early 1990s this included assisting with charters such as on 30 November 1991 for Hertfordshire Rail Tours 'The Peak Explorer' which ran from London Euston to Birmingham International, then to Manchester Piccadilly, Hindlow, Buxton, Disley and return and on 10 October 1992 for Pathfinder Railtours' 'The Gaerwen Grid' which originated at Bristol Temple Meads and ran to Birmingham New Street, Llandudno, Blaenau Ffestiniog, Holyhead, Chester and return.

From March 1993 her schedule was fully occupied with mainly Class 1 trains in the north west of England and to North Wales including services from Crewe or Birmingham which continued until her transfer to Motherwell in October 1997 after which she was allocated to trains north from Edinburgh to Fort William. Charter duties at this time included on 3 October 1998 for the SRPS 'The Glenfinnan Explorer' with 37428 from Berwick-upon-Tweed to Glenfinnan and return and again for the same operator on 10 June 2000 'The Heartbeat Special' with 37411 from Edinburgh to Tees Yard, Battersby, Whitby and return. Her move to Crewe Diesel Depot later that month saw her resume working services between the Midlands and the north west and then from August 2000 she was deployed in South Wales again with trains between Cardiff and Rhymney. She was employed on these Class 2 services on a daily basis until October 2006, interrupted only by the occasional appearance on a 'special' such as on 10 September 2005 for Arriva Trains West from Cardiff to Crewe, Llandudno, Blaenau Ffestiniog and return, then on 28 November 2005 a Private Charter 1Z37 between Cardiff and Bargoed and on 4 December 2005 for Arriva Trains Wales when a series of trains ran for the Rhymney Valley Diesel Extravaganza between Cardiff Central and Rhymney. On 15 April 2006 she was employed with 37419 by Kingfisher Tours for their charter 'The Snowdonia Explorer' which ran from Bedford to Machynlleth, Porthmadog and return and then again with 37419 on 29 April that year, the charter running as 1Z47 between Rugby and Whitby.

Whilst allocated to EWS Tactical Reserve from late October 2006 she and 37411 worked Pathfinder Railtours' 'The Bard & Birch' on 17 February 2007 from Bristol Temple Meads to Birmingham, Kingsbury, Birch Coppice Exchange Sidings, Stratford-upon-Avon, Oxford, Princes Risborough, Banbury and return. After that and until March 2009 her time was spent in store at Margam or Toton, then between 27 and 29 March 2009 she featured as a guest on the heritage Mid Norfolk Railway. She was then used by EWS on various duties as required before being sold to DRS in August 2011. A series of engagements followed including on 12 January 2013 'The Enigmatic Logistician' for Pathfinder Railtours when she, 37259 and 37611 had charge of the tour which ran from Crewe to Stafford, Nuneaton, Milton Keynes, Wolverton, Incline Siding, Haversham Bank and return. On 11 April 2014 she was paired with 37259 again for 'The S&C 25th Anniversary Express', a charter organised by The Settle-Carlisle Railway Development Company to celebrate twenty-five years since the iconic line was saved from closure.

Between these two, she was a guest at Kingmoor Open Day on 17 August 2013. From June 2015 she was employed in East Anglia with Class 2 services out of Norwich to Lowestoft and Great Yarmouth, taking several trains each day top and tail with classmates including 37405, 37419 and 37422. This continued until November 2015, a period which also featured on 24 September that year a Positioning Train from Eastleigh to Paignton for Pathfinder Railtours' 'The Autumn Chieftain', a four-day tour which began the following day from Exeter St Davids. She and 37218 had charge throughout. The tour ran first to Inverness, then on to Kyle of Lochalsh and return, followed on the third day to Thurso, Wick and return to Inverness and finally back to Exeter St Davids on day four, 28 September 2015.

A brief period working the Cumbrian Coast Line between Carlisle and Barrow-in-Furness followed then she resumed her East Anglian duties in December that year with 37422 until the latter was replaced by classmate 37419 in January 2016. In February 2016 she was returned to Cumbria to resume her duties there until going back again to Norwich in October. November brought another return to Carlisle until March 2017 when Norwich beckoned yet again, this time until May when she returned to Carlisle until August, during which time she was displayed at Kingmoor Open Days on 21 and 22 July 2017. In September she was back in East Anglia working top and tail with classmates again until July 2018 when she was moved back to Carlisle to work the Cumbrian Coast Line services one last time. Finally she was transferred back to Norwich in February 2019 until May of that year when she entered DRS Stored Fleet, later to become a part of their Supply Chain Operations.

During this period she was busy again with charter trains including on 3 and 4 September 2021 with day two and day three of GB Rail Freight's convoluted tour 'GBRf 2021–This Time it's Personal' which began and ended in London but ran as far as Oban taking in a mass of goods lines and minor routes on the way. On 7 March 2022 she was allocated to DRS Supply Chain Operations based at Kingmoor and thereafter embarked upon a series of 'special' engagements. On 12 March 2022 she was in action with 37218 for Pathfinder Railtours' 'The Pennine Wayfarer', Bristol Temple Meads to Bolton and return by way of Birmingham New Street, Derby, Chesterfield, Edale, Huddersfield and Manchester Victoria. She was involved with two further long tours during 2022, first on 9 April for day two of four for UK Railtours' 'The West Highland & Royal Deeside' when with 37422 she had charge between Dumbarton and Oban and return. Finally from 15 to 18 April 2022 she was busy with Pathfinder Railtours' 'The Easter Highlander' which originated at Eastleigh and ran to Skipton Class 68 hauled, there she and 37422 took over for a tour of Scotland by way of Paisley, Dumbarton, Oban, Dalmuir and Aberdeen before heading back south to York, after which the tour returned to Eastleigh by Class 68.

From 26 to 28 May 2023 she appeared on the heritage Bo'ness & Kinneil Railway working at times with classmate 37025 then continued in her role leading charter trains such as that for The Branch Line Society on 27 August, 'The Garsdale Growler', which she and 37401 Mary Queen of Scots headed from Derby to Carlisle via Ribblehead. During the autumn months of 2023 she and 37419 worked Rail Head Treatment Trains from York Thrall Europa to destinations including Scarborough and Hull. Allocated to HNRC at Crewe Gresty Bridge from May 2024. She visited the ELR and was on duty during their Diesel Gala held from 29 June to 1 July 2024, working with their own 37109.

**37426 (D6999, 37299)**
Released by EE Vulcan Foundry as D6999, Works Number EE/VF3559/D988 on 20 August 1965 and allocated to Canton.

Final depot: Toton, 5/07.

Names carried: Y Lein Fach/Vale of Rheidel, 5/86–4/91; Mt. Vesuvius, 7/93.

Status: Cut up at C.F. Booth, Rotherham, 3/13.

Notable movements:
Her work in South Wales during her early years was typical of her Class, being a mix of heavy freight related to the mining and steel industries of the Valleys, occasional passenger duties and time spent as a banker on the Lickey Incline.

**At Manchester** Victoria with a ballast train on 13 June 1992 is 37426.

Early 'special' turns included 1Zxx between Swansea and Clifton Down on 2 August 1979 and following her transfer to Laira she was involved with 1Z15 'The Penzance Pullman' organised by Railway Pictorial Publication Railtours on 26 April 1980. This was Class 50 hauled from London Paddington to Plymouth where she and Class 25 number 25155 took over to Par, Penzance and return to Plymouth for the Class 50 to complete the trip back to Paddington. This set the scene and further Class 1 services were taken during the next few years in the south west as well as freight and parcels trains.

She was soon involved with further charters including on 19 September 1982 for F+W Tours 'The Western Whistler' which ran from Crewe to Birmingham New Street, Gloucester, Totnes and Mount Gould Junction Class 40 hauled, where she and classmate 37206 took over to Plymouth, Lostwithiel and Carne Point then back to Plymouth for the return to Crewe by Class 40. On 5 May 1984 she and 37296 were involved with the Marlow & Maidenhead Passenger Association railtour which ran as 1Z44 from Ealing Broadway to Gloucester by Class 47 then she and 37296 had charge to Shrewsbury, Cardiff Central and back to Gloucester for the Class 47 to return the tour to Ealing Broadway.

Following a series of depot transfers she spent some time back at Cardiff Canton from January 1986 and whilst there was regularly employed on passenger services both in the South Wales area and further afield to Bristol Temple Meads or to Shrewsbury, Crewe, North Wales and the north west of England. On 7 June 1986 she and classmate 37428 had charge of the Pwllheli to Shrewsbury leg of the Railtours charter 'The Welsh Thunderer' which ran from Stalybridge to Shrewsbury and return and on 1 November 1986 F+W Tours 'The Gargoylian Gasconader' ran from Plymouth to Bristol Temple Meads by Class 47 from where she had sole responsibility to Birmingham New Street, Chesterfield, Rotherham, Doncaster, Huddersfield and on to Manchester Victoria, Wigan North Western and back to Bristol by way of Crewe and Birmingham. From there a Class 50 took over back to Plymouth.

Even after her transfer to Immingham in November 1989 her duties still centred on Class 1 passenger services, regularly involving trains between Cardiff and Manchester Piccadilly or Liverpool Lime Street, these continuing following her move back to Canton in 1990, but her transfer to Tinsley in July 1991 saw her employed on services out of Manchester Victoria to Liverpool, Southport or to Blackpool until June 1992. From that time her duties became more varied as freight haulage returned to her schedule, but her transfer to Wigan Springs Branch in May 1995 saw her often involved with Class 1 services between Bangor or Holyhead and Crewe or Birmingham. On 23 March 1996 she and classmate 37211 had charge of The Class 37 Group/Shropshire Rail tour 'The Exhibitionist' which ran from Chester to Kensington Olympia (for the Ideal Home Exhibition) and to Alton (for the Mid Hants Railway) and return.

Her move to Crewe Diesel depot in November 1996 saw her Class 1 duties continue with trains mainly to the north west and North Wales until her transfer to Motherwell in

January 2001 saw her take charge of services between Edinburgh and Fort William. A brief return to Cardiff Canton involved her with Cardiff to Rhymney Class 2 trains during October that year but by November she was back at Motherwell to resume her duties in the Highlands. On 10 August 2002 she and 37206 took The Branch Line Society's 'The Circumforth Railtour' which meandered from Linlithgow to Millerhill, Falkirk, Clydebank Dock and Muirhouse to Perth and Dunfermline, then returned by the Forth Bridge to Linlithgow. Added to her regular Class 1 duties at this time were a number of 1Zxx 'specials' including on 6 October 2002 1Z64 Edinburgh to Oban and return with 37411 followed on 7 October with 1Z65 Edinburgh to Saltaire and Chester with 37057. Then between 11 and 14 October a series of workings with 37415 north of Edinburgh visiting Fort William, Mallaig, Perth and Kyle of Lochalsh before she returned light engine to Motherwell. On 12 April 2003 she and 37428 took 1Z62/63 between Edinburgh and Oban followed on 3 May by 1Z18/19 Glenrothes to Mallaig and return.

Charters also appeared in her schedule with day two of four for Hertfordshire Rail Tours 'The Easter West Highlander' (King's Cross to Oban and return) taking the Dumbarton to Oban and return legs with 37427. On 5 May 2003 she and 37411 had charge of the North East Railtours Newcastle to Oban and return charter and on 17 May she was in action again with the 'special' 1Z18/19 Ayr to York and return, again with 37411. For the remainder of May 2003 she was employed on freight trains throughout the Midlands and north of England until moving light engine to Motherwell to receive an 'A Exam' and brake block change, completed on 1 June after which she resumed Class 1 duties north from Edinburgh but she was transferred south by EWS and by February 2004 was in store. She was sold by DB Schenker to DRS and moved to Kingmoor in October 2011 only to be scrapped in March 2013 by CF Booth at Rotherham.

**37427 (D6988, 37288)** (See also 37427 in Class 37s in Colour)
Released by EE Vulcan Foundry as D6988, Works Number EE/VF3548/D977 on 14 June 1965 and allocated to Canton.

Final depot: Toton, 5/07.

Names carried: *Bont Y Bermo*, 4/86–4/93; *Highland Enterprise*, 5/93. Later unofficially renamed back to *Bont Y Bermo*, 10/03 (painted name).

Status: Cut up at C.F. Booth, Rotherham, 2/13.

Notable movements:
Typically for her Class she spent her early years in the Valleys of South Wales hauling a variety of trains including parcels, engineers' trains and the heavy freight associated with the coal and steel industries of that area. She was soon allocated passenger duties and also served a time banking on the Lickey Incline in the early 1980s, including on 23 September 1983 with 37204 helping F+W Railtours' 'The Skirl O' The Pipes 3' up the bank, that being a charter running from Plymouth to Aviemore. Though freight workings continued into the early 1980s her time was increasingly spent heading passenger services particularly when transferred to Scottish depots in 1985 when trains north from Glasgow and Edinburgh became her usual duties and her move back to Cardiff Canton in 1986 saw her continue in this manner with services to Bristol, the Midlands and North Wales.

As the 1980s continued her destinations increased to include trains to Manchester and Liverpool and this mix of Class 1 and Class 2 services continued until her transfer to Inverness in March 1993. Also included during this time were occasional charters such as on 16 January 1988 for Hertfordshire Railtours/NSE (Watford) 'The Glamorgan Valleys Explorer' which ran from Milton Keynes to Cardiff for a tour of branches and freight lines around Bridgend, Port Talbot and Swansea before returning to Cardiff and back to Milton Keynes. For the Welsh lines part of the tour she and 37162 were in charge. A brief appearance as a guest on the heritage SVR on 7 and 8 May 1988 and selection with 37430 to haul The Royal Train through South Wales on 20 April 1989 were the other highlights of this period.

Moving to Inverness saw her Class 1 passenger responsibilities turn to the line to Aberdeen or south to Edinburgh as well as Class 2 trains to Perth or Kyle of Lochalsh. Her transfer back to Canton in September 1995 had her reinstated onto charter duties including on 7 October that year for the Monmouthshire Railway Society 'The Garw Growlers', when she and 37902 ran from Newport to Cardiff, Port Talbot, Jersey Marine South Junction, Pontycymmer and Cwmbargoed before returning to Cardiff and Newport. On 13 January 1996 she was working for Pathfinder

Railtours, mostly top and tail with 59001 taking 'The Mendip Rail Meanderer', beginning at Birmingham New Street then on to Bristol Parkway and Westbury for a tour of freight lines in the Merehead area.

Much of the next two years was spent with services between Bristol Temple Meads and Weymouth or from Cardiff to Birmingham New Street or Manchester Oxford Road then a transfer to Motherwell in April 1998 involved her on the Edinburgh to Fort William route. Whilst there she was unofficially renamed back to *Bont y Bermo*. On 23 May 1999 she was involved with the Regency Railcruises three-day charter 'The Cock O' The North' which ran Class 47 hauled from Bristol Temple Meads to Motherwell for her and 37416 to take over to Inverness, Wick and return to Motherwell for the Class 47 to take the tour back to Bristol. Repeated transfers between Scotland and South Wales followed over the next five years seeing her working out of Cardiff between August and September 1999, Inverness from then until October 2000, Cardiff again from November to December 2000 and back to Inverness until December 2004.

During her times at Inverness she worked charters for the SRPS including between Newcastle and Fort William on 1 May 2000 with 37405, between Dumbar and Kyle of Lochalsh on 27 May 2000 with 37418 and again on 9 September 2000 with 37419. Two weeks later on 23 September she and 37405 ran between Berwick-upon-Tweed and Oban for the same tour operator. From 6 to 9 October she was paired with 37408 for the Scottish sections of Hertfordshire Rail Tours 'The Autumn Highlander' which ran between King's Cross and Edinburgh Waverley Class 90 hauled both ways, the Class 37s taking the tour on to Aberdeen, Kyle of Lochalsh and Dundee. Her time between April 2001 and her transfer to Toton in January 2005 was fully occupied with services north from Edinburgh to Fort William but inserted amongst these were numerous charters and special trains including between 13 and 16 April 2001 'The Easter Highlander' for Hertfordshire Railtours, on 22 September 'The Mallaig Centenarian' for the SRPS, on 25 May 2002 'The Kyle of Lochalsh' for the same operator. Others for the SRPS soon followed including on 31 August 2002 Ayr to Fort William, Mallaig and return, then on 7 September 'The Oban & Lorne Explorer' from Berwick-upon-Tweed and on 12 October 'The Galloway Special'. Working again for Hertfordshire Rail Tours on 19 April 2003 she was involved with 'The Easter West Highlander'. Back with the SRPS on 31 May she took 'The Crewe & Shrewsbury', aka 'The Shropshire Rambler' from Linlithgow. The on 11 October 2003 a charter for SRPS/North East Railtours between Edinburgh Waverley and Buxton.

In 2004 she began with involvement again with Hertfordshire Rail Tours four-day charter 'The Easter West Highlander' then on 1 May the SRPS tour to Fort William and Mallaig. Two days later she was in action for North East Railtours between Newcastle and Fort William and then on 4 July she had the VSOE Northern Belle 'Oban to the Isle of Mull' from Edinburgh to Dumbarton. The same honour came her way again on 15 August 2004 when she headed their 'Fort William from Edinburgh & Dumbarton' special train. Finally on 27 and 28 August 2004 she was involved with Pathfinder Railtours' 'The Northern Lights' which ran from Birmingham to Inverness and Kyle of Lochalsh and return, taking the sections north of Carlisle.

From January 2005 she was transferred to Toton but was still in demand to head charters in addition to her 'normal' duties. Examples included on 29 January 2005 'The Barmouth Barker' for Past Time Rail, followed on 5 February for Pathfinder Railtours' 'The East Ender', Crewe to London Liverpool Street, Southend and return. 'The High Peaks Hustler' on 26 February ran from Birmingham to Liverpool Lime Steet, then to Buxton and return then 'The Aggregated Syphons' on 12 March began at Derby and ran to Brentford, Haywards Heath, Acton and return, both these also for Pathfinder Railtours. On 26 March she was working for Hertfordshire Rail Tours again, being involved on day two of their 'Easter Highlander' charter between Dumbarton and Oban. Back with Pathfinder Railtours on 2 May 2005 for 'The Cumbrian Warrior' which ran from Cardiff to Workington Docks, Maryport and return. On 25 June 2005 she was enlisted to help D1015 with a

**Nameplate of** 37427.

section of Pathfinder Railtours' 'The Western Trident' and on 30 July, again for Pathfinder Railtours she was involved with 'The Snowdonian II' tour from Bristol Temple Meads to Pwllheli, Machynlleth and return.

She was employed by Arriva Trains Wales on 31 August with a Jewish Festival 'Additional' between Aberystwyth and Birmingham New Street and finally on 10 September 2005 for the 6024 Preservation Society's 'The Welsh Marches Express' from Birmingham Snow Hill to Bristol Temple Meads, the return journey being taken by steam loco 6024 *King Edward I*. From 21 September 2005 to 25 April 2006 she returned to the Highlands to take services between Edinburgh and Fort William, then in May 2006 entered EWS Tactical Reserve Pool. By September 2007 she had been put into store and she was sold by DB Schenker and transferred to Kingmoor for DRS in September 2011. She was later removed from stock and cut up by CF Booth at Rotherham in February 2013.

### 37428 (D6981, 37281)

Released by EE Vulcan Foundry as D6981, Works Number EE/VF3541/D970 on 12 May 1965 and allocated to Canton.

Final depot: Toton, 5/07.

Nameplate of 37428.

Names carried: *David Lloyd George*, 5/87; *Royal Scotsman*, 5/98.

Status: Cut up by C.F. Booth, Rotherham, 4/13.

### 37429 (D6600, 37300)

Released by EE Vulcan Foundry as D6600, Works Number EE/VF3560/D989 on 26 August 1965 and allocated to Canton.

Final depot: Toton, 5/07.

Names carried: *Sir Dyfed/County of Dyfed*, 4/87–7/87; *Eisteddfod Genedlaethol*, 8/87.

Status: Cut up by EMR, Kingsbury, 2/08.

Notable movements:
Following her early years in South Wales hauling the heavy freight

**At the** stops at Crewe station on 12 March 1988 is 37429 *Eisteddfod Genedlaethol*. (*Rick Ward*)

**Approaching Prestatyn** on 23 June 1993 is 37429 heading the 07.15 Birmingham International to Llandudno service. (*Jonathan Allen*)

**Approaching Rhyl** on 23 June 1993 is 37429 in Regional Railways livery with the 16.00 Holyhead to Stafford. (*Jonathan Allen*)

**Nameplate of** 37429.

associated with the area she was increasingly allocated to passenger services to the Midlands and north west of England as well as occasional charters taking her further afield. These included on 3 March 1984 for F+W Railtours' 'The Welsh Central Liner' which ran from Plymouth to Taunton, Bristol Temple Meads, Gloucester then on to Port Talbot, Craven Arms, Severn Tunnel Junction and Sudbrook before returning to Plymouth. She and 37266 had charge between Severn Tunnel Junction and Sudbrook both ways. On 17 July 1985 she took a 'Golf Extra' between Glasgow Central and Ayr. Between then and September 1994 she was employed first on services between South Wales and Bristol or to Crewe, Manchester Piccadilly or Liverpool Lime Street or into North Wales.

From the early 1990s she was primarily engaged with services between Manchester Victoria, Liverpool Lime Street and the Lancashire coast resorts of Southport and Blackpool, or to North Wales or to the Midlands. On 24 September 1994 she and 37158 took the charter for The Branch Line Society 'The Port Vale' which started and finished at Newport and ran to Cardiff Central for a tour of lines around Barry Dock, Bridgend, Swansea, Port Talbot and Margam. On 4 July 1998 she headed 'The Bournemouth & Beaulieu Belle' for Regency Railcruises, which ran from Preston to Bournemouth and return. Her duties from the late 1990s were mainly with Class 1 services between the Midlands and North Wales and this continued until her time in store for EWS in 2001 after which she was largely inactive until being scrapped in 2008.

**37430 (D6965, 37265)**
Released by EE Vulcan Foundry as D6965, Works Number EE/VF3525/D954 on 3 February 1965 and allocated to Darnall.

Final depot: Toton, 5/07.

Name carried: *Cwmbrân*, 5/86.

Status: Cut up at EMR, Kingsbury, 5/08.

**Nameplate of** 37430.

**37431 (D6972, 37272)** (See also 37431 in Class 37s in Colour) Released by EE Vulcan Foundry as D6972, Works Number EE/VF3532/D961 on 26 March 1965 and allocated to Canton.

Final depot: Doncaster, 4/99.

Names carried: *Sir Powys/County of Powys*, 6/87–5/91; *Bullidae*, 5/91–4/93.

Status: Cut up at Wigan CRDC, 1/00.

Notable movements:
While in the South Wales valleys during her early years her duties revolved around the heavy industries of that area and it was not until the mid-1980s that passenger work started to play a major part in her schedules. She was then employed on regular Class 1 services from Cardiff to the Midlands and the north west, as well as to Bristol Temple Meads from Swansea until mid-1991. During this time she was shown on display at Newport Station Rail Fair on 27 June 1987 and on 20 April 1989 was rostered as a spare loco for the Royal Train on its journey through South Wales. Her transfer to Eastfield in May 1991 saw her employed mainly on services between Inverness and Aberdeen.

Her allocation to Trainload Petroleum at Immingham involved her on freight duties for a short time but by March 1993 she was back in the Highlands working services to Aberdeen from Inverness or south as far as Edinburgh, with occasional Class 2 trains to Kyle of Lochalsh. This continued until early 1996 when she was transferred south again and into store for EWS. During this time in southern England she was employed by Regency Railcruises in the company of 37402, 37406 and 37410 for a three-day charter beginning at Bristol Temple Meads on 24 April 1998 and running to Motherwell, Inverness, Kyle of Lochalsh and returning via Edinburgh Waverley. She also spent a time from 30 May 1998 heading mainly Class 2 services from Bristol to Weymouth or Cardiff and between Cardiff and Rhymney until a brief return to Motherwell in November that year. By April 1999 she had been condemned and was scrapped at Wigan the following year.

**Sub-class 37/5**
Numbers 37501 to 37521 and 37667 to 37699 were converted from the original fleet between 1986 and 1988. They had no train heating. Tractive effort was increased to 55,590lb (248KN) and weighed 107 tonnes Those classified as 37/6 (numbers 37601 to 37612) were converted from the original fleet between 1994 and 1996. They were fitted with 'through wired' heating and were air braked. Their coupling type was modified to 'Blue Star/Special' for the European Passenger Services fleet and their maximum speed was increased to 90mph (145km/h) from the now standard 80mph (129km/h). They weighed 106 tonnes.

**37503 (D6717, 37017)**
Released by EE Vulcan Foundry as D6717, Works Number EE/VF2880/D596 30 May 1961 and allocated to Stratford.

Final depot: Toton, 5/07.

Name carried: *British Steel Shelton*, 7/87–7/93.

Status: Stored at Kingmoor by DRS, 1/14; Moved to Barrow Hill, 2/14; Allocated to EuroPhoenix

Nameplate of 37431.

### Table 4. Locos numbered as sub-class 37/5

**37/5**

| | | | |
|---|---|---|---|
| D6717: 37503 | D6739: 37603 | D6947: 37671 | D6934: 37685 |
| D6728: 37505 | D6707: 37604 | D6889: 37672 | D6872: 37686 |
| D6793: 37509 | D6736: 37605 | D6832: 37673 | D6905: 37688 |
| D6812: 37510 | D6790: 37606 | D6869: 37674 | D6895: 37689 |
| D6756: 37513 | D6803: 37607 | D6864: 37675 | D6822: 37692 |
| D6764: 37515 | D6722: 37608 | D6826: 37676 | D6910: 37693 |
| D6786: 37516 | D6815: 37609 | D6821: 37677 | D6892: 37694 |
| D6718: 37517 | D6881: 37610 | D6956: 37678 | D6857: 37695 |
| D6776: 37518 | D6871: 37611 | D6823: 37679 | D6928: 37696 |
| D6727: 37519 | D6879: 37612 | D6924: 37680 | D6943: 37697 |
| D6741: 37520 | D6851: 37667 | D6830: 37681 | D6946: 37698 |
| D6817: 37521 | D6957: 37668 | D6936: 37682 | D6953: 37699 |
| D6705: 37601 | D6829: 37669 | D6887: 37683 | |
| D6782: 37602 | D6882: 37670 | D6834: 37684 | |

**Giving up** the single line token at Achnasheen on 21 May 1984 is the crew of 37017 with the 07.10 Kyle of Lochalsh to Inverness service. Following a Heavy General Overhaul in March 1986 during which she was dual braked she was renumbered to 37505. *(Jonathan Allen)*

**Nameplate of** 37503.

Locomotives UK, 3/16; Moved to the Wensleydale Railway by road, 8/19 as a PODL; Moved to Pontefract by road, 3/21.

Notable movements:
Her career was weighted more towards passenger services than freight workings from the start with trains out of London Liverpool Street featuring heavily into the 1970s to destinations including Cambridge, Kings Lynn and Lowestoft. By the early 1980s she was spending time in Scotland working services north from Glasgow as well as in the Highlands from Inverness, but by 1985 she was transferred south to Canton and worked trains in South Wales until her move to Thornaby in 1987. As she was transferred regularly between depots over the following years her duties took her on a variety of routes to destinations including Manchester Victoria, Liverpool Lime Street, Llandudno Junction, Holyhead, Blackpool North, Barrow-in-Furness, Carlisle as well as into the Midlands to Crewe and Birmingham International and south as far as Exeter and Plymouth.

By March 2000 she was back at Motherwell but only briefly as by the end of the year she was returned to Crewe and worked passenger services in the Midlands and South Wales again. During this period she was also called upon to work a number of charters including on 11 October 1986 for F+W Railtours' 'The Red Dragon' which ran from Crewe to Cardiff for a tour of South Wales lines before returning to Crewe. She and 37699 were involved top and tail between Penarth and Cardiff. On 25 February 1989 she worked on Pathfinder Railtours' 'The Warcop Warrior' which originated at Swindon and ran to Settle then Appleby, Warcop and back to Appleby before going on to Carlisle to return to Swindon via the WCML and Gloucester. On 5 August 2000 for the SRPS she worked 'The West Highlander' between Fort William and Mallaig, the tour having begun and ended at Edinburgh Waverley. Finally, and again for Pathfinder Railtours, she was involved with 'The Crewe Invader Train 1' on 31 May 2003, Salisbury to Crewe and return and 'The Crewe Invader Train 2' the following day from Bristol Temple Meads to Crewe, Shrewsbury and return.

After having spent time in store at Toton and at Barrow Hill she made a guest appearance on the heritage NVR from 30 September to 2 October 2011 before being moved to Barrow Hill in April 2012. In March 2016 she was allocated to EuroPhoenix Locomotives UK and in August 2019 moved by road to the Wensleydale Railway as a PODL. She was transferred by road from there to Pontefract in March 2021 into the care of the Shires Removal Group.

## 37505 (D6728, 37028)

Released by EE Vulcan Foundry as D6728, Works Number EE/VF2891/D607 22 September 1961 and allocated to Stratford.

Final depot: Toton, 5/07.

Name carried: *British Steel Workington*, 4/87–4/91.

Status: Cut up at EMR, Kingsbury, 2/08.

Notable movements:
From her early days passenger duties dominated her schedules especially following her move to Scotland in 1979 when she was engaged on services from Glasgow to such destinations as Edinburgh, Dundee, Perth, Oban, Fort William and Inverness. During this time she was occasionally employed on 'specials' duty such as on 1 September 1979 when she took 1Z40, a train from Ramsgate to Edinburgh Waverley for the Edinburgh Military Tattoo, being in charge between Carstairs and Edinburgh Waverley. On 22 September 1984 she was involved on day two of three for F+W Railtours' 'The Skirl o' the Pipes 5'. This originated at Plymouth and ran to Crewe, Carlisle and Mossend Yard where the train split. 'Portion 1' went to Fort William, Mallaig, Kyle of Lochalsh and on to Inverness before heading for Edinburgh Waverley, while 'Portion 2' took the route to Perth then Inverness, Kyle of Lochalsh, Mallaig and Fort William before also heading for Edinburgh where the train recombined to travel to Glasgow Central, Carlisle, Derby, Bristol Temple Meads and finally back to Plymouth. She was used between Perth and Inverness on 'Portion 2'. From July 1993 she was regularly used to take Anglo-Scottish trains from London Euston north from Edinburgh to Aberdeen or Inverness, work which kept her fully occupied until May 1995 when she was transferred south again first to the Midlands at Bescot.

On 14 December 1996, she was on charter duty again for Pathfinder Railtours' 'The Rooster Booster' which originated at Bristol Temple Meads and ran to Stratford-upon-Avon, Guildford and Kensington Olympia, then on to Northampton, Birmingham New Street and back to Bristol. She was in charge between Northampton and Birmingham in partnership with Class 20 number 20075. After this she worked for EWS Transrail (Infrastructure) from Crewe Diesel depot from January 1997, Immingham's North of England pool from September 1997, Toton's EWS Systemwide pool from November 1998 and Toton's Sandite pool from September 2000. Periods in store and on contract hire in France followed before she was sold by EWS and withdrawn from stock in July 2007 to be scrapped by EMR in February 2008.

**At Coombe** Junction, Cornwall with 6C18, a train of fuel tanks from Exeter Riverside to Moorswater on 12 October 1999 is 37505 *British Steel Workington*.

**Nameplate of** 37505.

## 37509 (D6793, 37093)

(See also 37509 in Class 37s in Colour) Released by EE RSH as D6793, Works Number EE/RSH3220/8339 20 February 1963 and allocated to Gateshead.

Final depot: Doncaster, 12/01.

Name carried: None.

Status: Cut up at Cardiff Canton, 8/05.

Notable movements:
Amongst her early passenger workings were a 'special', 1Z28 between Hinckley and Whitby

on 3 July 1983 and services from Sheffield to Scarborough or Skegness the following year. On 20 March 1993 she was involved with the Black Cat Railtours' 'Farewell to Eastgate' charter which ran from Crewe to York then on to Eastgate Cement Works, County Durham and return. She took part between York and Eastgate with 37707 and 37708. On 17 September 1994 she was working for Pathfinder Railtours with 'The Lancastrians', which originated at Crewe and ran to Manchester Piccadilly, then to Buxton and back to Manchester before going on to Chester then Liverpool Lime Street, Wigan Wallgate, Warrington Bank Quay, Wigan North Western, Preston and finally Blackpool North. She was involved between Warrington Bank Quay and Blackpool North.

During the next two years she headed Class 1 services between Crewe and Holyhead then on 20 September 1997 she worked for RT Railtours with 'The Slate & Narrow', a charter from Skipton to Manchester Victoria, Warrington Bank Quay then on to Blaenau Ffestiniog and return to Skipton via Wakefield Kirkgate and Leeds. She and 37211 had charge from Warrington Bank Quay to Blaenau Ffestiniog and back to Skipton. In June 1998 she featured on Class 1 services between Birmingham and Holyhead and from Crewe to Bangor and Holyhead but by this time her passenger hauling days were coming to an end. She was allocated to EWS Systemwide at Toton in November 1998 and after some time in store was Sandite fitted for working Rail Head Treatment Trains. A further period in store was ended in August 2005 when she was scrapped at Cardiff Canton.

**37510 (D6812, 37112)** (See 37112 in sub-class 37/0)

**37513 (D6756, 37056)**
Released by EE Vulcan Foundry as D6756, Works Number EE/VF3048/D710 on 28 September 1962 and allocated to Thornaby.

Final depot: Toton, 5/07.

Name carried: None.

Status: Cut up at C.F. Booth, Rotherham, 2/08.

**37515 (D6764, 37064)**
Released by EE Vulcan Foundry as D6764, Works Number EE/VF3056/D718 on 7 November 1962 and allocated to Thornaby.

Final depot: Kingmoor, 2/05.

Name carried: None.

Status: Cut up at T.J. Thomson's scrapyard, Stockton, 7/10.

*Below left*: **At Eaglescliffe** near Stockton on Tees on 14 October 1989 with a train of loaded ballast wagons is 37510.

*Below right*: **Passing through** Barnetby station in May 1992 are 37515 and 37516 with a train of coal empties.

Locomotive Histories • 105

**37516 (D6786, 37086)** (See also 37516 in Class 37s in Colour)

Released by EE RSH as D6786, Works Number EE/RSH3213/8332 on 28 December 1962 and allocated to Gateshead.

Final depot: Toton, 5/07.

Name carried: *Loch Laidon*, for WCRC

Status: Operational with WCRC, Carnforth from 2/09.

Notable movements:
Early freight duties in the Yorkshire and north east of England included iron and steel movements (including the 'torpedo' trains) between Lackenby and Consett, ore and ballast workings between Derbyshire and Lincolnshire and later cement and other heavy freight trains in South Wales. By the mid-1970s she was being more regularly required to head Class 1 passenger trains anywhere in the east and north east of England but by 1979 following her transfer to March depot her workload was centred on services out of London Liverpool Street to Cambridge, Kings Lynn or Lowestoft, workings which would keep her busy until the mid-1980s. Around this time she was beginning to be called upon to head charter trains and 'specials' including on 4 July 1981 for BR (Eastern Region) 'The Joint Line Venturer' which ran from King's Cross to Lincoln, March, Lowestoft, Ipswich and on to London Liverpool Street, when she had charge between March and Liverpool Street. Then on 26 February 1983 for F+W Railtours' 'The Essex Explorer I' which originated at Plymouth and ran to Enfield, London Liverpool Street, Southminster, Fenchurch Street, Shoeburyness, Tilbury and Reading before returning to Plymouth by way of Bristol Temple Meads. She was in charge from London Liverpool Street to Tilbury.

By 1987, now working out of Thornaby depot, her workload was more varied including freights from Teesside. Similarly, when transferred to Immingham and later to Canton, freight duties continued to occur regularly in her schedule. She was still occasionally used on charters such as on 20 September 1993 when she was involved paired with 37515 for the Sheffield, York, Thornaby and return to Sheffield leg of Pathfinder Railtours' 'The Tees-Side Tornado' (see 'Notable Movements' for 37511 for further tour details) and on 15 June 1997 she was entrusted with the Bradford to Scarborough via Bridlington leg of the VSOE luxury service.

It was not until her transfer to Carnforth as a PODL in February 2009 that her career as a charter loco really took off. From May of that year, she was virtually in full time employment with 1Zxx trains for West Coast Railways. In 2009 alone she worked north from Edinburgh into the Highlands, over the S&C route and to the south coast at Swanage. During 2010 she visited East Anglia, the north east of England and the Scottish Highlands again. The following year saw her employed in the south from London Euston and in 2012 she headed 'specials' north from Newcastle to Oban, between Birmingham and the south west, to Scarborough and in the Glasgow area. During 2013 she was called upon to assist with 'The Scarborough Spa Express' and later that year spent time working trains in the Highlands, notably to Kyle of Lochalsh and between Edinburgh,

**Near Haxby** on the Scarborough line from York, 37516 *Loch Laidon* is helping on the rear of the steam-hauled 'The Scarborough Spa Express' due to high fire risk conditions, the train headed by MN 35016 *British India Line* on 28 June 2018.

**Nameplate of** 37516.

**Passing South** Bank, Redcar with a Tees Yard to Skinningrove freight on 14 October 1988 is 37518.

**On 6 October** 2017 WCRC's 37518 and 37669 pass Shapbeck Gate near Little Strickland on the WCML in Cumbria with 1Z38, the Kettering to Fort William 'The West Highland & Jacobite Statesman'. WCRC's 47804 is on the rear. (*Jonathan Allen*)

Glasgow, Fort William and Mallaig. This continued through to June 2015 when she returned to duties out of Carnforth, notably to York and Scarborough.

These 'summer specials' kept her busy during the following years, combined with numerous other charters for West Coast Railways throughout the north of England and into Scotland as well as assisting the regular tourist train between Fort William and Mallaig, 'The Jacobite' during the summer of 2023. During May 2024 she and classmate 37075 were operational on the K&WVR hauling 'specials' in support of Martin House hospice. On 11 June 2024 she was employed for WCRC on 'The Dalesman' from Chester to Carlisle, outward via the S&C, returning by way of the WCML. She had charge between Preston and Hellifield Goods Loops on the outward journey and between Carnforth and Chester on the return.

**37517 (D6718, 37018)** (See also 37517 in Class 37s in Colour)
Released by EE Vulcan Foundry as D6718, Works Number EE/VF2881/D597 on 5 June 1961 and allocated to Stratford.

Final depot: Toton, 5/07.

Names carried: *St Aidan's CE Memorial School Hartlepool Railsafe Trophy Winners 1995*, 7/95.

Status: Operational with WCRC, Carnforth from 12/07.

**37518 (D6776, 37076)**
Released by EE RSH as D6776, Works Number EE/RSH3068/8322 on 8 October 1962 and allocated to Thornaby.

Final depot: Toton, 5/07.

Name carried: *Fort William/An Gearasdan*, 7/12–8/15.

Status: Bought for preservation, 2/07; Operational on the NVR, 9/07; Reinstated into traffic as a PODL, 8/10; Operational with WCRC, Carnforth from 11/13.

Notable movements:
Her early work with freight in the north of England was soon supplemented with passenger duties centred on Newcastle upon Tyne station, from where she often headed trains to the Yorkshire coast at Scarborough or to York. Class 1 services would continue to

dominate her schedule throughout the 1970s and 1980s, be they from London Liverpool Street to East Anglia or in the Scottish Highlands. In the early 1990s she became sought after for more 'special' duties including helping with 1Z42, a train from Swansea to Edinburgh on 1 February 1991 when she and 37285 were involved between Shap and Carlisle. On 4 October 1992 she worked for the Barry Open Day Committee on their charter 'The Taff Talisman' which ran from Cardiff Central to Bristol Temple Meads and return, then on to tour lines in South Wales before returning to Cardiff. From there they went to Gloucester, Newport and back to Cardiff again. She and 37077 were in charge between Cardiff Central and Newport. On 26 June 1993 she was involved with Hertfordshire Rail Tours 'The Castor & Pollocks', a tour which originated at King's Cross and ran to Barnetby via Grantham and Lincoln, followed by a tour of lines around Immingham, Leeds and Goole before returning to King's Cross by way of Doncaster and Peterborough. She and 37798 were involved between Barnetby and Doncaster.

Periods in store or working a mix of freight and passenger services followed, including a period in France at the turn of the century before she was saved into preservation in early 2007 and moved first to the NVR where she worked from October 2007 until October 2009. She then appeared as a guest on the heritage Mid Norfolk Railway in September 2010 before transferring to the ELR where she worked from October that year until March 2013, being named *Fort William/An Gearasdan* there on 30 July 2012. After a brief appearance on the North Norfolk Railway in that month she moved back north, this time to work on the NYMR from April to May that same year. Her move to West Coast Railways at Carnforth from November 2013 signalled the beginning of her new life in WCRC colours. Early duties for them included workings between Fort William and Mallaig during May 2014 followed by 1Zxx 'specials' from Liverpool Lime Street to North Wales on 17 August 2014 and from Newcastle to Linlithgow on 27 September that year. Then she worked Class 1 services in the Highlands until on 15 December 2015, now in WCRC maroon livery but with name removed she worked the Railway Touring Company charter 'The Sherborne Christmas Carol' from London Victoria to Sherborne (for the Sherborne Abbey carol service) then on to Yeovil before returning to London Victoria. The following day she was called upon to replace the failed steam loco 61306 *Mayflower* for Steam Dreams 'The Cathedrals Express' from King's Cross to York and return.

Returning to the Highlands in June 2016 she then worked Class 2 services between Fort William and Mallaig. Then from mid-June 2017 until the end of August that year she also worked regularly on the heritage Swanage Railway. On 24 and 25 March 2018 she was involved throughout with the Branch Line Society/84G Railtours charter 'The Sussex Salopian/Sunday Salopian'. On day one this ran from Carnforth to Crewe, then Birmingham International to Watford Junction for a tour of lines in the Wembley Yard, Willesden and Kensington Olympia areas before going on to Clapham Junction then Gatwick and to Bognor Regis, then Barnham, Fratton, Guildford, Reading and Birmingham New Street. A tour of lines near Bescot and Wolverhampton followed, then on to Shrewsbury and finally back to Crewe. Day two involved a return from Crewe to Carnforth by way of Warrington, Wigan North Western and Lancaster. From 26 May 2018 she was back on the Fort William to Mallaig route (assisting with 'The Jacobite' steam hauled tourist train) interrupted only by appearances on 10 August 2019 for the Branch Line Society's 'Type 3 to the Sea/Cosham Completer' tour from Crewe to Portsmouth Harbour, Eastleigh and return, with classmates 37669 and 37706 throughout.

The following day involved the locos with a positioning move back to Carnforth from Crewe, 'The Tri County Triple Tractor'. On 22 August 2019 she was involved with 'The Scarborough Spa Express' from Carnforth to Scarborough via York, when she and 37706 had the train between Carnforth and York both ways while steam loco 35018 *British India Line* took charge between York and Scarborough. On 19 October 2019 she and 37516 took North East Railtours' 'The Ayr & Stranraer' top and tail from Newcastle to Edinburgh Waverley and Stranraer, then to Carlisle, Newcastle, Edinburgh Waverley and Linlithgow. From April 2021 she has been working between Fort William and Mallaig, assisting with 'The Jacobite' for the WCRC, until September 2023. On 4 May 2024 she and classmate 37668 had charge of 1Z65/1Z66 the West Coast Railway Company charter for Pathfinder Railtours' 'The Spring Cornish Explorer' from Dorridge to Penzance and return. On 6 June 2024 she worked 'The Dalesman' for WCRC which ran from York to Carlisle, over the S&C in both directions. She headed the train between Leeds and Hellifield Goods Loops both ways.

**37519 (D6727, 37027)**
Released by EE Vulcan Foundry as D6727, Works Number EE/VF2890/D606 on 15 September 1961 and allocated to Stratford.

Final depot: Toton, 5/07.

Name carried: *Loch Eil*, 10/81–1/87.

Status: Cut up by C.F. Booth, Rotherham, 3/08.

**37520 (D6741, 37041)** (See also D6741 in Class 37s in Colour)
Released by EE Vulcan Foundry as D6741, Works Number EE/VF2904/D620 on 7 June 1962 and allocated to Hull Dairycoates.

Final depot: Toton, 5/07.

Name carried: None.

Status: Cut up at T.J. Thomson's scrapyard, Stockton, 10/07 as 37520.

**Nameplate of** 37519.

**37521 (D6817, 37117)** (See also 37521 in Class 37s in Colour)
Released by EE Vulcan Foundry as D6817, Works Number EE/VF3246/D771 on 6 March 1963 and allocated to Darnall.

Final depot: Kingmoor, 1/14.

Name carried: *English China Clays*, 6/97.

Status: Operational with Locomotive Services Ltd (LSL), based at Crewe Diesel depot from 1/20, painted in LSL 'retro green' livery and a regular on their 'specials', including on 4 May 2024 with D6851, 'The English Riviera Express'.

**37601 (D6705, 37005, 37501)** (See also 37601 in Class 37s in Colour)
Released by EE Vulcan Foundry as D6705, Works Number EE/VF2868/D584 on 12 January 1961 and allocated to March.

Final depot: Kingmoor, 2/08.

Names carried: *Teesside Steelmaster*, 2/87–1/91; *Class 37–Fifty*, 9/10; Later named *Perseus*.

Status: Operational for EuroPhoenix Locomotives UK, leased to the Rail Operations Group, Leicester from 4/17.

Notable movements:
Her freight duties in the early years were focussed on the heavy industries of north east England, Yorkshire and the South Wales valleys, being concerned with the movement of oil, steel and coal, though on 21 August 1982 she did have the 'honour' of hauling preserved 'Deltics' 55009 and 55019 from Thornaby to their new home at Grosmont on the NYMR. An early 'special' turn for her was a 'FootEx' service between Glasgow and Edinburgh on 14 August 1982, otherwise her passenger duties centred on Class 2 trains out of Newcastle to Middlesbrough or Carlisle. While based at Canton in the mid-1980s she had charge of Class 1 services from the Midlands to North Wales. From February 1987 to March 1989 while still running as 37501 she was painted into Teesrail 'Sky Blue' large logo livery. This British Steel livery was unique to her until she was repainted again into Rail Freight's triple-grey scheme. By the early 1990s she was beginning to be called upon for charter duty, such as on 19 August 1990 for Pathfinder Railtours' 'The Tees Maid' which ran from Bristol Temple Meads to Doncaster, Darlington, Saltburn, Redcar and return. She and 37502 were involved between Saltburn and Darlington on the return trip.

In February 1995 she was transferred to Bristol Phillips Marsh depot in connection with the failed European Passenger Services project. On 13 May 1995 she and 37602 worked for A1A Charters 'The Canterbury Tales' which originated at Preston and ran to London Victoria then on to Ashford, Folkestone and Stafford before returning to Preston. They had charge between London Victoria and Ashford. Next on 13 July 1996 she was paired with 37603 for Pathfinder Railtours' 'The Yorkshire Doodle Dandy', a charter from Bristol Temple Meads to Crewe, Bradford Interchange, Doncaster, Nottingham, Birmingham New Street and return to Bristol. They took the legs between Bristol and Crewe and then Birmingham and

Bristol on the return. While based at Old Oak Common she worked Class 1 services in the Birmingham area and following her move to North Pole depot she was reunited with charter duties in the shape of Pathfinder Railtours' 'The Atomic Harbour Master' on 20 October 2007, which ran from Crewe to Wembley Yard then London Euston, Clapham Junction, Ashford International, Folkestone Harbour then back to Ashford before going on to Dungeness British Energy, back to Ashford then Sevenoaks, Willesden, Wembley Yard and finally back to Crewe. She and 37603 were involved from and back to Wembley Yard.

She transferred to Carlisle Kingmoor for DRS in February 2008 and was used on their nuclear waste trains. Then on 20 March 2010, she returned to tour duty for Spitfire Railtours with 'The Cumbrian Crusader II' which began at Birmingham International and ran to Birmingham New Street then to Leeds and Carlisle via the S&C, on to Newcastle along the Tyne Valley line then to York, Sheffield and return to Birmingham International. She was involved (on the rear) between Carlisle and Newcastle then with 37608 from Newcastle to Birmingham International. A weekend as guest on the Mid Norfolk Railway saw her named *Class 37-Fifty* at Dereham on 25 September 2010 and then she resumed charter duties including on 30 October that year for Spitfire Tours 'The Jorvic Explorer II/Saltburn Smuggler' which ran from Taunton to York, then Saltburn and return, with 37038 throughout. On 12 February 2011 for Pathfinder Railtours' 'The Galloway Galloper' from Glasgow Central to Riccarton, Killoch, Ayr, Stranraer, Motherwell and return to Glasgow with 37607 throughout. Working again for Pathfinder Railtours on 15 October 2011 with 'The Ousing Dove' which began at Bristol Temple Meads and ran to Crewe, Thorne Junction, Goole, Wakefield, Sheffield then on to Tamworth, Birmingham New Street and back to Bristol Temple Meads. She and 37611 had charge between Bristol and Crewe. Between 26 April and 5 May 2012 she was used on a series of 1Zxx 'specials' which ran between Edinburgh and Southampton Docks. For the first train she and 37409 had charge between Barrow Hill and the Western Docks then on 2 and 5 May she was paired with 37608 from Edinburgh to the Eastern Docks and return.

On 17 August 2013 she was on display at Kingmoor for the DRS Open Day then on 29 August 2014 she and 37603 took another 1Zxx 'special' from Crewe to Kingswear (for Dartmouth) and return. A four-day tour to the Scottish Highlands followed from 30 September to 3 October 2016. Pathfinder Railtours' 'The Autumn West Highlander' began at Paignton and travelled to Fort William then to Mallaig, Crianlarich and Oban, back to Fort William and returning to Exeter St Davids. For this she was paired with 37612 throughout. Finally on 11 September 2021, now working for the Rail Operations Group/Retro Railtours she headed 'The Barrow Hill Rail Ale Festival' trains, two of which ran between Derby and Barrow Hill for the event. She continues in service allocated to the Rail Operations Group and during May and June 2024 was used to transfer new Class 730 units between various locations.

### 37602 (D6782, 37082, 37502)

Released by EE RSH as D6782, Works Number EE/RSH3209/8328 on 29 November 1962 and allocated to Hull Dairycoates.

Final depot: Kingmoor, 5/02

Name carried: *British Steel Teesside*, 3/87–1/91.

Status: In store for DRS at Eastleigh Yard from 9/19, deregistered by DRS in 1/20; Moved to Barrow Hill for HNRC, 6/23.

Notable movements:
Her early years were occupied with the usual mix of freight and passenger workings associated with the several depot areas to which she was allocated. It was not until after her conversion to sub-class 37/6 in February 1995 to work the European Passenger Services trains that she began to feature regularly on Class 1 services and on occasional charters. These latter included on 13 May 1995 'The Canterbury Tales' for A1A Charters which ran from Preston to London Victoria then to Ashford, Folkestone Harbour and on to Stafford before returning to Preston. She and 37601 were in charge between London Victoria and Ashford. On 11 March 2000 for Pathfinder Railtours she and 37604 were involved with 'The Medway Medicaster', a charter from Crewe to London Victoria then Dartford, Maidstone and back to London Victoria, then on to Richmond, Swindon and return to Crewe, the 37s having the London Victoria and return leg of the tour.

**At Pilmoor,** ECML on 11 April 1975 37082 travels south towards York with an engineers' train. She was renumbered to 37502 following a Heavy General Overhaul in March 1986 when dual braking was fitted, and again to 37602 in February 1995.

**Nameplate of** 37504.

She also appeared at depot Open Days during this period including at Old Oak Common in 2000 and at Carnforth in July 2008. Then on 23 May 2009 for Spitfire Railtours she and 37069 had charge of 'The Wessexman', a charter from Crewe to Oxford, Didcot, Eastleigh then on to Bournemouth, Weymouth and return to Crewe.

After then being employed by DRS in their nuclear fleet and spending some time in store she was in demand again for charter work including on 24 June 2013 for Compass Tours 'The Oban & Lorn Highlander' with 37607 from Crewe to Oban and return. She was working for Pathfinder Railtours on 28 November 2015 heading 'The Jolly Marketeer' from Derby to Salisbury and Portsmouth Harbour and return, with 37605 throughout. Then again for the same operator on 25 April 2016 for the final day of four for their tour 'The Spring West Highlander' which that day had come from Fort William to Carlisle with 37409 and 37610. She and 37610 then returned the tour to Eastleigh. On 15 July 2017 she was paired with 37606 for Retro Railtours' 'The Retro Welsh Dragon 2' from Huddersfield to Swansea and return, then on 12 August 2017 with 37609 for UK Railtours' 'The Edinburgh Military Tattoo/Highland Fling' day two of four, from Edinburgh Waverley to Oban and return. Finally on 22 September 2018 she and 37606 were paired again for Pathfinder Railtours' 'The Marches Cornishman' which ran from Shrewsbury to Penzance and return. From September 2019 she was put into store by DRS and deregistered the following January before being moved by road to Barrow Hill in June 2023.

**37603 (D6739, 37039, 37504)** (See also 37603 in Class 37s in Colour) Released by EE Vulcan Foundry as D6739, Works Number EE/VF2902/D618 on 18 May 1962 and allocated to Hull Dairycoates.

Final depot: Kingmoor, 2/08.

Names carried: *British Steel Corby*, 3/87–8/91; *Fort William/An Gearasdan*, 8/91.

Status: Allocated to HNRC, locomotives for lease at Barrow Hill from 4/22.

**37604 (D6707, 37007, 37506)** (See also 37604 in Class 37s in Colour) Released by EE Vulcan Foundry as D6707, Works Number EE/VF2870/D586 on 3 February 1961 and allocated to March.

Final depot: Kingmoor, 10/07.

Names carried: *The Third East Anglian Regiment*, 4/63–9/63; *British Steel Skinningrove*, 3/87–4/95.

Status: Allocated to HNRC, locomotives for lease at Barrow Hill from 4/22.

Notable movements:
Her freight duties were limited to occasional oil, chemicals and general freight workings as passenger services occupied her from her early days, including 'Footex' trains and the Harwich Boat train but by the early 1980s she was being called

upon more frequently to head Class 1 services anywhere from the north of England to Scotland. On 7 April 1985 she was sent to rescue the SLOA charter 'The Great Western Limited' which originated at London Paddington and ran to Bristol Temple Meads, Taunton, Exeter St Davids, Plymouth and return. Following the failure of two steam locos she and 37178 took the tour from Exeter St Davids to Plymouth after which the journey was completed by a Class 50. Her transfer to Immingham and subsequent Heavy General Overhaul was followed by regular passenger work between the Midlands and Wales, including time spent banking on the Lickey Incline during 1986 but during the late 1980s to mid-1990s she became a 'maid of all work', operating throughout the country from Cardiff to Carlisle.

In April 1995 she was transferred to Bristol Phillips Marsh depot in connection with the failed European Passenger Services project. On 1 June 1996 she was back on charter duty with Pathfinder Railtours' 'The Cumbrian Coaster' which ran from Bristol Temple Meads to Crewe, Carnforth, Workington, Sellafield and return with her and 37611 operating between Bristol and Crewe outward and Carnforth to Bristol on the return, the remainder being handled by Class 20s. She appeared as a guest on the heritage K&WVR for two days from 31 July 1999 then after that her routine was regularly interrupted by charters, including on 4 September 1999 for Mercia Charters 'The Best of Both Worlds' from Preston to Littlehampton, Brighton and return with 37612 throughout.

On 11 March 2000 she was working for Pathfinder Railtours again with 'The Medway Mediator' which ran from Crewe to London Victoria then on to Lewisham, Maidstone and back to London Victoria, then to Reading, Swindon Bath Spa and back to Crewe, being paired with 37602 from and back to London Victoria. On 7 May 2007, again for Pathfinder Railtours' 'The Ouse-Humberman', from Southampton Central to Didcot (Foxhall Junction], York and return, when she and 37603 worked from and back to Foxhall Junction. Then on 1 August 2009 for Spitfire Railtours' 'The Cumbrian Crusader' which began at Wolverhampton and ran to Leeds, Carlisle via the S&C then to Preston, Blackburn, Wakefield, Doncaster, Sheffield and finally Birmingham New Street where it terminated due to late running, buses then returning passengers to Wolverhampton. She was paired with 37607 between Leeds and Carlisle. Next was Retro Railtours' 'The Glasgow Avoider/A Stirling Effort' on 19 May 2012 where she and 37606 had the tour throughout from Crewe to Stirling and return. On 18 May 2013 she was working for Pathfinder Railtours again with 'The Northumbrian Explorer', from Bristol Temple Meads to Birmingham New Street, Alnmouth and return, paired with 37194 throughout.

She was on display at DRS Kingmoor Open Day on 17 August 2013 and on 21 December 2013 she was involved with a 1Zxx 'special' between Newport (South Wales) and Beverley. On 13 June 2014 for Pathfinder Railtours she, 37402 and 37423 were involved with 'The Purbeck Explorer' from Sheffield to Southampton, Swanage and return, then on 6 and 7 March 2015 for the same promoter 'Sabrina's Tea Train/The White Rose Kipper/The Lancs Links' which ran from Crewe to Ironbridge Power Station and return, then from Crewe to Glossop, Bradford, Leeds and return and finally from Crewe to Preston (for the docks), Wigan North Western, Edge Hill, Seaforth Container Terminal and back to Crewe. Over both days she worked with 37419 throughout.

Next was Retro Railtours' 'The Retro Cumbrian Coast Explorer' on 11 July 2015 which originated at Chesterfield and ran to Huddersfield, Blackburn, Preston, Ulverston, Workington and Carlisle, then to Carnforth by the WCML and return to Chesterfield with 37612 throughout. She then spent time working Class 2 services between Carlisle and Barrow-in-Furness before on 3 September 2016 she was involved with the *Railway Magazine*/ Virgin Trains/ DRS charter 'The Independent Yorkshireman' which ran from Chester to Crewe, Stafford, Warrington, Manchester Victoria then on to Wakefield, York and Scarborough. The return was by way of York, Sheffield, Derby then back to Crewe and Chester with her and 37603 having charge throughout. She transferred to Kingmoor into their Cumbrian Coast pool from June 2017 until being transferred to Barrow Hill in April 2022, available for lease from HNRC.

**37605 (D6736, 37036, 37507)**

Released by EE Vulcan Foundry as D6736, Works Number EE/VF2899/ D615 on 25 April 1962 and allocated to Hull Dairycoates.

**At Didcot** on 27 July 2001 is 37605 carrying her Channel Tunnel roundels. (*Steve Jones*)

**Passing Colton** Junction near York on 12 March 2013 is 37606 hauling a NR Multi-Purpose Vehicle (MPV). (*Rick Ward*)

Final depot: Kingmoor, 1/19.

Name carried: *Hartlepool Pipe Mill*, 12/87–6/92.

Status: Preserved by The Heavy Tractor Group on the GCR, 5/22; Scrapped by Chris Allsop Metal Recycling, Colwick, 7/23 after donating parts to the NRM's D6700 (37119/37350), Heavy Tractor Group's 37714 and others. She was the first of the twelve sub-class 37/6 locos (numbers 37601–37612) intended for the aborted the European Passenger Services Ltd. (EPS} 'Nightstar' service in the 1990s to be broken up.

**37606 (D6790, 37090, 37508)**
Released by EE RSH as D6790, Works Number EE/RSH3217/8336 on 28 January 1963 and allocated to Gateshead.

Final depot: Kingmoor, 2/18.

Name carried: None.

Status: Operational as a PODL, allocated to Loram Locomotives, Derby, from 10/22, later to be painted in Rail Freight Grey livery with Thornaby depot's Kingfisher logo, 1/23 and renumbered back to 37508, 3/24.

Notable movements:
Much of her early freight work involved trains between the major marshalling yards at Whitemoor in Cambridgeshire and Temple Mills in East London which continued until the 1980s, though equally important at this time was her passenger commitment with services out of London Liverpool Street to Cambridge and East Anglia. On 13 March 1982 she was employed on a charter for F+W Railtours' 'The Joint Line Bumper' which ran from Plymouth to Gloucester then on to Walsall, Spalding, March East Junction, Wisbech, Whitemoor Junction, Nuneaton, Birmingham New Street, Stourbridge and return to Plymouth. Her part was between March East Junction and Whitemoor Junction. After this her passenger duties became more variable and in addition to trains from London Liverpool Street also included such diverse services as between Swansea and Cardiff,

King's Cross and Newcastle and Glasgow and Carlisle.

Her transfer first to Thornaby and then to Eastfield during the early to mid-1980s saw her involved with Class 1 services between Sheffield and Manchester then north from Glasgow into the Highlands. This continued until her transfer to Cardiff Canton in 1986 when she was allocated to banking duty on the Lickey Incline and then moved back to Thornaby to work freight and passenger services including over the S&C to Carlisle. On 20 September 1992 she was at their Open Day and for the next four years was either in store or on various freight duties. In July 1995 she was transferred to Bristol Phillips Marsh depot in connection with the failed European Passenger Services project. On 21 June 1997 she was involved with A1A Charters 'The Longest Day', a tour from Preston to Crewe, Rugby, London Waterloo then on to Aldershot, Alton, Eastleigh, Plymouth Harbour, Southampton, Didcot, Nuneaton and back to Preston where she was used between Alton and Eastleigh and between Portsmouth Harbour and Didcot.

Her use on Class 1 services continued into the new millennium with trains between the south or south west of England and the Midlands, then her allocation to nuclear traffic whilst based at Kingmoor saw her enter a new era which would eventually involve more regular charter work. This included on 24 March 2012 with 37603 for Pathfinder Railtours' 'The Coal Grinder' from Crewe to Cardiff then a tour which took in Tondu Garw Goods Loop, Llanelli, Gwaun-Cae-Gurwen, Swansea Burrows Sidings, Cwmgwrach, Jersey Marine South Sidings and then back to Crewe. This was followed on 19 May that year for Retro Railtours' 'The Glasgow Avoider/A Stirling Effort' with 37604 from Crewe to Stirling and return. Then on 9 June for Pathfinder Railtours' 'The 3-2-C' with 37609 from Crewe to Plymouth then to Parkandillack and back to Plymouth, then on to Heathfield, Newton Abbott and return to Crewe. Finally for 2012 on 30 June for Cheshire Cat charters 'The York & Scarborough', with 37611 from Cardiff Central to Crewe, Sandbach, then Wakefield, York, Scarborough and return.

On 16 May 2015 she resumed charter duty for Pathfinder Railtours with 'The Heart of Wales Explorer' which started at Tame Bridge Parkway and ran to Worcester, Cardiff Central, Port Talbot, Carmarthen, Craven Arms, Wolverhampton, Kidderminster, Worcester and on to Bristol Parkway. A time spent working Class 2 services between Carlisle and Barrow-in-Furness then followed until July 2015 when after a couple of 'failures' she was transferred to Crewe Gresty Bridge depot. She resumed charter duties on 23 July 2016 for Pathfinder Railtours with 'The Cheshire Cat' with 37609 from Eastleigh to Stockport, Crewe and return, then on 15 July 2017 for Retro Railtours' 'The Retro Welsh Dragon 2' with 37602 from Huddersfield to Cardiff Central, Swansea and return. She was on display at Crewe Gresty Bridge Open days on 20 and 21 July 2018 and then on 22 September that year worked again with Pathfinder Railtours on 'The Marches Cornishman' which ran from Shrewsbury to Bristol Temple Meads then on to Taunton, Exeter St Davids, Plymouth, Penzance and return, again in the company of 37602. During these latter years she was kept busy between charters with freight including nuclear traffic, the occasional Rail Head Treatment Train or maintenance train movements for Network Rail until being allocated to Loram UK in October 2022.

**37607 (D6803, 37103, 37511, 37607)**
Released by EE Vulcan Foundry as D6803, Works Number EE/VF3232 on 9 January 1963 and allocated to Darnall.

Final depot: Kingmoor, 2/17.

Name carried: *Stockton Haulage*, 2/88–6/94.

Status: Operational for HNRC at Barrow Hill, 7/17; Allocated to Colas Rail Freight, 5/18; Returned to HNRC at Barrow Hill, 5/21, operational and painted into HNRC orange livery.

Notable movements:
During her days in Yorkshire she was frequently employed on Class 1 passenger services from Sheffield to the Midlands or to coastal towns such as Skegness or Scarborough. Her transfer to Stratford in 1980 and then to March depot the following year saw this type of work continue with trains from London Liverpool Street to Cambridge or the East Anglian coast, especially to Kings Lynn. She was not a frequent performer on 'specials' during this time but on 24 May 1985 did head 1Z06 from York to Birmingham and on 11 June 1989 was involved

**114** • THE ENGLISH ELECTRIC CLASS 37: CO CO DIESEL ELECTRIC LOCOMOTIVES FROM DESIGN TO DEMISE

**Receiving attention** at Crewe Works during 1988 is 37511. She was renumbered to 37607 in preparation for working the EPS in November 1995. (*Rick Ward*)

*Below left*: **Operational on** the K&WVR on 4 August 2001 is 37607. (*Douglas Todd*)

*Below right*: **At Keighley** on the Worth Valley Railway on 4 August 2001 is 37607. (*Douglas Todd*)

with Hertfordshire Rail Tours 'The Coalville Cobler' which ran from London Euston to Nuneaton, Coalville (for their Open Day) then on to Leicester and return. She and 37504 took the section between Coalville and Leicester.

While based at Thornaby she was also called upon for freight duties including steel between Corby and Lackenby. In late April 1990 she appeared as a guest on the heritage NYMR and on 20 September 1992 she featured on Pathfinder Railtours' 'The Tees-Side Tornado', a charter from Salisbury to Bristol Temple Meads then on to Sheffield, York, Thornaby (for their Open Day) and return. She and 37513 were in charge between Thornaby and Sheffield on this tour which was class 37 hauled throughout and also included 37225, 37262, 37513, 37515 and 37516.

Following periods in store and a brief transfer to Bristol Phillips Marsh for EPS during the mid-1990s she was transferred to Cumbria and worked freight and passenger trains in that area. On 27 March 1999 she was involved with Eagle Railtours' 'The Cumbrian Mountain Explorer & Hadrian's Wall Explorer' which originated at Leamington Spa and ran to Birmingham New Street, Crewe, Blackburn and on to Carlisle via the S&C. A pair of Class 20s then took the train along the Tyne Valley line to Newcastle and return to Carlisle for the journey back to Leamington Spa, otherwise she and 37610 had charge throughout. Between 26 and 28 May

2001 she was paired with 37608 for a series of Regional Railways 'Football Additionals' between Cardiff Central and Manchester Oxford Road, between Crewe and Cardiff Central and between Cardiff Central and Manchester Oxford Road again. On 4 and 5 August 2001 she appeared on the heritage K&WVR following which she resumed her duties for DRS in Cumbria. On 1 August 2009 she was in action for Spitfire Railtours with 'The Cumbrian Crusader' which ran from Wolverhampton to Leeds, then Carlisle via the S&C before heading to Lancaster by the WCML, then to Blackburn, Wakefield, Sheffield and Birmingham New Street where buses conveyed passengers back to Wolverhampton due to the late running of the train. She and 37604 had charge between Leeds and Carlisle. She was employed by the same tour operator on 27 February 2010 for their charter 'The White Rose' with 37038 from Crewe to York then on to Bishop Auckland, Stanhope and return, followed by UK Railtours' 'The Easter West Highlander' on 3 and 4 April that year, which ran from King's Cross to Wakefield then to Carlisle via the S&C before going on to Dumbarton and Oban, returning to King's Cross by way of Paisley, Stranraer and Edinburgh Waverley. She was involved between Dumbarton and Paisley with 37423.

From 6 April to 27 April 2010 she worked Class 2 passenger services between Maryport and Workington on the Cumbrian Coast line and then was busy with a series of charters including on 5 June 2010 for Pathfinder Railtours' 'The Powys Chugger' which ran from Bristol Temple Meads to Birmingham International then on to Crewe, Welshpool (for the Welshpool & Llanfair Railway), Newtown, Wolverhampton, Bescot, Coventry and return. She and 37423 took the Crewe to Bescot section. On 12 February 2011 she was in action again for Pathfinder Railtours with 'The Galloway Galloper' paired with 37601 from Glasgow Central to Kilmarnock, Ayr, Stranraer and return, then from 22 to 25 April 2011 for the same operator 'The Easter Highlander', a tour from Salisbury to Carlisle then Inverness, Aberdeen and return, with 37218 between Carlisle and Inverness. On 24 June 2013 she and 37602 took Compass Tours 'The Oban & Lorn Highlander' from Crewe to Oban and return and then on 20 June 2015 she was involved with Pathfinder Railtours' 'The Heart of Wales Rambler' which began at Exeter St Davids and ran to Shrewsbury for a tour of lines in mid and south Wales before heading back by way of Cardiff Central and Bristol Temple Meads, working with 37608 between Shrewsbury and Bristol. She was then transferred to HNRC and based at Barrow Hill. The November 2022 edition of the *Railway Magazine* noted that she had been painted into HNRC orange and black livery and acquired on loan by Colas Rail Freight.

### 37608 (D6722, 37022, 37512)

Released by EE Vulcan Foundry as D6722, Works Number EE/VF2885/D601 on 13 July 1961 and allocated to Ipswich.

Final depot: Doncaster, 3/16.

Names carried: *Thornaby Demon*, 5/87–7/95; *Andromeda*, 1/17.

Status: Transferred from DRS at Kingmoor to Leicester for EuroPhoenix Locomotives UK, 3/16; Allocated to the Rail Operations Group, 9/17. Renumbered to 37508, 3/24. Repainted into Rail Operations Group green livery, 4/24.

**With classmate** 37218 in York station Parcels Sidings on 31 January 2013 is 37608.

**Leaving York** behind and passing through Colton Junction is 37608 on 21 February 2013. (*Rick Ward*)

**Passing through** Millom station, Cumbria on 14 May 2014 are 37608 and 37607 with the Sellafield to Crewe Coal Sidings nuclear flask train.

Notable movements:
Her duties whilst based in the south of England during her early years consisted of a mix of freight and passenger work, the latter most often out of London Liverpool Street station to Cambridge or East Anglia. She was occasionally used on 'specials' and charters at this time including on 10 July 1977 with 1Z12, from Chesterfield to Sheffield and on 6 May 1978 'Football Specials' between Ipswich and Wembley. On 20 July 1980 she was involved with a day excursion for BR (Birmingham Division) from Wolverhampton to Birmingham New Street, Norwich, Great Yarmouth and return between Norwich and Great Yarmouth. This work continued until her transfer to Eastfield in January 1981 when her regular duties became Class 1 services north from Glasgow to Oban or Fort William and taking over the Scottish sections of trains from London Euston to the Highlands. She took part in the three-day charter for F+W Tours 'The Skirl o' the Pipes 4' which originated at Plymouth on 11 May 1984 and ran to Bristol Temple Meads, Crewe and Mossend Yard where the train split into two portions. Portion One went to Fort William, Mallaig, Inverness and on to Edinburgh Waverley while Portion Two ran to Perth, Inverness, Kyle of Lochalsh, Mallaig then Fort William, Cowlairs and to Edinburgh. There the train was recombined and returned to Plymouth by way of Glasgow Central, Carlisle, Birmingham and Bristol. Her involvement was between Fort William and Mallaig (Portion One) and Mallaig and Cowlairs (Portion Two).

Her transfer to Thornaby in August 1986 saw her freight duties increase with workings in the Yorkshire area occupying much of her time. On 3 April 1993 she featured on NENTA Traintours' 'The Weardale Valley Ghost' which ran from Norwich to Ipswich then to York, Shildon, Eastgate, Darlington and return, being used

Locomotive Histories • 117

between York and Darlington. Moving to Kingmoor in May 2000 resulted in a more varied work pattern, beginning with a charter for First North Western/*Railway Magazine* 'The Class 37 Farewell' on 20 May 2000. This all-37 hauled tour ran from Crewe to Llandudno Junction then Blaenau Ffestiniog, Holyhead, Stockport, Manchester Piccadilly and back to Crewe. Her involvement was between Llandudno and Holyhead with 37612. On 22 and 23 July 2000 she was a guest on the heritage K&WVR, then on 26 and 28 May 2001 she took 'Football Additionals' for Regional Railways between Cardiff Central and Manchester Oxford Road and between Crewe and Cardiff Central, on both occasions in the company of 37607.

She worked on the heritage ELR on the 5 and 6 July 2003 but by September 2005 freight workings were occupying her again including nuclear traffic for DRS in Cumbria. On 24 May 2009 she appeared at 'Eastleigh 100' Open Day and then began a period of charter activity including on 20 March 2010 for Spitfire Railtours' 'The Cumbrian Crusader II' which originated at Birmingham International and ran to Birmingham New Street, Leeds then Carlisle via the S&C, Newcastle, Sheffield and return to Birmingham. She and 37601 had charge between Carlisle and Birmingham International. Then from 18 to 21 June that year she and 37610 worked 'The Highlander', again for Spitfire Railtours and again from Birmingham International. It ran from there to Carlisle, Inverness, Kyle of Lochalsh, Wick, Thurso and back to Inverness before returning to Birmingham. Spitfire Railtours were the promoters again on 31 July 2010 for 'The Cumbrian Crusader III', Birmingham International to Birmingham New Street then Sheffield, Carlisle by the S&C, then to Newcastle, York, Sheffield and return. She was paired with 37259 between Newcastle and Birmingham International. Then

**Crossing Arnside** Viaduct, Cumbria on 15 May 2014 are 37608 and 37607 with the nuclear waste flasks from Sellafield to Crewe Coal Sidings.

**At Doncaster** on 27 February 2020 is 37608 *Andromeda*.

from 7 to 9 August 2010 she and 37409 had charge of the Scottish sections of the VSOE 'Northern Belle' which ran from King's Cross to Inverness and return.

On 2 September 2011 she and 37607 took 1Z59, a 'special' from Glasgow Central to Southampton Eastern Docks, then between 6 and 9 April 2012 she worked with 37069 on a charter from Exeter St Davids to Penrith, Dumbarton, Oban and return via Glasgow Central. On 2 May 2012 she and 37601 worked another 'special' to Southampton Eastern Docks, this one from Edinburgh, returning on 5 May. Then on 29 and 30 September that year she and 37605 took a charter from Dumbarton Central to Oban and return, then to Glasgow Central, Stranraer, though this terminated at Girvan due to line closure. The next day saw them continue from Dumbarton to Salisbury as 1Z38. Into 2013 and the charter work continued with 1Z38 on 9 February from Carlisle to Bristol Temple Meads accompanied by 37609. The tour continued the next day to destinations in the South West including Exeter St Davids, Liskeard and Plymouth, joined by 37218. On 21 June she and 37259 worked another 1Zxx 'special' from Carlisle to Barrow-in-Furness then from there to Fort William, then on 20 July she was involved for Compass Tours with 'The Jolly Fisherman' a charter from Hooton to Crewe, Sheffield, Lincoln, Skegness and return, working between Hooton and Crewe. Her 'day-job' on the Cumbrian Coast route for DRS continued until on 20 June 2015 for Pathfinder Railtours she and 37607 were involved with 'The Heart of Wales Rambler' which began at Exeter St Davids and ran to Shrewsbury then Craven Arms for a tour of lines to Port Talbot, Cardiff Central and on to Bristol Temple Meads and return.

After her repainting into EuroPhoenix livery and being named *Andromeda* during January 2017 she worked a series of 1Zxx 'Specials' between Barrow Hill and Chesterfield during mid-May before continuing her duties for the Rail Operations Group, then on 18 July 2021 she was employed by Transport for Britain with 37884 on their charter 'The Buxton Spa Express' which ran from Lichfield City to Chesterfield, Edale, Buxton and return. During October 2023 she and 37716 were hired in by DRS for Rail Head Treatment Train duties in the Hebden Bridge–Huddersfield–Skipton area, after which she transferred to similar workings in East Anglia and was noted at Stowmarket on 11 November 2023. During early 2024 she was regularly used to move units or coaching stock between depots including on 9 May 2024 as 5Q56 between Asfordby and Oxley, from Derby Litchurch Lane to Oxley as 5Q65 on 11 May 2024 and from Crewe to Landore as 5W79 with 37884 on the rear on 13 May 2024. She featured as a guest loco for the Mid Norfolk Railway's Spring Diesel Gala on 25–27 May and for the North Yorkshire Moors Diesel Gala from 14 to 16 June 2024.

**37609 (D6815, 37115, 37514)** (See also 37609 in Class 37s in Colour) Released by EE Vulcan Foundry as D6815, Works Number EE/VF3244/D769 on 22 February 1963 and allocated to Darnall.

Final depot: Kingmoor, 5/00.

Name carried: None.

Status: Deregistered by DRS after storage at Kingmoor, 1/20; Operational for HNRC, Barrow Hill, locomotives for lease from 4/22.

Notable movements:
Early duties included freight in the Yorkshire area and passenger services centred on Sheffield, though with her transfer to Stratford in 1977 her activities became focussed on London Liverpool Street, with trains to Cambridge and East Anglia which would occupy her until late 1984, interrupted only by the occasional venture into wider territory, including on 18 July 1983, 1Z62 between Glasgow Central and Edinburgh, services between Glasgow and Carlisle during April 1984 and between Sheffield and Manchester Piccadilly in October that year.

The mid- and late 1980s saw her working a variety of passenger and freight trains mainly in the north of England though she did feature at Thornaby Open Day on 20 September 1992. On 31 October that year she was used by the Branch Line Society on their tour 'The Tyne-Tees Wanderer IV' which began at Derby and ran to Deepcar, Sheffield Victoria, York, Billingham Junction, Seal Sands Junction, Newcastle, Jarrow and return, including branch lines near Sheffield, Billingham and Newcastle, all in the company of 37422. She was paired with the same classmate on 6 March 1993 for Pathfinder Railtours' 'The Coker-Coaler' from Manchester Piccadilly to Derby, Bolsover

Colliery, Doncaster, Wakefield Kirkgate, Sheffield then to Birmingham New Street and return to Manchester Piccadilly, including tours of colliery lines in Derbyshire, Nottinghamshire and South Yorkshire.

In April 1995 she was transferred to Bristol Phillips Marsh depot in connection with the failed European Passenger Services project. She was a guest at the heritage K&WVR Diesel Gala on 1 and 2 August 1998 and then on 24 October that year she and 37610 worked an Eagle Charters rail tour between Worcester Shrub Hill and Workington and return. On 5 August 2000 she featured on Pathfinder Railtours' 'The Anglian Capitalist' which began at Preston and ran to Wembley Central, on to Ipswich and return. She was employed by Regional Railways on 'Rugby Additionals' between Crewe and Cardiff Central on 11 and 18 November 2000, then on 12 May and 12 August 2001 on 'Football Additionals' between Liverpool Lime Street and Cardiff Central and Manchester Piccadilly and Cardiff Central respectively.

Her duties for DRS based at Kingmoor kept her busy until on 2 April 2005 she worked the 'special' 1Z37, 'The Wedding Belle' with 37606 from Crewe to Stafford and return. She then appeared at Kingmoor Open Day on 11 June that year before returning to her nuclear traffic role from Kingmoor until 28 November 2009 when she and 37259 took Spitfire Railtours' 'The Yuletide York/The Geordie Growler' charter from Birmingham International to York, Newcastle and return. Then on 9 June 2012 she was paired with 37606 for Pathfinder Railtours' 'The 3-2-C' from Crewe to Gloucester, Plymouth, Parkandillack and return.

She was a guest at Gresty Bridge Open Day on 18 August that year then on 9 February 2013, again for Pathfinder Railtours she was involved with 'The Winter Whistler' from Bristol to Birmingham New

**Leaving Keighley** on the Worth Valley Railway on 2 August 1998 are 37609 and 37029. (*Douglas Todd*)

**At Doncaster** on 24 April 2014 with a NR track testing train is 37609.

Street then Crewe, Wigan North Western, Blackburn and on to Carlisle via the S&C, returning by the WCML to Bristol, in the company of 37218 and 37608 throughout. Next day the three were in action again for the same promoter with 'The Hullaba-Looe', Bristol Temple Meads to Exeter St Davids, Liskeard, Looe and return. On 24 July 2013 she and 37603 headed 'The Pennine & North Eastern Explorer' for Compass Tours, Milton Keynes Central to Durham and return. Then on 17 August that year she appeared at the DRS Open Day at Kingmoor and on 28 and 29 December was a guest at the heritage Mid Norfolk Railway. Pathfinder Railtours were the promoter yet again on 21 and 22 February 2014 for their tour 'The Curried Goyt/The Red Rose Kipper/ The Clay Box' which also featured 37402, 37409 and 37703. It began at Crewe and ran to Manchester Victoria, Guide Bridge, Rose Hill Marple and return. Then resumed from Crewe to Preston, Windermere, back through Preston to Blackpool South, Blackburn, Colne, Bolton, Manchester Piccadilly and back to Crewe. The final stage was from Crewe to Shrewsbury, Wolverhampton, Birmingham International, Daventry, Stoke-on-Trent, Warrington Bank Quay and return to Crewe by way of Wolverhampton and Birmingham International.

After spending 2015 in store or hauling Class 2 services between Carlisle and Barrow-in-Furness she moved 'light engine' to DRS Coal Sidings at Crewe. On 23 July 2016 she and 37606 took Pathfinder Railtours' 'The Cheshire Cat' from Eastleigh to Crewe (for DRS Open Day) then to Stockport and return. Her next major outing was 'The Spring Highlander', a four-day charter for Pathfinder Railtours between 14 and 17 April 2017 which involved her, 37259 and 37605 from Eastleigh to Inverness for a tour of the Highlands. She was paired with 37605 again from 15 to 17 June that year for another long-distance tour beginning at Crewe and running to Bangor, then to Ravenglass for the narrow gauge Ravenglass & Eskdale Railway, back to Barrow-in-Furness then on to Fort William and back to Crewe via Carlisle. She was then involved in day two of the four-day charter for UK Railtours' 'The Edinburgh Military Tattoo/ Highland Fling' on 12 August 2017 when she and 37602 ran between Edinburgh and Oban and return. Then on 10 February 2018 she was back working for Pathfinder Railtours again with 'The Blue Boys Ribble Rouser', a tour from Eastleigh to Nuneaton, Crewe, Preston Docks, Warrington Bank Quay and return when she and 37069 had charge between Eastleigh and Nuneaton and return. She then went into store for DRS at Kingmoor until being transferred to Barrow Hill for HNRC in April 2022, 'locomotives for lease'.

**37610 (D6881, 37181, 37687)**
Released by EE RSH as D6881, Works Number EE/RSH3359/8402 on 21 October 1963 and allocated to Canton.

Final depot: Kingmoor, 5/00.

Names carried: *The Malcolm Group*, 4/02; *T.S. Cassady*, 4/08.

Status: Operational as a PODL, HNRC, Barrow Hill; On loan to Colas Rail Freight from 9/18 and operating NR engineers' trains during spring 2024 painted in blue livery.

**Passing Shipton** by Beningbrough north of York on 14 April 2017 are 37609 and 37259 with 1Z37, day 1 of Pathfinder Railtours' 'The Spring Highlander', Eastleigh to Inverness.

## Locomotive Histories • 121

**37611 (D6871, 37171, 37690)**
Released by EE Vulcan Foundry as D6871, Works Number EE/VF3349/D835 on 17 September 1963 and allocated to Canton.

Final depot: Kingmoor, 5/00

Names carried: *Pegasus*, 4/17; *Denise*, 5/23.

Status: Moved from DRS Stored Locomotives to Leicester for EuroPhoenix Locomotives UK, 4/16; Operational in blue livery with the Rail Operations Group from 4/23.

**37667 (D6851, 37151)**
Released by EE Vulcan Foundry as D6851, Works Number EE/VF3326/D825 on 2 July 1963 and allocated to Canton.

Final depot: Kingmoor, 2/17.

Names carried: *Wensleydale*, 9/88; *Flopsie*, 11/21.

Status: In store for DRS at Kingmoor, 2/17; Transferred to Crewe Diesel Depot as a PODL, 5/17; Allocated to LSL Operational Locomotives, 11/18; Moved from Loram at Derby to Crewe DMD by road, 7/19; Operational for LSL from 9/19; With D6817 hauled 'The English Riviera Express' for LSL/Saphos Trains, 5/24; Guest loco for the Weybourne Traction Group on the North Norfolk Railway's 'Rails & Ales' mixed traction gala, 6/24 in LSL green livery.

**37668 (D6957, 37257)**
Released by EE Vulcan Foundry as D6957, Works Number EE/VF3514/D945 on 12 January 1965 and allocated to Canton.

Final depot: Toton, 5/07.

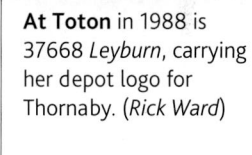

Name carried: *Leyburn*, 9/88–8/90.

Status: Bought by WCRC, Carnforth, 12/07; Reinstated to traffic as a PODL and operative with WCRC from 7/14.

Notable movements:
Her early days in South Wales were occupied with the usual mix of local passenger services and the heavy freight associated with the area and she would have to wait until the 1980s before 'specials' began to appear in her schedule. On 2 June 1982 she worked 1Z17 Cardiff to Barry Island, then 1Z22 on to Gloucester and return. During late 1983 she was employed as a

**At Toton** in 1988 is 37668 *Leyburn*, carrying her depot logo for Thornaby. (*Rick Ward*)

**On 24 October** 1989 37668 *Leyburn* leads 37667 *Wensleydale* through Gloucester with their steel train from South Wales.

**Parked alongside** 37401 in York station Parcels Sidings on 12 July 2018 is WCRC 37668.

Lickey Banker for a time and then was occupied with Class 1 services between Shrewsbury and North Wales or Crewe to Cardiff until her transfer to Thornaby in May 1988 after which she was involved with the movement of heavy freight again in the north of England as well as the occasional Class 1 service into Scotland.

She appeared at Doncaster Works Open Day on 12 July 1992 and after transferring to Canton in September 1991 continued freight work with China clay trains while based at St Blazey. On 3 April 1994 she and 37521 worked 'The Pixie' excursion for Pathfinder Railtours which ran from Bristol Temple Meads to Plymouth, Bere Alston, Calstock and return, but the tour was terminated early due to the failure of 37521 and re-run as 'The Pixie Returns' on 23 October that year featuring 37146 and 37412. On 31 December 1996 she and 37416 operated a series of special trains top and tail between Newton Abbot and Heathfield. Her China clay work continued until late 1999 when she was Sandite fitted by EWS and transferred first to Bescot in September and then to Toton in December that year. On 17 June 2000 she was called on to assist with Vintage Trains '4936 *Kinlet Hall*–Inaugural Run', a steam-hauled 'special' from Birmingham Snow Hill to Didcot Parkway and return when she hauled the ailing steam loco back from Didcot to Birmingham.

Her transfer to Crewe Diesel depot heralded the start of what would eventually become her new life in preservation with involvement in charters, beginning with Vintage Trains 'The Cathedrals Express' on 31 March 2002 when she assisted preserved steam loco 6024 *King Edward I* on the second of its return journeys between Birmingham Snow Hill and Worcester Shrub Hill. On 1 April 2002 she was required to assist Green Express Railtours with their charter 'Steam Along the Cumbrian Coast' which featured preserved steam loco 45112 from Milton Keynes, but its failure near Nuneaton meant that the tour could not proceed and was terminated at Stafford after its rescue by 37668. She was busy the following day for Regional Railways (Rugby Additionals) with a Crewe to Cardiff Central and return train. Another 'assist' followed on 13 July 2002 for Fishwick & Sons 'The Fishwick Fellsman' which ran from Crewe to Manchester Victoria, Preston, Blackburn and Carlisle via the S&C, returning by way of the WCML to Preston, then Manchester and Crewe, where her involvement followed the failure of a Class 47 near Manchester on the return journey. Then on 21 September 2002 she featured for Past Time Rail's 'The Spinnin' State IV' which ran from London Paddington to Newport, Hereford, Crewe, Nuneaton, Oxford and return to London Paddington. She and 37706 had charge from near Hereford to Crewe. On 29 December 2003 she worked Pathfinder Railtours' 'The Settle & Carlisle 2' from Crewe to

Chester, Sheffield, Settle, Carlisle and return, with 37698 throughout.

Short periods in store for EWS at Toton and on Sandite duties were followed in December 2007 by her purchase by WCRC. She appeared at Carnforth Open Day on 27 July 2008 and was later reinstated into stock as a PODL, thereby embarking on her new career as a 'heritage diesel'. Early duties for West Coast Railways were in the Scottish Highlands during late 2014 with trains to Kyle of Lochalsh, Boat of Garten, Oban and Inverness in the company of 37685 but it was from the summer of 2016 that she featured most often for the company with 'The Scarborough Spa Express', then with their other 'regulars' including 'The Waverley', 'The Cumbrian Mountain Express' and 'The Dalesman'. She was also in demand from other promoters and featured on Branch Line Society tours such as 'The Cliffe Hopper' on 7 October 2016, 'The 565 Special' organised by them and 565 Railtours on 1 September 2017 and later 'The Sunday Yicker' on 9 June 2019. She worked for Steam Dreams on 10 June 2018 assisting steam on 'The Cathedrals Express' and on 26 June that year replaced steam on Statesman Rail's 'The Fellsman' due to the heightened fire risk. On 5 May 2019 she featured on the final day of nine for the Railway Touring Company's extensive tour 'The Great Britain XII' when she was called upon to pilot the struggling steam loco 60103.

Pathfinder Railtours also made use of her services during 2022 including on 15 October with 37676 on 'The Settle & Carlisle' charter, on 29 October with 'The Cotswold Caper' and on 12 November with 'The Whistling Geordie'. Finally for 2022 she worked for the Railway Touring Company again on 'The York Yuletide Express'. In addition to all this regular work she was a guest on the collaboration between the WCRC and Ian Riley for 'The Flying Scotsman Christmas Dalesman' on 4 December 2019 and during June 2023 featured on 'The Jacobite' services between Fort William and Mallaig, assisting on the rear of the steam hauled train due to the high fire risk. On 29 October 2023 she and WCRC 37676 *Loch Rannoch* 'top and tail' took Pathfinder Railtours' 'The Cotswold Caper' which ran from Burton-on-Trent to Banbury. Working again for Pathfinder Railtours on 4 May 2024, she and 37518 worked 'The Spring Cornish Explorer' from Dorridge to Penzance and return.

**37669 (D6829, 37129)**
Released by EE Vulcan Foundry as D6829, Works Number EE/VF3274/D803 on 20 March 1963 and allocated to Canton.

Final depot: Toton, 5/07.

Name carried: None.

Status: Sold by DBS, 1/11; Reinstated to traffic for WCRC, Carnforth, as a PODL, 3/11; Operational from 7/14.

Notable movements:
Like so many of her classmates her early duties involved local passenger services and freight associated with the industries of her home depots though also like so many others her time in the south west of England involved her on banking duty on the Lickey Incline as well as taking her own Class 1 trains in that area. Time

**Passing through** York station on 11 August 2016 and heading for the NRM after bringing 'The Scarborough Spa Express' from Carnforth are WCRC 37669 and 37516.

**In the** livery of the West Coast Railway Company, 37669 assists on the rear of 'The Scarborough Spa Express' on 5 July 2018, the train being hauled between York and Scarborough by steam loco 35018 *British India Line*.

spent in Scotland in the mid-1980s saw her in charge of services to Perth and Inverness while when sent to Laira in January 1988 she took Class 1 trains in the Plymouth and Bristol area. She was a guest on the heritage Bodmin & Wenford Railway on 19 and 20 September 1992 then on 26 September 1993 she and 37413 were involved with BR (Inter-City, Plymouth Area) on a tour carrying 'The Royal Duchy' headboard, running between Plymouth and Bere Alston then between Plymouth and Penzance.

Her transfer to Canton in January 1994 was followed by a period in store followed by one hauling China Clay trains when allocated to St Blazey from March 1995. By this time though she was also becoming more sought after for charter train duties including for Pathfinder Railtours on 8 May 1995 'The Grockle Grid' which ran from Wolverhampton to Bristol Temple Meads, Plymouth, Carne Point, Lostwithiel, Penzance, St Ives and return, when she and 37696 were in charge between Plymouth and Penzance. Pathfinder Railtours were the promoter again for 'The Cornish Gnome' on 3 May 1998, from Cardiff Central to Bristol Temple Meads, Plymouth, Par, Falmouth Docks, Coombe Junction, Looe, Liskeard, Plymouth, Exeter St Davids and back to Cardiff. She was paired with 37403 from Par to Plymouth. After transferring to Motherwell in December 2000 she next took Green Express Railtours' 'GER Tour No.186' from Moston to Wakefield Kirkgate, Carlisle via the S&C, Edinburgh Waverley and return to Moston by way of York, with 37682 throughout. On 14 February 2004 for Pathfinder Railtours again she and 37521 were in action with 'The Tyneside Valentine' which ran from Cardiff Central to York, Newcastle, Durham, York and return to Cardiff. They had the train from York to Newcastle and return.

She then moved to Toton and there followed a series of charters including on 31 July 2004 for Pathfinder Railtours' 'The Moorlander' from Crewe to Birmingham New Street, Grantham, Finsbury Park, Wembley EFOC, Dolland's Moor Yard, Kensington Olympia, Acton Reception, Kettering, Wigston North Junction then back to Crewe via Birmingham, with 37689 between Crewe and Grantham and Acton Reception and Crewe. For Pathfinder Railtours again on 11 December 2004 with 'The Anglian Angel', Birmingham New Street to Derby, Peterborough, Ferne Park Sidings, Leicester North Junction, Nuneaton and return to

Birmingham, between Birmingham and Derby and Leicester North Junction and Birmingham with 37692. Then on 29 January 2005 for Past Time Rail 'The Barmouth Banker', Northampton to Birmingham International then on to Machynlleth, Pwllheli and return, paired with 37427 from Birmingham to Machynlleth and return. She was back with Pathfinder Railtours for 'The East-Ender' on 5 February 2005 which ran from Crewe to Reading Up Goods then to London Liverpool Street, Southend Victoria, Wembley EFOC and return to Crewe, with 37427 from Crewe to Reading Up Goods and from Wembley EFOC to Crewe. For the same operator on 26 February that year with 'The High Peaks Hustler', from Birmingham International to Chester North Junction then Liverpool Lime Street, Manchester Victoria, Rose Hill Marple, Buxton, Crewe and return to Birmingham International, top and tail with 37427 throughout.

Her reinstatement to active duties by WCRC at Carnforth in July 2014 following periods in store saw her activity increase dramatically with regular appearances on their 'Scarborough Spa Express', 'The Waverley' and 'The Dalesman' as well as appearing on a number of other tours including on 2 September 2017 for 565 Railtours/Branch Line Society 'The 565 Special' (see 37668 for details). On 16 September that year she was working for the SRPS on 'The Oban Excursion'. Inverurie to Aberdeen, Oban and return with 37685. On 15 April 2018 she worked on Charity Railtours' 'The Mayflower' which ran from Highbury & Islington to Sizewell CEGB, Ipswich, Halifax Junction, Griffin Wharf, Harwich Town, London Liverpool Street then to Bethnal Green and back to Highbury & Islington, top and tail with a Class 47 throughout. Between 17 and 21 June 2018 she headed regular Class 2 services between Windermere and Oxenholm, then she was back on charter duty for The Railway Touring Company on 24 July with 'The Welsh Mountaineer', assisting steam loco 48151 due to the high fire risk on the tour from Preston to Llandudno Junction, Blaenau Ffestiniog and return. On 15 May 2019 she worked for Steam Dreams on the rear of day seven of nine of 'The Highlands & Islands Explorer', between Fort William, Dumbarton Central, Coatbridge, Carstairs and Penrith North Lakes, with steam loco 61306 on the front.

On 20 July that year she worked top and tail throughout on the Branch Line Society tour 'The Luca Pezzulo Express' which ran from Lancaster to Wakefield Kirkgate, Tinsley, Hull Paragon then to Kellingley Colliery and return to Lancaster. Then on 10 August 2019 she was involved for the Branch Line Society on their tour 'Type 3 to the Sea/The Cosham Completer' which explored branch lines between Crewe, Portsmouth Harbour, Eastleigh and return in the company of 37518 and 37706. All these were fitted in between her regular work for the WCRC which also included appearances assisting steam on 'The Jacobite' between Fort William and Mallaig during periods of high fire risk as well as heading the diesel-hauled legs of 'The Scarborough Spa Express'.

### 37670 (D6882, 37182)

Released by EE RSH as D6882, Works Number EE/RSH3360/8403 on 28 October 1963 and allocated to Canton.

Final depot: Leicester (for EuroPhoenix Locos UK), 3/16.

Name carried: *St Blazey T&RS Depot*, 2/93–7/99.

Status: Cut up at Leicester LIP, 3/18.

**At Newport** South Wales on 4 June 1998 with a freight are 37670 *St Blazey T&RS Depot* and 37669.

**37671 (D6947, 37247)**
Released by EE Vulcan Foundry as D6947, Works Number EE/VF3504/D935 on 22 October 1964 and allocated to Canton.

Final depot: Toton, 5/07.

Name carried: *Tre Pol and Pen*, 7/87–7/99.

Status: Cut up by EMR, Attercliffe, 2/11.

**37672 (D6889, 37189)**
Released by EE RSH as D6889, Works Number EE/RSH3367/8410 on 9 January 1964 and allocated to Canton.

Final depot: Barrow Hill for HNRC, stored locomotives, 8/06.

Name carried: *Freight Transport Association*, 9/87.

Status: Cut up at T.J. Thomson's scrapyard, Stockton, 12/10.

**37673 (D6832, 37132)** (See also 37673 in Class 37s in Colour)
Released by EE Vulcan Foundry as D6832, Works Number EE/VF3277/D806 on 3 April 1963 and allocated to Canton.

Final depot: Toton, 5/07.

Name carried: None.

Status: Cut up at EMR, Kingsbury, 5/08.

**37674 (D6869, 37169)** (See also 37674 in Class 37s in Colour)
Released by EE Vulcan Foundry as D6869, Works Number EE/VF3347/D833 on 23 August 1963 and allocated to Landore.

Final depot: Toton, 5/07.

Name carried: *Saint Blaise Church 1445–1995*, 12/95.

Status: Sold from EWS stock, 5/07; Moved to the Wensleydale Railway, 5/14; Operational on the Strathspey Railway, arrived 11/21.

Notable movements:
Though she was involved with freight duties in the Yorkshire area in her early days it was with passenger services that she soon made her mark, heading Class 1 trains between the Midlands and the north of England. An early charter for her was on 12 May 1985 with classmate 37189 heading 1Z49, the returning 'Skirl O' the Pipes 6' three-day tour of Scotland for F+W Railtours, when they delivered the train back to Bristol Temple Meads. Her move to Laira in April 1987 involved her with services to Penzance and Plymouth including Class 1 trains out of Paddington from the late 1980s through to the mid-1990s. On 17 May 1997 she was involved for A1A Charters/Pathfinder Railtours with 'The Pirates of Penzance' charter from Preston to Birmingham New Street, Swindon, Bristol Temple Meads then on to Penzance, St Ives, Par and return. She had the train from Penzance to Birmingham New Street. On 31 July 1999 for Pathfinder Railtours she was paired with 37801 for 'The Spinning Haggis', a tour from Swindon to Birmingham New Street, Crewe then Motherwell, Glasgow Central, Stirling, Dundee and return, when they were in charge between Glasgow Central and Stirling. Then on 6 May 2000 for the SRPS 'The West Highlander' which ran from Dundee to Fort William, Mallaig and returned only as far as Drem due to engineering works. She and 37411 took the train between Fort William and Drem.

Her transfer to Crewe Diesel in December 2002 saw her involved with charters for Pathfinder Railtours again including on 12 April 2003 'The Wizard Express' which ran from Reading to Birmingham New Street,

**At the** platform at Leeming Bar, Wensleydale Railway on 23 August 2016 is 37674.

**Parked at** Leeming Bar on the Wensleydale Railway on 18 December 2016 is 37674.

Manchester Victoria, Preston, Wigan Springs Branch, Knowsley Freight Terminal, Crewe and return, with her and 37689 working between Crewe and Reading. On 31 May and 1 June that year she and 37503 were involved with 'The Crewe Invader I and II' also for Pathfinder Railtours. Train I ran from Salisbury to Crewe, then to Ironbridge and return while next day Train II ran from Bristol Temple Meads to Crewe and Shrewsbury and return. Both tours had the option of visiting the Open Days at Crewe Works. Then on 19 July 2003 for Hertfordshire Rail Tours she and 37670 took part in 'The Cat & Fiddle' charter which ran from London Paddington to Newport, Craven Arms, Chester, Toton, Nottingham, Grantham and Peterborough to London King's Cross. They had charge between Newport and Chester.

Working out of Toton depot from March 2004 she was a guest on the heritage East Somerset Railway during April that year before spending time either in store for EWS or in their 'tactical reserve'. After being sold and moved to the heritage Wensleydale Railway in North Yorkshire she worked there from November 2014 to June 2018 then was sent to the Strathspey Railway where she has worked since March 2022.

**37675 (D6864, 37164)**
Released by EE RSH as D6864, Works Number EE/RSH3342/8359 on 22 August 1963 and allocated to Landore.

Final depot: Toton, 5/07.

Name carried: *William Cookworthy*, 8/87–1/94.

Status: Cut up at EMR, Kingsbury, 10/10.

**37676 (D6826, 37126)**
Released by EE RSH as D6826, Works Number EE/RSH3271/8386 on 14 May 1963 and allocated to Canton.

Final depot: Toton, 5/07.

Name carried: *Loch Rannoch* from 7/08.

Status: Sold by EWS, 11/07; Operational as a PODL for WCRC, Carnforth from 3/08. During 2024, based at Fort William for use when required over the route of 'The Jacobite' to Mallaig.

**37677 (D6821, 37121)**
Released by EE RSH as D6821, Works Number EE/RSH3266/8381 on 19 April 1963 and allocated to Canton.

Final depot: Toton, 5/07.

Name carried: None.

Status: Cut up by C.F. Booth, Rotherham, 10/08.

**37678 (D6956, 37256)**
Released by EE Vulcan Foundry as D6956, Works Number EE/VF3513/D944 on 8 January 1965 and allocated to Canton.

Final depot: Doncaster, 12/00.

Name carried: None.

Status: Cut up by EMR, Kingsbury, 5/07.

**37679 (D6823, 37123)**
Released by EE RSH as D6823, Works Number EE/RSH3268/8385 on 25 April 1963 and allocated to Canton.

Final depot: Toton, 5/07.

Name carried: None.

Status: Sold by EWS, 5/07; Preserved on the Northampton & Lamport Railway from 7/07; Reinstated into traffic 8/07 and moved to Nemesis Rail by road, 6/11; Moved to Ian Riley Engineering, Bury for the ELR by road, 3/14; Moved to Railway Services Ltd, Wishaw by road, 12/20. For photo, see 37686.

**37680 (D6924, 37224)** (See also 37680 in Class 37s in Colour)
Released by EE Vulcan Foundry as D6924, Works Number EE/VF3410/D868 on 30 January 1964 and allocated to Landore.

Final depot: Doncaster, 9/03.

Name carried: None.

Status: Cut up at T.J. Thomson's scrapyard, Stockton, 12/10.

**At Hope** Cement Works, Derbyshire on 4 September 2008 is 37680. (*Phil Sangwell*)

**37681 (D6830, 37130)** (See also 37681 in Class 37s in Colour)
Released by EE Vulcan Foundry as D6830, Works Number EE/VF3275/D804 on 25 March 1963 and allocated to Canton. Final depot: Immingham, 9/90.

Name carried: None.

Status: Cut up by M.R.J. Phillips at Crewe Adtranz, 8/95.

Notable movements:
An early claim to fame came on 10 June 1964 when still numbered D6830 she headed the first diesel hauled excursion to travel down the Rhymney Valley line in South Wales from Rhymney near Merthyr through Caerphilly and on to Cardiff with her train for Clifton Down, Bristol. When working out of Stratford depot in the 1970s she had some freight duties in the form of oil trains as well as Class 1 passenger services from London Liverpool Street to East Anglia. Her move to Tinsley in early 1982 saw her often used on services between Sheffield and Blackpool during May and June, but apart from occasional Class 1 trains and the 'special' 1Z11 London Euston to Stirling on 27 March 1986, between Mossend Yard near Motherwell and Stirling, her work during the 1980s was mainly with freight, notably railway ballast from the quarries near Panmaenmawr to Salford Hope Street in 1987 and 1988 to improve the railway system in the Ordsall area of Greater Manchester and beyond. This type of work continued into the early 1990s in the Leeds area where she was often stabled at Holbeck, but her 'accident' at Skipton on 22 January 1992 when she was struck by a Pacer dmu effectively ended her career and she was cut up at Adtranz, Crewe Works in August 1995.

**37682 (D6936, 37236)**
Released by EE Vulcan Foundry as D6936, Works Number EE/VF3422/D880 on 29 April 1964 and allocated to Landore.

Final depot: Kingmoor, 12/08.

Name carried: None.

Status: Cut up at C.F. Booth, Rotherham, 11/16.

Notable movements:
Early freight workings in the South Wales area were typical of her class, being associated with the heavy industries of 'The Valleys'. While

in Scotland in the late 1960s she took occasional passenger services between Glasgow and Edinburgh but on transferring back to Canton and Landore she resumed freight work with very little variety. On 3 September 1978 she and classmate 37291 were on charter duty for the Lea Valley Railway Club heading 'The Severn Choppers Express' which ran from London Paddington to Maidenhead, Bath Spa, Bristol Temple Meads then on to Ebbw Vale, Newport, Chepstow, Gloucester and back to Paddington. They were in charge from Gloucester back to London Paddington. In the summer of 1979, she worked as a Lickey Banker but by the early 1980s was heading Class 1 services between Bristol, Cardiff and the Midlands, and to Leeds.

Heavy freight continued to occupy her through the 1980s although on 26 May 1984 she and 37177 were involved on a 'special' running as 1Z56 from Bristol to Glasgow Central, taking it as far as Wolverhampton. She was busy with the Panmaenmawr to Salford ballast trains during 1987 and early 1988, usually with 37681 or 37683 (see 37681 for more detail) but from mid-1988 was used regularly on services to Aberystwyth from the Midlands. This mix of passenger and freight work occupied her into the 1990s then on 22 June 1991 she worked for The Class 37 Group with 'The Brentford Bard', Manchester Piccadilly to Stratford-on-Avon, Brentford Goods, Southall West Junction, London Paddington, Birmingham International and return to Manchester Piccadilly, working throughout with 37685 except between Brentford Goods and Southall West Junction (Class 47).

**Approaching Colton** Junction, York on the ECML, DRS liveried 37682 runs light engine from Derby (NR) to Edinburgh Craigentinny Train & Rolling Stock Maintenance Depot on 15 April 2014.

Freight continued to dominate her duties until 14 and 15 May 1998 when she headed 'The Royal Scotsman' from Paddington to York and then York to Edinburgh with 37428. Then on 10 July 1999 she was involved for Worksop CTC with 'The Worksop Midlothian' which ran from Retford to York, Edinburgh Waverley, Dunfermline then on branch lines to Kincardine Power Station and Rosyth Dockyard before heading to Inverkeithing, Edinburgh Waverley and return to Retford. She featured between Dunfermline and Edinburgh Waverley. On 6 April 2002 she worked for Pathfinder Railtours on 'The Napier Navigator' which was 'Deltic' hauled from Crewe to York and return, with her and 37521 taking the train on from York to Scarborough ('Deltic' back from Scarborough to Crewe). Then on 20 July 2002 she was involved on day two of Pathfinder Railtours' 'The Ayr Receeder' which began at Newport and ran to Birmingham New Street, Crewe, Mossend Yard and then touring freight branches around Grangemouth to Paisley Gilmour Street, on to Glasgow Central followed by more freight lines to Motherwell, then to Carlisle and return to Newport via Crewe. She and 37667 were in charge for the branch line sections. She was employed by Green Express Railtours on 3 August that year with 'GER Tour No.186' with 37669 from Moston to Wakefield Kirkgate then to Carlisle via the S&C and to Edinburgh and return. After that she spent periods of time in store for EWS before being sold to HNRC in November 2007.

She worked for DRS nuclear traffic from Kingmoor until interrupted by an appearance as a guest on the heritage Keighley and Worth Valley Railway between 5 and 7 June 2009. Then on 12 September 2009 for Spitfire Railtours' 'The Cumbrian Coaster' which ran from Birmingham International to Birmingham New Street, Crewe Basford Hall, Preston, Carnforth to Carlisle by the WCML, then to Chester, Crewe and back to Birmingham. She and 37510 worked between Carlisle and Crewe. She continued with her nuclear traffic duties broken by periods in store until appearing on the heritage Mid Norfolk Railway on 31 March and 1 April 2012 and on the Wensleydale Railway on 20 September 2014. Then on 25 April 2014 she worked for Virgin Trains 'The Welsh Warrior' from Crewe to Chester, Holyhead, North Llanrwst, Llandudno Junction, Llandudno, Chester and return, with 37419 throughout. This was a farewell special for Virgin Trains Mk.3 set (also known as the 'Pretendolino') raising money for the British Legion Poppy Appeal. She was then allocated to DRS stored fleet until being cut up by CF Booth at Rotherham in November 2016.

**37683 (D6887, 37187)**
Released by EE RSH as D6887, Works Number EE/RSH3365/8408 on 31 January 1964 and allocated to Landore.

Final depot: Toton, 5/07.

Name carried: None.

Status: Cut up by C.F. Booth, Rotherham, 2/13.

**37684 (D6834, 37134)** (See also 37684 in Class 37s in Colour)
Released by EE Vulcan Foundry as D6834, Works Number EE/VF3279/D808 on 24 April 1963 and allocated to Canton.

Final depot: Toton, 5/07.

Name carried: *Peak National Park*, 9/91.

Status: Cut up by C.F. Booth, Rotherham, 1/10.

**37685 (D6934, 37234)**
Released by EE Vulcan Foundry as D6934, Works Number EE/VF3420/D878 on 10 April 1964 and allocated to Landore.

Final depot: Toton, 5/07.

Name carried: None.

Status: Preserved as a PODL, WCRC, Carnforth, 12/07: Short-term hire to Colas Rail Freight from 10/23; Operational on the West Highland line for WCRC during 4/24, assisting 'The Jacobite', between Fort William and Mallaig.

**37686 (D6872, 37172)** (See also 37686 in Class 37s in Colour)
Released by EE Vulcan Foundry as D6872, Works Number EE/VF3350/D836 on 6 September 1963 and allocated to Canton.

Final depot: Doncaster, 7/00.

Name carried: None.

Status: Cut up by C.F. Booth, Rotherham, 4/06.

**37688 (D6905, 37205)**
Released by EE Vulcan Foundry as D6905, Works Number EE/VF3383/D849 on 5 November 1963 and allocated to Landore.

Final depot: Kingmoor, 2/06.

Names carried: *Great Rocks*, 6/88; *Kingmoor TMD*, 7/07.

Status: Preserved on the Mid Norfolk Railway, 3/17 by the D05 Preservation Society; Transferred to Doncaster, 7/17 and operational as a PODL, available for hire from D05 Preservation Ltd.

Notable movements:
The usual mix of freight and passenger work kept her busy during her first years in South Wales, Scotland and later in Yorkshire. On 8 April 1978 she took part in the Main Line Steam Trust's 'Great Central Wanderer' charter which ran from London Marylebone to Stockport, Penistone, Sheffield and Dinting (for the Dinting Railway Centre) then on to Birmingham New Street and return to Marylebone. She had charge between Penistone and Sheffield.

After her transfer to Bristol in 1979 she spent some time as a Lickey Banker until moving to Canton in March 1981 when she was engaged with passenger work in the Bristol and south west area and into the Midlands. On 5 May 1985 she was involved with day three of three for the RESL charter 'The Sutherland Highlander' which began at Cardiff and ran to Derby, York, Edinburgh, Inverness, Wick and back to Edinburgh. Then on to Mossend, Dumbarton, Glasgow Queen Street, York, Sheffield, Leicester, Southall East Junction and back to Cardiff via Bath Spa. She and 37216 were in charge between Southall and Cardiff.

During 1987 and 1988 she was involved in the ballast movements from Panmaenmawr to Salford (see 37681 for more detail). She was present at Tinsley Open Day on 29 September 1990 and after that was occupied with freight haulage mainly in Yorkshire and the Humber region until on 12 July 1997 when she worked for Hertfordshire Rail Tours on 'The Dungeness Pebbledasher' which ran from Finsbury Park to Kensington Olympia, then from Ashford International to Dungeness and return followed by a freight lines tour around Seven Oaks,

**In Rail** Freight Construction livery, 37688 is stabled at Tinsley on 25 April 1988. (*Rick Ward*)

Kensington Olympia, Wembley Freight Centre and Willesden before returning to Finsbury Park. Her involvement was from Finsbury Park to Dungeness and Ashford International. Her usual mix of freight workings and occasional passenger services continued until on 2 February 2002 she was involved with Pathfinder Railtours' 'The Spider's Web' which began at Reading and ran to Birmingham International, Toton Centre, Lincoln, Grantham, Stratford, Kensington Olympia and back to Reading and Birmingham International. She and 37797 were in charge from Reading to Toton. On 23 August 2003 she took the 'special' 1Z33 from Crewe to Cardiff via Wrexham and the return but after that was transferred to Toton for EWS and in November 2003 allocated to their 'Tactical Reserve'.

After working for DRS at Kingmoor she was a guest on the heritage Mid Norfolk Railway on 22 and 23 September 2007 and after a time in store was busy with a series of charters and 1Zxx 'specials' in addition to her usual duties for DRS. On 8 March 2008 for Spitfire Railtours' 'The Cumbrian Explorer' which ran from Birmingham New Street to Manchester Victoria then to Lancaster, Carlisle and return, with 37667 throughout. Next on 5 May 2008 for North East Railtours' 'The Argyll Invader' from Newcastle to Oban and return with 37248 throughout. On 24 September 2009 she headed the 'special' 1Z55 Whitehaven to Carlisle and on 30 April 2011 another 1Zxx, from Preston to Carmarthen and return with 37194. On 17 September 2011 she was in charge of 1Z36 from Birmingham International to Carlisle between Derby and Carlisle with 37194 again. Then from 8 to 11 June 2012 she was paired with 37667 for 1Z20–1Z26, a series of days touring from King's Cross to Dumbarton Central, Dumbarton Central to Mallaig, Mallaig back to Dumbarton Central, Helensburgh Upper to Oban, Oban to Dumbarton Central, Dumbarton Central to Edinburgh and Edinburgh to King's Cross. This was followed on 22 and 23 June that year by 1Z52–1Z54, a tour from Bangor to Ravenglass between Carlisle and Ravenglass, then Ravenglass to Fort William and Fort William to London Euston between Fort William and Carlisle. On 29 November 2014 she was working on Pathfinder Railtours' 'The Festive Portsmouth Explorer' from Stafford to Portsmouth Harbour via Eastleigh and return, with 37218 throughout, then on 6 December for the Railway Touring Company 'The Bath Christmas Market' assisting on the rear of steam loco 34067 *Tangmere* from Three Bridges to Bath Spa, Bristol Temple Meads and return. Finally that year again for the Railway Touring Company, 'The Christmas Sussex Belle' London Victoria to Eastbourne and return, and again on the rear of the train headed by 34067 *Tangmere*.

In early June 2016 she was employed on Class 2 services between Carlisle and Barrow-in-Furness, after which in February 2017 she was bought for preservation by D05 Preservation Ltd. Between March and December 2017 she worked on the heritage Mid Norfolk Railway then from May 2018 to December 2019 on the SVR and on 17 and 18 September 2021 on the ELR. Three days later on 21 September she was called upon to assist steam loco 35018 *British India Line* with her charter 'The Pendle Dalesman' for the West Coast Railway Company. The train ran from Lancaster to Hellifield then over the S&C to Carlisle and return, but needed help on the rear from Hellifield due to slippery rail head conditions. Between 14 and 19 April 2022 she was involved with a six day private charter for Locomotive Services Limited (LSL), running from Edinburgh Waverley to Wansford (for the NVR), Wansford to Watlington, Dereham (Mid Norfolk Railway) to Canterbury West, Canterbury West to Ashford International and Beechbrook Farm Loop and return, Canterbury West to Crewe Down Refuge Siding (all these with 37667 throughout) then finally from Crewe Down Refuge Siding to Wigan North Western, Hellifield, Carlisle by the S&C then to Carstairs, Edinburgh Waverley and Alnmouth for Alnwick, with 37521 throughout (running as D6817).

She followed that with another six day private charter also for LSL and also paired with 37521 beginning on 19 May 2022 from Crewe to Chester and Llandudno, then on day 2 from Llandudno to Blaenau Ffestiniog and return on her own, then on day three from Llandudno

Nameplate of 37688.

to Crewe, Church Stretton and Llandrindod, followed on day four by Llandrindod to Cardiff Central, Bath Spa and Weymouth, then on day five from Weymouth Jersey Sidings to Weymouth and return and finally on day six from Weymouth to Eastleigh, Oxford and back to Crewe. On 19 October that year she was working for InterCity with 'The Torbay Delight', York to Paignton and return, again with 37521. This was followed by a five-day private charter for LSL starting from Crewe on 28 October 2022, again in the company of 37521 throughout. From Crewe it ran to London Euston, then to Keighley for the Worth Valley Railway, then from Keighley to Carnforth and on to Perth, Aviemore and Boat of Garten. Day three was from Boat of Garten to Aviemore and Kyle of Lochalsh, then on day four from Achnasheen to Inverness and on to Carnforth and Hellifield and finally on day five from Hellifield to Wakefield Kirkgate and Peterborough where it terminated due to very late running.

A well-deserved break from charter work then until 24 June 2023 when she was reunited with 37521 for Saphos Tours 'The English Riviera Express' from Shrewsbury to Taunton, Paignton, Kingswear and return, when they were in charge between Shrewsbury and Taunton and return. On 29 October 2023 she and D6817 (37521) hauled a private charter for LSL, 1Z71, from the K&WVR to Boat of Garten on the Strathspey Railway, which delighted visitors to the Class 37 Running Day at the Bo'ness & Kinneil Railway as they passed at speed. On 15 November

2023 she and WCRC 37685 *Loch Arkaig* on short-term hire to Colas Rail Freight hauled a rake of TTA tanks from Grangemouth Oil Refinery to Gascoigne Wood (North Yorkshire) for storage.

**37689 (D6895, 37195)**
Released by EE RSH as D6895, Works Number EE/RSH3373/8416 on 17 March 1964 and allocated to Landore.

Final depot: Toton, 5/07.

Name carried: None.

Status: Cut up at EMR, Kingsbury, 2/11.

**37692 (D6822, 37122)**
Released by EE RSH as D6822, Works Number EE/RSH3267/8382 on 25 April 1963 and allocated to Canton.

Final depot: Toton, 5/07.

Names carried: *The Lass O'Ballochmyle*, 9/93; *Didcot Depot*, 11/02.

Status: Cut up by C.F. Booth, Rotherham, 7/09.

**37693 (D6910, 37210)** (See D6910 in Pre-TOPS Days)

**37694 (D6892, 37192)**
Released by EE RSH as D6982, Works Number EE/RSH3370/8413 on 20 February 1964 and allocated to Landore.

Final depot: Toton, 5/07.

Name carried: *The Lass O'Ballochmyle*, 10/90–7/93

Status: Cut up at EMR, Kingsbury, 1/08.

## Locomotive Histories • 133

**37695 (D6857, 37157)**
Released by EE Vulcan Foundry as D6857, Works Number EE/VF3332/D831 on 25 July 1963 and allocated to Canton.

Final depot: Toton, 5/07.

Name carried: None.

Status: Cut up at Hull's scrapyard, Rotherham, 4/08.

**37696 (D6928, 37228)**
Released by EE Vulcan Foundry as D6928, Works Number EE/VF3414/D872 on 28 February 1964 and allocated to Landore.

Final depot: Toton, 5/07;

Name carried: None.

Status: Cut up by C.F. Booth, Rotherham, 11/14.

**37697 (D6943, 37243)**
Released by EE Vulcan Foundry as D6943, Works Number EE/VF3500/D931 on 17 September 1964 and allocated to Canton.

Final depot: Doncaster, 4/99.

Name carried: None.

Status: Cut up by C.F. Booth, Rotherham, 3/06.

**37698 (D6946, 37246)** (See also 37698 in Class 37s in Colour)
Released by EE Vulcan Foundry as D6946, Works Number EE/VF3503/D934 on 12 October 1964 and allocated to Canton.

Final depot: Toton, 5/07.

Name carried: *Coedbach*, 9/88–3/93.

Status: Cut up at C.F. Booth, Rotherham, 1/10.

Notable movements:
Her duties during her first ten years consisted of the usual mix of freight and passenger workings but by the late 1970s she was being allocated to more Class 1 trains particularly from Birmingham New Street. Her move to Stratford saw her working services out of London Liverpool Street to East Anglia but when transferred to Tinsley in 1982 she took trains from Sheffield to Manchester and

**At Portway,** Worcestershire, on 15 August 2003 is 37694. (*Steve Jones*)

**At Bristol** Temple Meads during 1988 37698 awaits her next duty. (*Rick Ward*)

Blackpool as well as to Carlisle and on to Glasgow. Working from Cardiff from July 1985 involved her with heavy freight in South Wales but also saw her sought after for charter duty including on 7 June 1987 for the Branch Line Society with 'The Meldon Quarryman' which ran from Birmingham New Street to Westbury, Exeter St Davids, Meldon Quarry, Crediton, Barnstable and return to Birmingham. On 5 May 1991 she was employed by Trainload Metals on a series of trains which ran from locations including Basingstoke, Newport, Ledbury, Worcester, Craven Arms, Abergavenny and Birmingham New Street to the Hereford Rail Festival. Then on 23 June that year she and 37702 were involved with shuttles between Cardiff Bute Road and Merthyr Tydfil for the Taff Valley Railway's 150th Anniversary celebrations and Cathays Railway Works Open Day at Cardiff.

After periods in store at Immingham she and 37694 worked for Pathfinder Railtours on 10 July 1994 with 'The Donny Deviator' which originated at Derby and ran via Sheffield to Doncaster and Silverwood Colliery for a tour of freight lines before returning to Derby. A mix of freight and passenger work kept her busy throughout the 1990s and until on 21 July 2002 when she had charge of the 'special' 1Z53 from York to Scarborough, then on 12 April 2003 for Pathfinder Railtours she was paired with 37712 for 'The Wizard Express' which ran from Reading to Birmingham New Street then Preston, Wigan, Crewe and back to Reading, the 37s having charge from Reading to Preston. More work for Pathfinder Railtours followed that year, first with 'The Grampian Gyrator' on 19 July, originating at Stafford the previous day then running to Crewe and Carlisle.

From there to Inverness (for the Strathspey Railway) then to Edinburgh Waverley and return to Stafford. She and 37707 were in charge between Inverness and Edinburgh. Finally on 29 December 2003 'The Settle & Carlisle Circular 2' from Crewe to Chester and on to Carlisle via the S&C and return with 37668 throughout. On 4 and 5 August 2004 she and 37408 were busy with 'specials' between Knaresborough, Leeds and Carlisle before she was put into store at Toton, then Doncaster and finally sold by EWS from Margam Yard to CF Booth at Rotherham for scrapping in January 2010.

## The Channel Tunnel European Passenger Services project.

In November 1990 the EPS was set up with the intention of managing services through the Channel Tunnel, including a number of overnight sleeper trains designated 'Nightstar'. Services originating in the north of the UK would be hauled by electric locos operating on the WCML and the ECML, but those from the south-west and Wales would require diesel traction to reach London. To operate these latter services twelve Class 37 locos were chosen from the Trainload Freight sector, overhauled and modified at Doncaster Works and renumbered for their new role as the Nightstar trains. The locos involved were:

The twelve were not to be restricted to use on the former 'Great Western' lines but could also be drafted into service whenever a diesel alternative to electric traction was required. They were allocated to Bristol St Phillips Marsh depot from 31 January 1995 and though the first of the twelve was outshopped in a livery of 'Executive Grey' on the upper third of the bodyside and light grey below the former was replaced by 'Flint Grey' from October the same year. The roof was dark blue and they carried EPS branding below the cab window together with cast Channel Tunnel roundels on both sides.

The Channel Tunnel project and its 'Eurostar' services soon encountered financial difficulties and by 1997 cost-cutting became inevitable, with the result that both Nightstar and the proposed Regional Eurostar schemes were suspended. By July 1999

### Table 5. Channel Tunnel EPS locos

| Original Number | Replacement EPS Number |
|---|---|
| 37501 | 37601 |
| 37502 | 37602 |
| 37504 | 37603 |
| 37506 | 37604 |
| 37507 | 37605 |
| 37508 | 37606 |
| 37511 | 37607 |
| 37512 | 37608 |
| 37514 | 37609 |
| 37687 | 37610 |
| 37690 | 37611 |
| 37691 | 37612 |

both had been cancelled. The Class 37/6 fleet was disbanded, a process begun in 1997 when the project was initially put on hold. Numbers 37607 to 37612 were transferred to DRS, to be followed by 37602, 37605 and 37606 during 2002. Numbers 37601, 37603 and 37604 were kept at North Pole depot as 'Thunderbird' locos but by 2008 these too had joined the DRS fleet. Later DRS sold a number of their Class 37s to the spot-hire company EuroPhoenix, which also took others from DB Schenker and preserved 37906 from the Ruston 906 Group. By 2018 the whole fleet had been given a full rebuild and returned to service.

### Sub-class 37/7

These were converted from the original fleet between 1986 and 1988. They had no train heating. They were fitted with modified traction alternators and additional ballast, increasing their weight to 120 tonnes and producing a tractive effort of 61,910lb (276kN). They had a RA of 7.

**37701 (D6730, 37030)**
Released by EE Vulcan Foundry as D6730, Works Number EE/VF2893/D609 on 16 October 1961 and allocated to Hull Dairycoates.

Final depot: Toton, 5/07.

Name carried: None.

Status: Cut up at EMR, Kingsbury, 1/08.

**37702 (D6720, 37020. 37702, L30)**
(See also 37702 in Class 37s in Colour)
Released by EE Vulcan Foundry as D6720, Works Number EE/VF2883/D599 on 30 June 1961 and allocated to Stratford.

Final depot: Doncaster, 3/01.

Name carried: *Taff Merthyr*, 11/89.

Status: Cut up at Puig Vert, Spain, 7/07.

**37703 (D6767, 37067, 37703, L023, L25)**
Released by EE Vulcan Foundry as D6767, Works Number EE/VF3059/D721 on 21 November 1962 and allocated to Thornaby.

Final depot: Kingmoor, 7/17.

Name carried: None.

Status: In store for DRS at Kingmoor, 8/13; Moved to Bo'ness & Kinneil Railway by road, 7/14; Transferred to Barrow Hill for HNRC, 1/22; On hire to the Dartmouth Steam Railway from 6/24.

**37704 (D6734, 37034)**
Released by EE Vulcan Foundry as D6734, Works Number EE/VF2897/D613 on 26 March 1962 and allocated to Hull Dairycoates.

Final depot: Toton, 5/07.

Name carried: None.

Status: Cut up at T.J. Thomson's scrapyard, Stockton, 6/09.

**37705 (D6760, 37060)** (See also 37705 in Class 37s in Colour)
Released by EE Vulcan Foundry as D6760, Works Number EE/VF3052/D714 on 19 October 1962 and allocated to Thornaby.

Final depot: Toton, 5/07.

Name carried: None.

Status: Cut up at T.J. Thomson's scrapyard, Stockton, 8/07.

**Passing through**
Eastleigh in the summer of 1994 is 37705 with an oil tanks train.
(*Terry Fougler*)

### Table 6. Locos numbered as sub-class 37/7

**37/7**

| | | | |
|---|---|---|---|
| D6730: 37701 | D6802: 37712 | D6761: 37799 | D6933: 37889 |
| D6720: 37702 | D6752: 37713 | D6843: 37800 | D6868: 37890 |
| D6767: 37703 | D6724: 37714 | D6873: 37801 | D6866: 37891 |
| D6734: 37704 | D6721: 37715 | D6863: 37802 | D6849: 37892 |
| D6760: 37705 | D6794: 37716 | D6908: 37803 | D6937: 37893 |
| D6716: 37706 | D6750: 37717 | D6876: 37883 | D6824: 37894 |
| D6701: 37707 | D6784: 37718 | D6883: 37884 | D6819: 37895 |
| D6789: 37708 | D6733: 37719 | D6877: 37885 | D6931: 37896 |
| D6714: 37709 | D6805: 37796 | D6880: 37886 | D6855: 37897 |
| D6744: 37710 | D6781: 37797 | D6820: 37887 | D6886: 37898 |
| D6785: 37711 | D6706: 37798 | D6835: 37888 | D6861: 37899 |

**In October** 1994 37705 takes a very short oil tanks train through the same station. (*Terry Fougler*)

**In WCRC** maroon livery, 37706 pilots 'Black 5' 44932 from York to Scarborough with 'The Scarborough Spa Express' near Haxby on 9 August 2011. The 'Black 5' had suffered a faulty injector prior to the first leg to Wakefield and back, which was taken by 37706. This was repaired at the NRM but insufficient steam pressure could be built up in time for the run to Scarborough, though 44932 would take the return leg with 37706 running light engine back to York earlier in the afternoon.

**37706 (D6716, 37016)** (See also 37706 in Class 37s in Colour)
Released by EE Vulcan Foundry as D6716, Works Number EE/VF2879/D595 on 16 June 1961 and allocated to Stratford.

Final depot: Toton, 5/07.

Name carried: *Conidae*, briefly from 4/91.

Status: Withdrawn from stock by EWS, bought and reinstated to traffic by WCRC, Carnforth as a PODL, 12/08, now working charter trains for WCRC.

Notable movements:
She was engaged in passenger work from her earliest days, taking trains from London Liverpool Street including a charter between Norwich and Wroxham (known as 'The Capital of the Norfolk Broads'). On transferring to Yorkshire from the late 1960s she continued to work both Class 1 services and also freight in the area including north into Tyneside. On 2 September 1978 she worked a combined charter from Newcastle to Edinburgh (one portion having originated at Saltburn) and in July and August 1979 headed a series of Class 1 trains between Peterborough and Norwich. Her mix of passenger and freight duties continued until her move to Stratford depot in January 1982 when she was used regularly on services between Liverpool Street, Cambridge and East Anglia until the mid-1980s. She appeared at Colchester depot Open Day on 2 May 1988 then was transferred to Immingham and then to Crewe Diesel in December 1990.

Regular freight duties followed from both Crewe and Immingham depots until on 21 September 2002 she headed Past Time Rail's 'The Spinnin' State IV', a charter from London Paddington to Newport, Hereford, Brecon Curve GF then to Crewe, Nuneaton, Banbury, Oxford, Didcot and return to Paddington. She and 37668 had charge between Brecon Curve GF and Crewe. On 26 July 2003 she worked for Pathfinder Railtours with 'The Doncaster Detour/York Excursion, which ran from Westbury to Bath, Birmingham New Street, Doncaster (for the Railway Works 150th Anniversary Open Day) then on to York and return, with 37890 throughout. Working mainly from Toton or Doncaster over the next five years, with regular periods in store or 'reserve' her purchase by WCRC and transfer to Carnforth saw her schedule change dramatically.

She was on display at Carnforth Open Day on 27 July 2008 and then after being reinstated into traffic

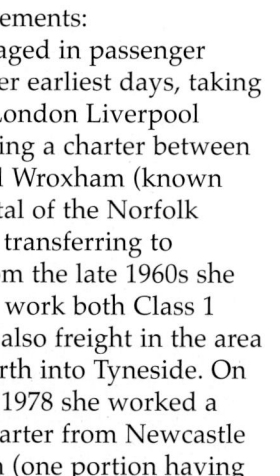

**Awaiting her** next duty at York station Parcels Sidings on 4 October 2022 is WCRC 37706.

was employed regularly on charters and 'specials'. On 24 May 2009 she appeared at 'Eastleigh 100' Open Day, then on 20 September that year for Spitfire Railtours' 'The Purbeck Growler', Crewe to Swanage and return with 37516 throughout. On 3 October 2009 she was working for Spitfire Railtours again on their circuitous charter 'The Witch Way/Cotton Mill Loop Circuit/ Oldham Loop Circuit & Oldham Loop Diesel Mini-tour. This ran from Preston to Manchester Victoria then round the Oldham Loops and eventually back to Preston. She was involved from Manchester Victoria back to Preston. On 22 April 2010 she worked a private charter with steam loco 48151 from Wakefield Kirkgate to Crewe, Shrewsbury, Aberystwyth and return.

During 2010 she was involved with Spitfire Railtours' 'The Shepherd Neame Brewery Spitfire' on 16 May, London Victoria to Faversham, Sheerness and return with 37516 followed on 29 May for the same operator 'The Prisoner', Preston to Crewe, Pwllheli and return. On 24 and 25 September that year she was a guest on the Mid Norfolk Railway then from 2011 she was busy with several charters and 'specials' including regular appearances on WCRC's 'The Scarborough Spa Express', 'The Dalesman' and 'The Pendle Dalesman', the Railway Touring Company's 'The Dorset Coast Express', 'The Cumbrian Mountain Express' and 'The Winter Cumbrian Mountain Express' and for Steam Dreams 'The Cathedrals Express'. Occasional charters for Spitfire Railtours, the SRPS, the Branch Line Society and the A1 Steam Locomotive Trust added to a very busy life in preservation. Her full schedule of duties for WCRC continued throughout the coming years and from the summer of 2023 she has been busy with 'The Cumbrian Mountain Express' and 'The Dalesman' charters as well as assisting on the rear of 'The Tynesider' propelled by steam loco 'Black 5' number 44932 on 10 June 2023 for the Railway Touring Company.

### 37707 (D6701, 37001)
Released by EE Vulcan Foundry as D6701, Works Number EE/VF2864/ D580 on 12 December 1960 and allocated to Stratford.

Final depot: Toton, 5/07.

Name carried: None.

Status: Cut up at EMR, Kingsbury, 9/11.

### 37708 (D6789, 37089)
Released by EE RSH as D6789, Works Number EE/RSH3216/8335 on 18 January 1963 and allocated to Gateshead.

Final depot: Toton, 5/07.

Name carried: None.

Status: Cut up by C.F. Booth, Rotherham, 3/08.

### 37709 (D6714, 37014)
Released by EE Vulcan Foundry as D6714, Works Number EE/ VF2877/D593 on 24 March 1961 and allocated to Stratford.

Final depot: Toton, 5/07.

Name carried: None.

Status: Cut up at EMR, Kingsbury, 9/11.

### 37710 (D6744, 37044)
Released by EE Vulcan Foundry as D6744, Works Number EE/VF3036/ D698 on 29 June 1962 and allocated to Darnall.

Final depot: Toton, 5/07.

Name carried: None.

Status: Bought by WCRC, Carnforth, 12/07; Partly cut up at Carnforth, 4/21.

Notable movements: During the early 1960s in Yorkshire, she worked a mix of freight and passenger services based on Sheffield but her move south first to March and then to Stratford saw her regularly used on Class 1 trains

**On 3 September** 1995 37710 waits at Hull Paragon in Rail Freight Metals livery.

out of London Liverpool Street to Cambridge or East Anglia, work which would occupy her until July 1984 when she was admitted to Doncaster Works and had her boiler isolated. On 4 July 1987 she was involved with 37091 (37358) for Hertfordshire Rail Tours on 'The Independent', a charter from Finsbury Park to Kidderminster (for the SVR) then on to Loughborough and back to London Euston. From then until late 1996 her work consisted largely of heavy freight first in southern Scotland, then in South Wales and finally in Yorkshire and The Humber region. This was interrupted on 23 November 1996 by a charter for Hertfordshire Rail Tours 'The Grimsby Reaper' which ran from King's Cross to Barnetby, Grimsby Marsh Junction, Brick Pit Siding then back to King's Cross via Doncaster.

Freight work then resumed until a brief appearance on the heritage West Somerset Railway in July 1997 and then on 7 July 2001 she worked for Pathfinder Rail Tours 'The Galloway Princess' charter which ran from Birmingham International to Carlisle, Polmadie, Glasgow Central and return, between Polmadie and Glasgow Central. On 17 November 2001 again for Pathfinder Rail Tours she was paired with 37685 for 'The Catherine Wheel' from Crewe to Derby, St Catherine's Junction, Bolsover and return. A year passed with her regular duties until her next charter, for Past Time Rail 'The Spinnin' State V' on 23 November 2002 which originated at London Victoria and ran to Bristol Temple Meads and return. She was involved between Victoria and Westbury Down Reception paired with 37890. Her next five years were spent either in reserve for EWS, in store or working Sandite trains until being bought by WCRC in December 2007 and officially withdrawn from stock in January 2008. She appeared at Carnforth Open Day on 27 July that year but was put into store and eventually partly cut up there in April 2021.

**37711 (D6785, 37085)**
Released by EE RSH as D6785, Works Number EE/RSH3212/8331 on 19 December 1962 and allocated to Gateshead.

Final depot: Doncaster, 12/99.

Name carried: *Tremorfa Steel Works*, 11/88–1/93.

Status: Cut up at EMR, Kingsbury, 11/05.

**37712 (D6802, 37102)**
Released by EE Vulcan Foundry as D6802, Works Number EE/VF3231/D756 on 4 January 1963 and allocated to Darnall.

Final depot: Toton, 5/07.

Names carried: *Cardiff Rod Mill*, 11/88–7/92; *Teesside Steelmaster*, 9/92.

Status: Sold by EWS; Preserved and operational with WCRC Carnforth as a PODL, 12/07; In store for WCRC, 'non-active Locomotives', at Carnforth, 1/13.

Notable movements:
Like so many of her Class her early duties consisted of a mix of passenger and freight associated with her region but it was not long before she was heading long distance trains of both types. On 6 May 1978 she was used on BR 'Football Specials' between Ipswich

*Above left*: **Nameplate of** 37712.

*Above right*: **Later nameplate of** 37712.

and Wembley and on 20 May that year on a charter for DAA/DEG 'The East Coast Pullman Salute' which ran from King's Cross to Leeds, York, Scarborough, Beverley, Goole, Doncaster and back to King's Cross. She and 37037 were in charge from Leeds back to King's Cross.

Her move to March depot in 1975 led to her work being dominated by Class 1 services from London Liverpool Street to Cambridge and East Anglia, then in mid-1984 she spent a time in the Scottish Highlands operating Class 2 trains between Georgemas Junction and Thurso and between Inverness and Wick, although during this period she was much travelled, being also used between Glasgow and Fort William, from Manchester Piccadilly and standing in for DMU services from Newcastle to Carlisle, Sunderland or Middlesbrough. On 6 April 1985 she was involved with 'football extras' between Glasgow Queen Street and Edinburgh and on 9 April that year had responsibility for the service 1E97, Edinburgh to King's Cross, a distance of almost 393 miles (632 km), then not long after on 15 April she headed 1N13, Yarmouth to Newcastle between Norwich and Newcastle, almost 276 miles (444 km).

During May 1986 she took over the Scottish sections of services from London Euston to Glasgow at Carlisle as well as working her own duties in the Highlands to Aberdeen or Inverness. From the late 1980s freight work occupied more of her time including oil, ore and steel workings in South Wales and later in north-east England, then her transfer to Motherwell in 1993 involved her again in taking over Anglo-Scottish services from Euston, now between Edinburgh and Aberdeen or Inverness. On 21 June 1997 she was involved with 37714 for RT Railtours on the Scottish sections of 'The Highland Explorer' which ran from Leeds to Motherwell, Inverness and return.

From late 1998 she was based in the south of England again and occupied mainly with freight work there and in the Midlands, with a short time in 2001 working passenger services between Cardiff and Rhymney. On 14 December 2002 she and 37798 worked Pathfinder Railtours' 'The Merry Widow', a charter from Gloucester to Leeds and return between Crewe Sorting Sidings North, Leeds and the return to Gloucester. On 12 April 2003 she was involved again for Pathfinder Railtours with 'The Wizard Express' which ran from Reading to Preston and return. She was paired with 37698 on the outward leg from Reading to Preston, the remainder of the tour also being Class 37-hauled by 37047, 37308, 37674 and 37689.

Her purchase by WCRC in December 2007 and subsequent transfer to Carnforth where she was reinstated into traffic saw her on 'specials' duty again with 1Z51 Manchester Victoria to Hellifield and return on 16 July 2008, then a charter for the SRPS 'Dundee to Scarborough' on 16 August that year with 'Deltic' 55022 *Royal Scots Grey* throughout. On 6 September 2008 she assisted with 1Z74 Leicester to Carlisle as far as Hellifield, then 1Z79 Carlisle to Leicester from York to Leeds. Finally that year on 27 September for Spitfire Railtours' 'Settle for Edinburgh' charter from Sheffield to Edinburgh Waverley and return with 37248 throughout, going outward by the S&C and returning by the Tyne Valley and ECML, a round trip of over 583 miles (939 km) in the day. She was then put in store at Carnforth for WCRC and from January 2013 was allocated to their 'non-active locomotives' pool.

**37713 (D6752, 37052)** (See also 37713 in Class 37s in Colour) Released by EE Vulcan Foundry as D6752, Works Number EE/VF3044/D706 on 6 September 1962 and allocated to Darnall.

Final depot: Doncaster, 3/00.

Name carried: *British Steel Workington*, 8/92–7/94.

Status: Cut up at Crewe DMD, 6/06.

**Below: Nameplate of** 37714.

**Bottom: Stabled at** Loughborough on 16 April 2022 is 37714 *Cardiff Canton*. THT Rail 2013.

**37714 (D6724, 37024, 37714, L031, L26)**
Released by EE Vulcan Foundry as D6724, Works Number EE/VF2887/D603 on 25 August 1961 and allocated to March.

Final depot: Kingmoor, 8/13.

Names carried: *Thornaby TMD*, 9/92–2/93; *Cardiff Canton*, 3/17.

Status: Preserved on the GCR at Loughborough from, 3/16, operated by The Heavy Tractor Group in Rail Freight Metals livery; Guest appearance at the Kent & East Sussex diesel gala, 12–14 April 2024.

**37715 (D6721, 37021)**
Released by EE Vulcan Foundry as D6721, Works Number EE/VF2884/D600 on 6 July 1961 and allocated to Norwich.

Final depot: Doncaster, 6/99.

Names carried: *British Steel Teesside*, 1/93–8/93; *British Petroleum*, 9/93–8/00.

Status: Cut up at EMR, Kingsbury, 11/05.

**37716 (D6794, 37094, 37716, L034, L23)**
Released by EE RSH as D6794, Works Number EE/RSH3221/8341 on 27 February 1963 and allocated to Gateshead.

Final depot: Toton, 5/07.

Name carried: *British Steel Corby*, 7/92.

Status: Transferred to Kingmoor for DRS (stored locos), 8/13; Moved to GCR by road, 3/16; Allocated to DRS Supply Chain Operations, 3/22; Allocated to DRS Locomotives Stored/For Disposal, 2/24; Sold to HNRC and transferred to Barrow Hill, locomotives for lease, 3/24; Moved to Worksop, 5/24.

Notable movements:
Her early years were characterised by repeated transfers between depots throughout the north of England and her workload reflected her itinerant nature at this time. By the summer of 1982 she was based at Stratford and occupied mainly with passenger services from London Liverpool Street to Cambridge or East Anglia. Her move to Cardiff Canton in July 1988 saw her taking trains to the Midlands or the north west of England then on 28 December 1992 she was working for Pathfinder Railtours' 'The Wensleydale Explorer' which ran from Swindon to Derby, York, Redmire and return, paired with 37884 from York. The following day her partnership with 37884 continued for Black Cat Railtours' 'The Redmire Farewell Railtour' from Crewe to York, Redmire and return, again in charge from York. Freight and passenger work continued until on 5 December 1998 she was called

and 37425. Then on 7 August 2021 she was paired with 37069 for Pathfinder Railtours' 'The Blue Boys Merrymaker' charter from Eastleigh to Bescot, Crewe, Stafford and return, between Bescot and Crewe after which she was allocated to DRS Supply Chain Operations Locomotives pool. During October 2023 she and EuroPhoenix 37608 *Andromeda* were occupied with Rail Head Treatment Train duties in the Hebden Bridge–Huddersfield–Skipton area but by February 2024 she had been listed as 'Stored, for disposal'. Sold to HNRC in March 2024 and made available for lease. Stored at their Worksop 'hub'.

**Near the** village of Shipton by Beningbrough north of York 37094 trundles northwards with a train of fuel tanks in May 1975. Following refurbishment she would become 37716 from December 1988.

**Stabled in** York station Parcels Sidings on 9 December 2016 is 37716.

upon to rescue Railtours North West's 'The Southport–Settle Scotsman' charter which ran from Southport to Wigan, Settle, Carlisle, Edinburgh and return by the WCML. She came to their aid from Lancaster on the return journey after the failure of both train locos, 37414 and 37428.

She was sent to work in Spain in May 2001. After her return from Spain where she was involved in the building of new high-speed lines she worked for a short time for DRS on the Cumbrian Coast line from Carlisle then was a guest at the heritage SVR from 19 to 21 May 2016. On 31 March and 1 April 2017 she and 37069 worked Pathfinder Railtours' 'The Evening Lark/Night Owl/Round Robin' tour top and tail throughout from Derby to Crewe, Matlock to Crewe, Long Marston and return to Crewe. From August 2017 to July 2019 she was fully occupied with Class 2 services in East Anglia, working top and tail with various classmates including 37405, 37407, 37419, 37423, 36424

**37717 (D6750, 37050)**
Released by EE Vulcan Foundry as D6750, Works Number EE/VF3042/D704 on 24 August 1962 and allocated to Darnall.

Final depot: Toton, 5/07.

Names carried: *Stainless Pioneer*, 8/92–7/96; *Maltby Lilly Hall Junior School Rotherham Railsafe Trophy Winners 1996*, 7/96; *St Margarets Church of England Primary School City of Durham Railsafe Trophy Winners 1997*, 7/97; *Berwick Middle School Railsafe Trophy Winners 1998*, 7/98.

Status: Cut up by C.F. Booth, Rotherham, 4/09.

**37718 (D6784, 37094, 37718, L021, L22)**
(See also 37718 in Class 37s in Colour)
Released by EE RSH as D6784, Works Number EE/RSH3211/8330 on 12 December 1962 and allocated to Gateshead.

Final depot: Kingmoor, 8/13.

Name carried: *Hartlepool Pipe Mill*, 7/92.

Status: Cut up by C.F. Booth, Rotherham, 7/15.

**37719 (D6733, 37033)**
Released by EE Vulcan Foundry as D6733, Works Number EE/VF2896/D612 on 20 March 1962 and allocated to Hull Dairycoates.

Final depot: Toton, 5/07.

Name carried: None.

Status: Cut up at EMR, Kingsbury, 1/08.

**37796 (D6805, 37105)**
Released by EE Vulcan Foundry as D6805, Works Number EE/VF3234/D759 on 16 January 1963 and allocated to Darnall.

Final depot: Toton, 5/07.

Name carried: None.

Status: Cut up by C.F. Booth, Rotherham, 2/09.

**37797 (D6781, 37081)**
Released by EE RSH as D6781, Works Number EE/RSH3208/8327 on 22 November 1962 and allocated to Hull Dairycoates.

Final depot: Crewe Diesel, 11/00.

Name carried: *Loch Long*, 10/81–5/86.

Status: Cut up by C.F. Booth, Rotherham, 2/06.

Notable movements:
Early freight duties included heading oil tanks, ballast, car transporters and parcels trains in the north of the country, while passenger services at this time featured her with rugby specials between Hull and Manchester and 'holiday extras' between Filey holiday camp and Manchester Victoria, and on 10 May 1975 she headed a 'special', 1Z21 Ramsgate to Spalding for the flower show. Whilst based at March depot from the mid-1970s she was kept busy with services from London Liverpool Street to Cambridge and East Anglia.

**Stabled at** Didcot on 21 September 2002 is 37717 *Berwick Middle School Railsafe Trophy Winners 1998*. (*Steve Jones*)

Moving to Scotland in 1979 saw her heading passenger trains north from Glasgow Queen Street or Edinburgh Waverley which continued until May 1986. During this time she featured on a BR 'RugEx' special between Glasgow and Edinburgh on 16 February 1980, a Steam Locomotive Operators Association (SLOA) rail tour from Craigendoran, near Helensburgh to Fort William, Mallaig and return on 15 and 16 January 1983 with 37027, then a BR 'Merrymaker Excursion' on 16 April 1983 from Peterborough to Cowlairs East Junction, Fort William, Mallaig and return, working between Cowlairs East Junction, Fort William and Mallaig with 37075.

A series of Day Excursions for Scotrail between Edinburgh and Oban followed, running on 3, 10, 17, 24, 31 July and 11 September 1983. On 26 May 1984 she was working for the SLOA again, featuring on the three-day charter 'The West Highlander' which originated at London Euston and ran to Fort William and Mallaig. She was in action between Mossend Yard and Fort William with 37264 out and 37112 back, steam haulage operating between Fort William and Mallaig. On 12 August 1984 she repeated the Day Excursion for Scotrail between Edinburgh and Oban then on 1 June 1985 she was called upon by the SLOA to assist with 'The West Highlander' again, this time running from Edinburgh Waverley to Oban, Crianlarich, Fort William, Mallaig and return when she worked with 37111 throughout. She continued working passenger services north from Glasgow into the Highlands during the summer of 1985 until her transfer south. After her conversion to sub-class 37/7 at Crewe Works during May 1986 and subsequent transfer to Cardiff Canton she was employed on a variety of freight and passenger duties throughout South Wales, the Midlands, Eastern and Northern England which included an appearance for Pathfinder Railtours on their charter 'The Cymric Gallivant' on 15 April 1995. On 12 February 2000 she was required to bank steam loco 35005 *Canadian Pacific* out of London Victoria with Past Time Rail's 'The Bournemouth Belle' then on 2 February 2002 she worked on Pathfinder Railtours' 'The Spiders Web' which ran from Reading to Toton and Lincoln for a tour of branch lines. She and 37688 had charge between Reading and Toton Centre. She was then held in 'Tactical Reserve' for EWS until finally being sold for scrap to C.F. Booth of Rotherham and cut up there in February 2006.

**37798 (D6706, 37006)**
Released by EE Vulcan Foundry as D6706, Works Number EE/VF2869/D585 on 20 January 1961 and allocated to Norwich.

Final depot: Toton, 5/07.

Name carried: None.

Status: Cut up by C.F. Booth, Rotherham, 7/09.

**37799 (D6761, 37061, 37799, L030, L27)**
Released by EE Vulcan Foundry as D6761, Works Number EE/VF3053/D715 on 24 October 1962 and allocated to Thornaby.

Final depot: Toton, 5/07.

Name carried: *Sir Dyfed/County of Dyfed*, 11/87.

Status: Cut up at Vilafranca del Panedes, Spain, 12/11.

**37800 (D6843, 37143, 37800, L33)**
Released by EE Vulcan Foundry as D6843, Works Number EE/VF3318/D817 on 29 May 1963 and allocated to Canton.

Final depot: Toton, 5/07.

Names carried: *Glo Cymru*, 9/86–3/94; *Cassiopeia*, 1/18.

Status: Withdrawn from EWS stock, 7/13; Operational with EuroPhoenix from 8/13; Leased to the Rail Operations Group (ROG) from 1/16; Reliveried and operational in ROG colours from 11/23. During May 2024 she was used to transfer new Class 730 units between various locations.

**37801 (D6873, 37173, 37801, L032, L29)**
Released by EE Vulcan Foundry as D6873 Works Number EE/VF3351/D837 on 12 September 1963 and allocated to Landore.

Final depot: Toton, 5/07.

Name carried: *Aberddawn/Aberthaw*, 9/86–3/93.

Status: Cut up at Vilafranca del Panedes, Spain, 12/11.

**Nameplate of** 37799.

**In Rail** Freight grey livery 37801 *Aberddawn/Aberthaw* takes her train through Cardiff Central station on 12 June 1989. (*Phil Richards*)

**Passing the** signal box at Pilmoor on the ECML north of York with a mixed freight during May 1975 is 37163 heading north. Later to become 37802 from October 1986 following refurbishment at Crewe Works.

**37802 (D6863, 37163, 37802, L32)**
Released by EE RSH as D6863, Works Number EE/RSH3341/8394 on 1 August 1963 and allocated to Landore.

Final depot: EWS HQ, Doncaster before being sent to Spain.

Name carried: None.

Status: Cut up at Calatayud, Spain, 7/03.

Notable movements:
Very much a typical 'mixed traffic' loco in her early days, with freight trains in South Wales, the Midlands and Yorkshire as well as passenger services anywhere from Cardiff to southern Scotland. Her move to Canton in 1984 involved her on banking duties on the Lickey Incline and Class 1 and Class 2 trains from Bristol Temple Meads to the south west and along the South Wales coast. Freight continued to dominate her work through the 1980s and into the late 1990s punctuated by occasional 'specials' including on 30 May 1993, Regional Railways 'Special Trains for Shrewsbury and Hereford Open days' when several ran between Crewe, Shrewsbury and Hereford. On 6 June 1999 she was in action for The Cardiff Railway Company's 'Barry Transport Festival Specials' when a number of trains ran between Rhymney, Barry Town and Cwm Bargoed, for which she was paired with 37796. After working a section of 1V98, the Glasgow Central to Paddington service between Carlisle and Preston via the S&C on 22 October 1999 she was transferred to Doncaster for EWS, initially into storage but then allocated to 'Special Projects', which in her case meant a move abroad. Her transfer to Spain with 37702 in July 2001 where she was renumbered to L32 marked the end of her life in the UK as she was scrapped without returning home, in July 2003.

## Locomotive Histories • 145

**37803 (D6908, 37208)**

Released by EE Vulcan Foundry as D6908, Works Number EE/VF3386/D852 on 20 November 1963 and allocated to Landore.

Final depot: Toton, 5/07.

Name carried: None.

Status: Cut up at EMR, Kingsbury, 7/07.

**37883 (D6876, 37176, 37883, L028, L28)**

Released by EE Vulcan Foundry as D6876, Works Number EE/VF3354/D840 on 14 October 1963 and allocated to Canton.

Final depot: Toton, 5/07.

Name carried: None

Status: Cut up at Vilafranca del Penedes, Spain, 12/11.

**37884 (D6883, 37183, 37884, L34)** (See also 37884 in Class 37s in Colour) Released by EE RSH as D6883, Works Number EE/RSH3361/8404 on 7 November 1963 and allocated to Landore.

Final depot: Toton, 5/07.

Name carried: *Gartcosh*, 8/92.

Status: Withdrawn from EWS stock, 7/13; Reinstated into traffic for EuroPhoenix Locomotives UK, 8/13; Allocated to the Rail Operations Group from 1/16 and to ScotRail from 6/23. During May 2024 she was used to transfer new Class 730 units between various locations.

**37885 (D6877, 37177, 37885, L033, L24)**

Released by EE Vulcan Foundry as D6877, Works Number EE/VF3355/D841 on 3 October 1963 and allocated to Canton.

Final depot: Doncaster, 2/01.

Name carried: None.

Status: Cut up at Vias Y Construcciones, Madrid, Spain, 7/03.

**37886 (D6880, 37180)**

Released by EE RSH as D6880, Works Number EE/RSH3358/8401 on 24 October 1963 and allocated to Landore.

Final depot: Toton, 5/07.

Names carried: *Sir Dyfed/County of Dyfed*, 5/81–1/87; Re-named *Sir Dyfed/County of Dyfed*, 6/01.

Status: Cut up at EMR, Kingsbury, 9/11.

Notable movements:
Her early years in South Wales were uneventful, being occupied with the usual mix of freight and passenger services of the area. On 1 March 1974 she stood in for failed classmate 37190 on a LNER Society railtour from Port Talbot to Shrewsbury, then on 29 July 1975 headed the special excursion 1Z38 Batley to Llandrindod Wells between Shrewsbury and Llandrindod Wells. On 24 August 1977 she was in charge of a BR Day Excursion from Swansea to Clifton Down and return, which was repeated on 16 August the following year. On 25 November 1978 she worked for Railway Pictorial Publications Railtours on 'The Welsh Wonder' which ran from London Paddington to Reading, Blaenavon, Uskmouth, Bargoed then Cardiff Central, Reading and return to Paddington. Her contribution was between Cardiff Central and Paddington with 37182. On the morning of 16 December 1978 she took the 'special' 1Z71 Swansea to Cardiff and the return 1Z60 in the afternoon. From then on she was

**At Thrimby** near Tebay on the WCML in Cumbria, 37886 heads south with a Mossend to Llanwern Rail Freight on 23 May 1992 (*Jonathan Allen*)

occupied regularly with Class 1 services mainly between Bristol Temple Meads and the cities of South Wales until on 22 March 1980 she was involved for Severnside Railtours on 'The Tyne-Tees Ltd' which began at Cardiff and ran to Gloucester, Birmingham New Street, York, Washington, Consett Steelworks, then Newcastle, Middlesbrough and back to York before returning to Cardiff. She was in charge from Cardiff to York and return.

Her work from then until early 1993 centred on services in South Wales, between there and the Midlands and periods banking on the Lickey Incline. This regular schedule was interspersed with charters including for Severnside Railtours on 17 March 1984 'The Tyne-Tees Explorer' which ran from Swansea to Bristol Temple Meads, Gloucester, Toton Centre then on to York, Durham and Middlesbrough before returning to York then Sheffield, Derby Bristol Temple Meads and Port Talbot, the journey back to Swansea being completed by bus. She worked with 37266 from Swansea to Bristol and from Derby to Port Talbot. On 28 April 1984 she was involved with 37189 for the Lea Valley Railway Club's 'The Pembroke Coast Freighter' which began at London Paddington and ran to Cardiff Central for a tour of freight lines in the Carmarthen and Fishguard Harbour areas before returning to Paddington. Then on 10 May 1985 she featured with 37189 on day two of three for F+W Railtours' 'The Skirl o' the Pipes 6' between Bristol Temple Meads and Derby (see 'Notable movements' for 37259 for details of the route). On 22 August 1987 she was working for Pathfinder Railtours on 'The Northumbrian', a charter from Swindon to Bristol Temple Meads, Birmingham New Street, Skipton, Carlisle by the S&C then on to Newcastle, Sunderland, back to Newcastle and to Carlisle, Birmingham New Street via the WCML then on to Gloucester, Bristol and back to Swindon. Her involvement was between Carlisle and Newcastle and return.

For the remainder of the 1980s and into the early 1990s she worked passenger and freight services mainly in South Wales, the Midlands and into Lancashire, Cambridgeshire or South Yorkshire until on 22 October 1994 she took Pathfinder Railtours' 'The Citadel Centurian' which began at Bristol Temple Meads and ran to Carlisle and return via Preston over the WCML outwards and the S&C back, when she and 37519 had charge between Preston and Carlisle and return. After periods in and out of storage and working freights for EWS Systemwide her transfer to Crewe Diesel depot in November 2000 saw her on charter duty once more for Pathfinder Railtours on 2 June 2001 with 'The (N) Onllwyn Orbiter' from Crewe to Ebbw Vale and return, including branch lines in 'The Valleys' with 37707 throughout. Then on 14 July 2001 again for Pathfinder Railtours, 'The Ayr Liner', Birmingham International to Ayr and return, including freight lines around Ayr, again with 37707 between Crewe and Carlisle. On 8 March 2003 for Hertfordshire Rail Tours 'The Wig & Weasel', Finsbury Park to Blackburn and return, working with 37517 from Doncaster to Blackburn, then on 30 August 2003 she headed the 'special' 1Z37 Hereford to Fishguard between Cardiff and Fishguard, then continued as 1Z38 Fishguard to Crewe. Periods spent at Doncaster and Toton in reserve for EWS followed by in store at Millerhill were ended in October 2010 when she was sent for scrapping at Kingsbury, being officially withdrawn from stock in January 2011 and cut up in September of that year.

### 37887 (D6820, 37120)

Released by EE RSH as D6820, Works Number EE/RSH3265/8380 on 29 March 1963 and allocated to Canton.

Final depot: Toton, 5/07.

Name carried: *Castell Caerffili/ Caerphilly Castle*, 8/92.

Status: Cut up at C.F. Booth, Rotherham, 4/08.

### 37888 (D6835, 37135, 37888, L024, L31)

Released by EE Vulcan Foundry as D6835, Works Number EE/VF3280/D809 on 24 April 1963 and allocated to Canton.

Final depot: Doncaster, 4/01.

Name carried: *Petrolea*, 5/88–5/95.

Status: Cut up at Puig Vert, Spain, 7/07.

### 37889 (D6933, 37233)

Released by EE Vulcan Foundry as D6933, Works Number EE/VF3419/D877 on 1 April 1964 and allocated to Landore.

Final depot: Doncaster, 6/99.

Name carried: None.

Status: Cut up at Crewe DMD, 3/07.

**Passing Redbridge** on 5 August 1994 with her train of oil tanks is 37891.

**37890 (D6868, 37168)**
Released by EE RSH as D6868, Works Number EE/RSH3346/8399 on 4 October 1963 and allocated to Canton.

Final depot: Toton, 5/07.

Name carried: *The Railway Observer*, 2/94–8/99.

Status: Cut up at Hull's scrapyard, Rotherham, 8/10.

**37891 (D6866, 37166)**
Released by EE RSH as D6866, Works Number EE/RSH3344/8397 on 9 September 1963 and allocated to Canton.

Final depot: Toton, 5/07.

Name carried: None.

Status: Cut up at EMR Attercliffe, 5/11.

Notable movements:
Early freight work included mineral traffic in Yorkshire in the late 1960s and Freightliner trains from Harwich Parkston Quay in the early 1970s, and freight continued to dominate her schedule through the 1970s and into the early 1980s. Her work included coal trains in the Newcastle upon Tyne area and cement trains around Warrington. In the mid-1980s she worked passenger services from London Liverpool Street but freight still dominated and included oil trains while based at Immingham. On 4 August 1991 she was involved with Pathfinder Railtours' 'Gloucester Rail Day' special trains. Originating at Manchester Piccadilly and bound for Gloucester, there followed a series of shuttles between there and Kemble, Sharpness and Westerleigh Yard before running to Nuneaton and back to Manchester Piccadilly. Her involvement was between Gloucester and Westerleigh Yard. She then headed Class 1 services form Manchester Victoria during April 1992 and from Crewe in the summer of 1998, otherwise freight continued to dominate until she was sent to France in August 1999. On her return she spent much of her time in store for EWS before being sold in January 2011, withdrawn from stock a month later and scrapped at Attercliffe, Sheffield in May 2011.

**37892 (D6849, 37149)**
Released by EE Vulcan Foundry as D6849, Works Number EE/VF3324/D823 on 21 June 1963 and allocated to Canton.

Final depot: Toton, 5/07.

Name carried: *Ripple Lane*, 10/87.

Status: Cut up at EMR, Kingsbury, 1/08.

**37893 (D6937, 37237)**
Released by EE Vulcan Foundry as D6937, Works Number EE/VF3423/D881 on 13 May 1964 and allocated to Canton.

Final depot: Toton, 5/07.

Name carried: None.

Status: Cut up at Hull's scrapyard, Rotherham, 4/12.

**37894 (D6824, 37124)** (See also 37894 in Class 37s in Colour)
Released by EE RSH as D6824, Works Number EE/RSH3269/8384 on 29 April 1963 and allocated to Canton.

Final depot: Toton, 5/07.

**Class 37s stabled** at Barry Depot during July 1991 include 37894 alongside 37803.

**Working a** freight train in June 1983 is 37283, later in February 1987 to become 37895 following refurbishment at Crewe Works.

Name carried: None.

Status: Cut up at EMR, Kingsbury, 8/08.

Notable movements:
Her early duties involved a mix of freight and passenger services including a football 'special' from Sheffield in August 1978 and Class 1 trains from Norwich during the summer of 1979. Her transfer to Eastfield in 1982 saw her busy with services north from Glasgow and when moved back to South Wales in 1985 she became involved with passenger work to the Midlands including a time spent banking on the Lickey Incline during the summer of that year as well as being busy with the heavy freight of the area. On 11 March 1995 she and 37887 worked for Hertfordshire Rail Tours with 'The Welsh Rarebit' which ran from London Paddington to Cardiff Docks for a tour of South Wales freight lines before returning to Paddington. Her freight workings continued to dominate through the 1990s until she was sent to work in France in September 1999. When finally returning to the UK she was put into store by EWS at Toton from September 2007 but was soon sold for scrap and withdrawn from stock in June 2008, to be cut up two months later.

### 37895 (D6819, 37283)

Released by EE RSH as D6819, Works Number EE/RSH3264/8379 on 27 March 1963 and allocated to Canton.

Final depot: Toton, 5/07.

Name carried: None.

Status: Cut up at EMR, Kingsbury, 9/11.

Notable movements:
Her freight duties in the early 1970s saw her heading Freightliner trains to Harwich Parkeston Quay and later oil tanks in the Yorkshire and Humberside area, work which continued into the 1980s. Passenger services at this time included Class 1 trains to York from North Wales and

Newcastle from Lincolnshire. She also headed services out of London Liverpool Street to Harwich and Lowestoft while based at Stratford and on 27 March 1982 assisted Hertfordshire Rail Tours 'The Wigan Enigma' charter which began at London St Pancras and ran to Bradford Exchange, Blackpool North, Wigan North Western and return via Toton. On 19 June that year she headed SVR Railtours' 'The Galloway Ranger' between Leeds and Ayr, the tour having started at Wolverhampton and run to Leeds, Carlisle via the S&C and on to Ayr and return.

Throughout the 1980s she was busy with Class 1 services as well as freight in the Midlands and north of England, then on 19 August 1990 she worked for The Growler Group's 'The Barry Bucketeer' which ran from Crewe to Cardiff and return for shuttles to Barry organised by the Barry Open Day Committee. On 2 March 1996 she featured for Pathfinder Railtours on 'The Glamorgan Freighter' which originated at Birmingham New Street and ran to Newport and return for a tour of freight lines in the Cardiff and Bridgend area in the company of 37412. She was reputed to be the last Class 37 to work to Aberthaw when she visited on 23 January 1997 and then on 30 January 1999 for Hertfordshire Rail Tours she headed the Carlisle to York leg of 'The Settle & Carlisle Circular/ City of York Bargain' which ran from King's Cross to York then on to Appleby, Carlisle and return to York and London, then on 7 December 2000 she featured on 1Z44, the VSOE between Carlisle and Manchester Victoria. After returning from Italy in March 2003 she worked freights in the south of England and in the Midlands but spent much of her time in store for EWS before being sold for scrap and eventually cut up at EMR Kingsbury in September 2011.

**37896 (D6931, 37231)**
Released by EE Vulcan Foundry as D6931, Works Number EE/VF3417/D875 on 12 March 1964 and allocated to Landore.

Final depot: Toton, 5/07.

Name carried: None.

Status: Cut up at Hull's scrapyard, Rotherham, 8/10.

**37897 (D6855, 37155)**
Released by EE Vulcan Foundry as D6855, Works Number EE/VF3330/D829 on 18 July 1963 and allocated to Landore.

Final depot: Toton, 5/07.

Name carried: None.

Status: Cut up at EMR, Kingsbury, 2/08.

**37898 (D6886, 37186)**
Released by EE RSH as D6886, Works Number EE/RSH3364/8407 on 29 November 1963 and allocated to Landore.

Final depot: Doncaster, 12/99.

Name carried: *Cwmbargoed DP*, 4/93.

Status: Cut up at EMR, Kingsbury, 9/11.

**37899 (D6861, 37161, 37899, L022, L21)**
(See also 37899 in Class 37s in Colour)
Released by EE RSH as D6861, Works Number EE/RSH3339/8392 on 19 July 1963 and allocated to Landore.

Final depot: Doncaster, 4/01.

Name carried: *Sir Gorllewin Morgannwg/County of West Glamorgan*, 5/91.

Status: Cut up at Vias Construcciones, Madrid, Spain, 7/03.

**Stabled at** Swindon on 15 September 1997 is 37895.

Notable movements:
Though some freight duties and parcels trains occupied her early years she was entrusted with Class 1 services in Yorkshire and the north east during the 1960s and early 1970s. She was also variously busy on passenger trains to East Anglia, from Edinburgh and between Crewe and Holyhead during the 1980s. On 5 May 1991 she was employed by Trainload Metals for the Hereford Rail Festival, when a series of trains ran to the event from such places as Newport, Ledbury, Worcester, Craven Arms and Abergavenny, with her being involved between Abergavenny and Hereford with 37698. Then on 1 September 1991 she was working for Pathfinder Railtours' 'The Bolsover Balladeer' which ran from Worcester Shrub Hill to Bristol Temple Meads, Doncaster Decoy Yard, Worksop and Bolsover for a tour of colliery lines in North Nottinghamshire, with classmate 37896. After that she returned to freight duties in the Midlands and South Wales with occasional Class 2 services in the Bristol and Cardiff areas until she was sent to work in Spain in April 2001. Her days were ended there as she was cut up in July 2003.

### Sub-class 37/9
These were converted from the original fleet during 1986 and 1987

### Table 7. Locos numbered as sub-class 37/9

| 37/9 | |
|---|---|
| D6850: 37901 | D6825: 37904 |
| D6848: 37902 | D6836: 37905 |
| D6949: 37903 | D6906: 37906 |

and fitted with Mirrlees MB275T engines (locos 37901 to 37904) or Ruston RX270T engines (locos 37905 and 37906). They had no train heating but like the 37/7s had modified traction alternators and additional ballast fitted. Their tractive effort was 62,680lb (279kN). Also like the 37/7s they weighed 120 tonnes with an RA of 7.

**37901 (D6850, 37150) (See also 37901 in Class 37s in Colour)**
Released by EE Vulcan Foundry as D6850, Works Number EE/VF3325/D824 on 1 July 1963 and allocated to Canton.

Final depot: Leicester, 10/18

Name carried: *Mirrlees Pioneer*, 12/86.

Status: In store for EWS, for disposal, 6/02; Reinstated into traffic as a PODL, 6/08; Worked on the ELR from 6/08; Allocated to Colas Rail (stored locos) from 5/16; Transferred to Leicester for EuroPhoenix Locomotives UK, 10/18; Allocated to Rail Operations Group Locomotives, 6/22; Allocated to EuroPhoenix Locomotives UK, from 11/22.

**37902 (D6848, 37148)**
Released by EE Vulcan Foundry as D6848, Works Number EE/VF3323/D822 on 19 June 1963 and allocated to Canton.

Final depot: Doncaster, 12/98.

Name carried: *British Steel Llanwern*, 6/91–9/92.

Status: Cut up at Sims Metals UK, Newport, 4/05.

Notable movements:
While based in Scotland from the mid-1960s she worked heavy freight including oil and iron ore trains but by the 1970s it was passenger duties in the Glasgow area which occupied her schedule and her use on passenger services continued through to the 1990s both in Scotland and further south. On 15 March 1992 she and 37227 were involved with a charter for DC Tours' 'The Hamworthy Quay Phoenix' which ran from London Waterloo to Eastleigh, Bournemouth, Hamworthy Quay, Brockenhurst, Southampton, Woking and back to Waterloo. On 7 October 1995 she worked with 37427 throughout on the Monmouthshire Railway Society charter 'The Garw Growlers', from Newport to Jersey Marine South Junction, Onllwyn, Pontycymmer, Cwmbargoed and return. Then on 16 November 1996 for Pathfinder Railtours' 'The Dyfed Docker', when she and 37412 assisted on the tour from Birmingham New Street to Cardiff Central, Carmarthen, Milford Haven, Fishguard Harbour and return, though sadly on this occasion neither '37' completed their shift successfully. Freight workings and local passenger services in South Wales and the Bristol area followed until periods in store during the late 1990s led to her being sold to DRS and later scrapped.

**37903 (D6949, 37249)**
Released by EE Vulcan Foundry as D6949, Works Number EE/VF3506/D937 on 9 December 1964 and allocated to Canton.

Final depot: Doncaster, 7/99.

Name carried: None.

Status: Cut up at Crewe DMD, 10/05.

**Passing Marshbrook** Crossing near Church Stretton on 9 July 1988 is 37902 with her freight train.

Notable movements:
Although involved with heavy freight workings in Yorkshire and the north east of England in the 1960s she was soon employed on passenger services, including Class 1 trains and charters. On 10 March 1979 she was involved for the DAA Railtour Society on 'The West Riding Limited' which ran from London Bridge to Doncaster, Healey Mills, York and then to Finsbury Park and finally London Victoria. She and 37245 were in charge between Healey Mills and York.

A mix of freight and passenger duties kept her busy until on 15 July 1984 she worked for Severnside Railtours with 'The South Yorkshireman' charter form Cardiff Central to Bristol Temple Meads, Birmingham New Street then to Sheffield, Huddersfield and return. She and 37248 led between Sheffield, Huddersfield and back to Sheffield. While based at Tinsley in the mid-1980s she headed Class 1 and Class 2 services in the area and when back at Canton resumed heavy freight workings in South Wales. She also appeared at the Open Day at Bescot on 9 October 1988 and at the Gloucester Rail Day on 17 September 1989. On 21 August 1994 she was involved for Pathfinder Railtours on their charter 'The Crewe Cruiser' which began at Bristol Temple Meads and ran to Birmingham New Street then to Nuneaton, Crewe and Manchester Piccadilly. It then returned to Crewe and ran from there first to Shrewsbury and return then to Chester and return before heading back to Bristol. She and 37906 were in charge from Bristol to Crewe. The remainder of the 1990s were spent with freight workings based on Cardiff depot or later in store at Doncaster before being condemned for disposal and scrapped in October 2005.

**37904 (D6825, 37125)** (See also 37904 in Class 37s in Colour) Released by EE RSH as D6825, Works Number EE/RSH3270/8385 on 8 May 1963 and allocated to Canton.

Final depot: Doncaster, 8/97.

Name carried: None.

Status: Cut up at C.F. Booth, Rotherham, 11/04.

**Stabled at** Carlisle station on 25 February 1992 are 37903 and 37235.

Notable movements:
During the early 1960s she worked coal trains in South Wales followed in the early 1970s by freight in Yorkshire then parcels from East Anglia and Freightliner trains to Harwich Parkston Quay. Passenger work at this time included Class 1 services to and from Sheffield and to York, duties which continued into the 1980s. On 31 May 1982 she was involved with the special trains 1Z22 and 1Z23 operated for the visit of Pope John Paul II to Edinburgh and on 7 July 1984 another 'special additional', 1Z13 from Kilmarnock to Blackpool as far as Carlisle.

After this she spent much of her time working Class 1 trains in the Edinburgh and Glasgow region until transferring south again in 1986. During this period she headed the 'special' 1Z12 Birmingham New Street to Edinburgh on 21 September 1984, though her regular work consisted of a mix of freight and passenger services across the network. On 4 May 1992 she took part in DC Tours 'The Six-Five Special & Regional Railways (North & West) Enthusiasts Day' when a series of trains converged on Hereford to then run between there and Shrewsbury and Crewe for Regional Railways 'Welsh Marches Day'. She and 37203 were involved between Hereford and Crewe. Further freight workings occupied her into the mid-1990s until she was put into store by EWS for component recovery in September 1998 after which she was cut up in November 2004.

**37905 (D6836, 37136)** (See also 37136 in Sub-class 37/0 and D6836 and 37905 in Class 37s in Colour)

**On display** at Old Oak Common Open Day on 5 August 2000 is 37906. (*Terry Fougler*)

**37906 (D6906, 37206)**
Released by EE Vulcan Foundry as D6906, Works Number EE/VF3384/D850 on 8 November 1963 and allocated to Landore.

Final depot: Leicester, 7/15.

Name carried: *Star of the East*, 9/99–9/99; *Star of the South*, 2/00.

Status: Bought by BREL Ltd from EWS for preservation, 6/06; Bought by Ruston 906 Group for preservation, 8/06; Re-registered for Network Rail as a PODL, 8/06; Transferred to Leicester for UK Rail Leasing, stored, not main line, from 10/15; Transferred to Shackerstone by road for the Battlefield Line, 10/19.

**Sub-class 97/3**
These four were refurbished from Class 37/0 locomotives and renumbered during 2008 at Barrow Hill by Network Rail. They have been fitted with the ERTMS signalling equipment, the system of standards for management and interoperation of signalling for railways by the European Union. This is achieved by replacing the existing national signalling equipment and operational procedures with a single new Europe-wide standard for train control and command systems.

They were intended for use primarily on the Cambrian lines from Shrewsbury to Aberystwyth and Pwllheli, which require an ERTMS-capable fleet but as mentioned earlier are now more widely used by Network Rail and others. The locomotives were formerly 37100, 37170, 37178 and 37217 respectively. A new inspection shed was built in 2008 at

# Locomotive Histories • 153

### Table 8. Locos numbered as sub-class 97/3

**97/3**

| | |
|---|---|
| D6800: 97301 | D6878: 97303 |
| D6870: 97302 | D6917: 97304 |

Coleham (Sutton Bridge Junction) in Shrewsbury specifically for these locos.

**97301 (D6800, 37100)** (See also 97301 in Class 37s in Colour) Released by EE Vulcan Foundry as D6800, Works Number EE/VF3229/D754 on 20 December 1962 and allocated to Darnall.

Final depot: Doncaster for Network Rail, 9/07.

Name carried: None.

Status: Withdrawn from stock by EWS, 11/05; Re-registered for Network Rail and transferred to Barrow Hill for the HNRC, 8/06; Allocated to Network Rail Diesel Locomotives, 9/07; Renumbered to 97301, 2/08; Stored at Derby RTC until 2001; Moved from Derby RTC to Nottingham Eastcroft by road, 5/23; Donated its power unit to 97303 then moved by road to Peak Rail, Rowsley, in store possibly for component recovery (no power unit). Moved to Boden Rail, Colwick TMD by road, for component recovery, 4/24.

Notable movements:
During her early years in Yorkshire, she featured on passenger services from Sheffield and York, mainly to the Midlands, then in the summer of 1983 spent time working out of London Liverpool Street before returning to the north of England, working as far as Carlisle (and at times beyond into Scotland). On 11 June 1984 she had charge of a 1Zxx 'Additional' between Edinburgh Waverley and Aberdeen and return, then on 25 May 1987 she took 1Z45 Derby to Skegness 'Relief' and the return as 1Z46. She worked for Hertfordshire Railtours on 1 July 1990 with their charter 'The Double Gloucester' which ran from London Paddington to Gloucester to include Gloucester depot Open Day, then to Sharpness and return to Gloucester before heading back to Paddington. She also featured on the 'Open Day Shuttles' between Birmingham New Street and Gloucester organised by Pathfinder Railtours.

The following almost three years were spent either in store or working freights until her transfer to Scotland from April 1993 saw her involved with Anglo-Scottish services from London Euston to Aberdeen or Inverness, taking them on from Edinburgh, or her own trains from Edinburgh to the Highlands. In June 1998 she was back in England for EWS before her visit to France in August 1999 after which she spent time in store awaiting disposal.

She was officially withdrawn from stock in November 2005 but re-registered for Network Rail shortly after and renumbered to 97301 after conversion at Barrow Hill. On 9 May 2009 she was involved with the Network Rail (Bristol & Swindon ICC) tour 'The Cambrian Mountaineer & Aber Dabble Doo' which ran from Bristol Temple Meads to Shrewsbury then on to Aberystwyth. From there it was steam hauled to Devil's Bridge and return before heading back to Bristol via Crewe. She and 37676 were in charge from Shrewsbury to Aberystwyth and return. She then

**At Banbury** with a NR Structure Gauging Train in March 2012 is 97301.

spent the summer of 2010 working on the heritage Mid Norfolk Railway before operating Network Rail's ERTMS signalling test train over the network until September 2014. She then spent a few days at the Midland Railway Centre at Butterley before resuming her duties for Network Rail. On 18 March 2017 she worked for Pathfinder Railtours' 'The Heart of Wales Wanderer' which ran from Eastleigh to Newport, Llandrindod Wells and return, with 97302 between Newport and Llandrindod Wells. Network Rail duties were then resumed once more based at Derby until she moved to Peak Rail in May 2023 to be stored, having donated her power unit to 97303.

### 97302 (D6870, 37170)

Released by EE Vulcan Foundry as D6870, Works Number EE/VF3348/D834 on 30 August 1963 and allocated to Landore.

Final depot: Doncaster, for Network Rail, 9/07.

Name carried: *Rheilffyrdd Ffestiniog ac Eryri/Ffestiniog and Welsh Highland Railways*, 4/19.

**Working for** NR on the Cambrian Coast line on 13 July 2012 is 97302. (*Peter Broster*)

Status: Withdrawn from stock by EWS, 10/05; Re-registered for Network Rail and transferred to Barrow Hill for HNRC, 8/06; Renumbered to 97302, 10/08; Operational in Network Rail Yellow livery from 8/11. Later she was regularly involved for Pathfinder Railtours with their charter 'The Cambrian Coast Express' between Shrewsbury and Pwllheli, operating with sister locos 97303 or 97304.

### 97303 (D6878, 37178)

Released by EE Vulcan Foundry as D6878, Works Number EE/VF3356/D842 on 9 October 1963 and allocated to Canton.

Final depot: Doncaster, 9/07.

Names carried: *Meteor*, 12/89–9/91; *Dave Berry*, 12/21.

Status: Sold by EWS from Eastleigh Yard, 7/05; Re-registered for Network Rail and transferred to Barrow Hill for HNRC, 8/06; Renumbered to 97303, 5/08; Operational in Network Rail Yellow livery from 9/07. Charter use followed including for Pathfinder Railtours' 'The Cambrian Coast Express'.

Notable movements:
Her years in South Wales were characterised by involvement with the heavy freight of the area, especially coal, which dominated along with Class 2 passenger services between Newport, Swansea and Cardiff and banking duties on the Lickey Incline. By the end of the 1970s though she was becoming sought after to head the more prestigious Class 1 trains to Bristol Temple Meads or to the Midlands and charter duties were also beginning to feature in her busy schedule. These included on 13 April 1979 for F+W Railtours' 'The Pixieland Express' which ran from Cheltenham Spa to Gloucester, Bristol Temple Meads, Penzance, Par, Newquay and return, taking over between Bristol and Par, then from Par to Worcester Shrub Hill, with 37084. Then on 17 June 1979, for the same tour operator 'The Doncaster Derby' which originated at Exeter St Davids and ran to Bristol Temple Meads, Birmingham New Street, Doncaster, Peterborough and return, when she and 37294 were in charge between Bristol and Birmingham both ways. Next was Hertfordshire Rail Tours 'The Valley Basher', from London Paddington to Newport and return for a tour of South Wales lines with 37190 and then on 20 August 1980 she headed a 1Zxx 'special' from Swansea to Clifton Down and on 9 May 1982 she took 1Z47, a 'special' from Wick to Plymouth between Birmingham New Street and Plymouth with 37188.

From then until August 1982 she was busy with Class 1 and Class 2 passenger services in South Wales and to Bristol, with occasional coal trains and oil tanks for Milford Haven, then in October 1982 she transferred to Eastfield and her attention shifted to services north from Glasgow and into the Highlands, a period which included a 'Football Extra' on 30 April 1983 between Dundee and Aberdeen and on 9 April 1984 a Tay Rail 'Day Excursion' from Dundee to Blackpool North, between Dundee and Mossend Yard.

She continued working in Scotland until visiting Crewe Works in October 1984 after which she assisted the charter 1Z47, the SLOA's 'The Great Western Limited' which ran from London Paddington to Bristol Temple Meads, Taunton, Tiverton, Exeter St Davids, Plymouth and back to Paddington, she and 37007 being required following the failure of the two steam locos involved in the tour. She then returned north and resumed her work mainly in Scotland until transferring to Stratford in November 1987 and then Tinsley in May 1989. She was a guest at Tinsley Open Day in September 1990 and on 4 May 1992 she and 37026 headed a 1Zxx 'Special' between Crewe and Hereford and return. Then on 8 November 1992 she was paired with 37278 for DC Tours 'The Exe-Solent Explorer' which ran from London Waterloo to Exeter St Davids, Exmouth and return, the '37s' being involved between Salisbury and Waterloo on the return.

Her passenger work then continued, centred on South Wales and the South West and from Crewe to North Wales for much of the 1990s, including the charter 1Z37 The 'Syphon Symphony' for Pathfinder Railtours, which began at Finsbury Park and ran to London Victoria then Horsham, Littlehampton, Haywards Heath, Brighton, Eastbourne, Hastings and return to Victoria and Finsbury Park. She and 37154 had charge between Victoria and Hastings. After being put into store by EWS in December 1999, designated for component recovery, in July 2000 she was sold, destined for scrapping until re-registered by Network Rail and brought back into use as 97303, now ERTMS fitted for working Cambrian lines.

On 2 September 2009 she was superficially damaged when involved in a fatal accident at Penrhyndeudraeth on the Cambrian Coast line, when travelling 'light engine', as she struck a car on a user-worked level crossing. From mid-2011 following repairs she was busy with a series of 1Zxx Network Rail test train workings centred on the Aberystwyth area, often accompanied by 97302 or 97304 and occasional charters including for Spitfire Railtours on 16 July 2011 'The Cambrian Coast Express', London Euston to Aberystwyth, Shrewsbury and return with 97304. For Pathfinder Railtours on 31 May 2013 she was involved with their 'Cambrian Coast Express' which ran from Bristol Temple Meads to Pwllheli and return, then on 20 July 2013 for UK Railtours' 'The Cardigan Bay Panorama' which began at London Euston and ran to Bescot then Shrewsbury, Aberystwyth and return. After a brief appearance on the Midland Railway Trust's line at Butterley in June 2015 she continued her NR operations interspersed with charters including on 10 October 2017 Pathfinder Railtours' 'The Cambrian Coast Express', Bristol Temple Meads to Shrewsbury, Pwllheli and return, a tour repeated on 13 May 2022. On 17 December 2021 she was named *Dave Berry* at Network Rail's Coleham depot, Shrewsbury. With 97302 ran light from Crewe Basford Hall to Rectory Junction (Colwick, Colas) east of Nottingham on 19 February 2024.

**97304 (D6917, 37217)** (See also 97304 in Class 37s in Colour) Released by EE Vulcan Foundry as D6917, Works Number EE/VF3395/D861 on 2 January 1964 and allocated to Landore.

Final depot: Doncaster, for Network Rail, 5/07.

Names carried: *John Tiley*, 11/08; *Rheilffyrdd Talyllyn Railway*, 5/24

Status: Sold by EWS, 5/07 and allocated to Network Rail; Operational in Network Rail Yellow livery from 5/07; Renumbered to 97304, 7/08; Hired out for charter work thereafter including regularly for Pathfinder Railtours' 'The Cambrian Coast Express' with 97302 or 97303.

**At Craven** Arms on 10 September 2020 are 97303 and 97302 *Rheilffyrdd Ffestiniog ac Eryri/ Ffestiniog & Welsh Highland Railways* heading the 16.00 Knighton to Crewe Basford Hall departmental train. *(Jonathan Allen)*

**156** • THE ENGLISH ELECTRIC CLASS 37: CO CO DIESEL ELECTRIC LOCOMOTIVES FROM DESIGN TO DEMISE

Chapter 4
# CLASS 37s IN COLOUR

**Class Leader, D6700 (37119, 37350)** (See also 37350)

**Preserved and** displayed at the National Railway Museum in York at their 'Railfest' on 5 June 2012 is class leader D6700.

## Class 37s in Colour • 157

**D6741 (37041, 37520)** (See also 37520 in sub-class 37/5)

**At Doncaster** during May 1963 is D6741.

**D6836 (37136, 37905)** (See also 37905 in sub-class 37/9)

**Passing Newark** in BR green with a freight on 16 June 1967 is D6836, later to be renumbered to 37136, then to sub-class 37/9 as number 37905.

**6961 (37261)** (See also 37261 in sub-class 37/0)

**At Manningtree** in August 1970 is 6961, later to be renumbered to 37261.

**6987 (37287, 37414)** (See also 37414 in sub-class 37/4)

**Stabled at** Aberdare in April 1972 is 6987.

**Class 37s in Colour • 159**

**37003 (D6703, 37003, 37360, 37003)** (See also 37003 in sub-class 37/0)

**Temporarily renumbered** to 37360 for her visit to Dereham, Mid Norfolk Railway is 37003 on 25 September 2010. (*Dan Davison*)

**37010 (D6710)** (See also 37010 in sub-class 37/0)

**37010 with** 37074 and 37077 stabled at Toton on 25 April 1988. (*Rick Ward*)

# 160 • THE ENGLISH ELECTRIC CLASS 37: CO CO DIESEL ELECTRIC LOCOMOTIVES FROM DESIGN TO DEMISE

**37011 (D6711)** See also 37011 in sub-class 37/0

**Damaged 37011** at BREL Crewe on 12 March 1988, after which she never returned into traffic. (*Rick Ward*)

**37019 (D6719)** (See also 37019 in sub-class 37/0)

**Passing Winchester** with a Freightliner train in October 1992 is 37019. (*Terry Fougler*)

Class 37s in Colour • 161

**37025 (D6725)** (See also 37025 in sub-class 37/0)

**Passing Colton** Junction near York on 8 December 2016 is 37025 *Inverness TMD Quality Approved* in charge of Network Rail's Structure Gauging Train.

**At Armathwaite** near Carlisle on the scenic S&C line on 21 February 2018 37025 *Inverness TMD Quality Approved* is in charge of Network Rail's Ultrasonic Test Unit, forming the 11.27 Mossend Down Yard to Derby RTC. *(Jonathan Allen)*

**Receiving attention** at Doncaster on 25 April 1988 is 37029. (*Rick Ward*)

**37029 (D6729)** (See also 37029 in sub-class 37/0)

**37032 (D6732, 37353, 37032)** (See also 37032 in sub-class 37/0)

**At Weybourne,** North Norfolk Railway on 22 June 2021 is 37032, aka D6732.

## 37038 (D6738)

**At Colton** Junction York on 12 October 2017 a DRS convoy from Barrow Hill LIP to York Thrall Europa is led by 20205 and 20312 dragging 37038 in DRS 'Compass' logo. DRS is owned by the Nuclear Decommissioning Authority, established in 1995, parent company of British Nuclear Fuels. DRS was created to provide the company with a rail transport service and initially carried only loads related to the nuclear industry, though in recent years has diversified into more general work.

## 37042 (D6742) (See also 37042 in sub-class 37/0)

**After taking** over from steam loco 35005 *Canadian Pacific* on Past Time Rail's 'The Bournemouth Belle', London Victoria to Poole charter on 12 February 2000, 37042 departs from Salisbury.

**37059 (D6759)** (See also 37059 in sub-class 37/0)

**Approaching Ribblehead** on the S&C line are 37059 and 37058 on 20 July 1996 with 1Z37, the Class 37 Group's 'The Settle Syphons'. The charter ran from King's Cross to Doncaster Decoy North Junction with 37051 and 37057 in charge, then on to Carlisle via the S&C as seen above. This pairing then took the train on to York by way of Hexham and Low Fell Junction before the original pair was re-united for the return to King's Cross.

**37079 (D6779, 37079, 37357)** (See also 37079 in sub-class 37/0)

**Awaiting their** fate at Barrow Hill on 14 July 2001 are Class 37s including 37079.

Class 37s in Colour • 165

**37099 (D6799, 37324)** (See also 37099 in sub-class 37/0)

**Colas liveried** 37099 with a NR test train from the Railway Technical Centre, Derby, to the Erewash Valley line on 8 September 2022. (*Geoff Sheppard*)

**37104 (D6804)** (See also 37104 in sub-class 37/0)

**Light engine** at Newcastle upon Tyne on 6 May 1993 is 37104.

**166** • THE ENGLISH ELECTRIC CLASS 37: CO CO DIESEL ELECTRIC LOCOMOTIVES FROM DESIGN TO DEMISE

**Passing through** Kensington Olympia on 3 September 2003 is 37109. (*Jonathan Allen*)

**37109 (D6809)** (See also 37109 in sub-class 37/0)

**37150 (D6850, 37901)** (See also 37901 in sub-class 37/9)

**At Aviemore** on 23 August 1978 is 37150. She was modified and renumbered to 37901 in October 1986. (*Steve Jones*)

Class 37s in Colour • 167

**37158 (D6858)** (See also 37158 in sub-class 37/0)

**37179 (D6879, 37691, 37612)** (See also 37179 in sub-class 37/0)

**Passing Westbury** near Trowbridge, Wiltshire with her freight on 14 May 1988 is 37158.

**Near Rose** Heyworth Colliery, Gwent, South Wales 37179 and 37182 head 'The Welsh Collieries Rambler' on 13 April 1980. This Oxford Publishing Company tour departed Oxford as 1Z37 with 47079 in charge as far as Newport where the 37s took over to Rose Heyworth Colliery, then via Ebbw Junction and Cardiff Central to Cwm Bargoed. There 37275 and 37280 were involved to Dowlais Furnace Top Branch. 37179 and 37182 took charge again there for the return journey to Newport by way of Blaenavon and Cardiff Central. The Class 47 resumed for the final leg back to Oxford. Rose Heyworth Colliery was sunk in 1874 and closed in 1985 with the loss of 450 jobs. The name lives on as that of the general area of Abertillery around the old colliery.

**At Rose** Heyworth Colliery the two 37s pose for pictures at the head of 1Z37 from Oxford. Both 37179 and 37182 were later modified and renumbered into sub-class 37/5.

**37185 (D6885)** (See also 37185 in sub-class 37/0)

**Stabled at** St Blazey on 1 July 1984 are 37185 and 37181.

**37190 (D6890, 37314, 37190, 37314)** (See also 37190 in sub-class 37/0)

**Passing Rothley** Carriage Works on the GCR on 26 April 2009 is 37314 *Dalzell*. She was renumbered to 37314 in July 1986 but not modified, so returned to 37190 in October 1988. After being withdrawn from stock in July 1993 and saved for preservation she was renumbered again to 37314. (*Duncan Harris*)

**37203 (D6903)** (See also 37203 in sub-class 37/0)

**At Toton** depot in ex-works Mainline blue livery is 37203 on 19 November 1995.

**170** • THE ENGLISH ELECTRIC CLASS 37: CO CO DIESEL ELECTRIC LOCOMOTIVES FROM DESIGN TO DEMISE

**37218 (D6918)** (See also 37218 in sub-class 37/0)

**In the** Parcels Sidings at York station on 6 March 2020 37218 awaits her next duty.

**Passing Cummersdale** near Carlisle on the Cumbrian Coast Line from Barrow-in-Furness on 8 April 2017 are 37218 and 37609 with a nuclear waste flasks train, 6K73, Sellafield to Crewe Coal Sidings. (*Jonathan Allen*)

Class 37s in Colour • 171

**37232 (D6932)** (See also 37232 in sub-class 37/0)

**In what** became known as 'Dutch' livery, 37232 *Institute of Railway Signal Engineers* manoeuvres at Perth station on 4 August 1991. The grey and yellow was said to resemble that of certain locomotives in the Netherlands and by 1992 thirty-five locos had been so painted.

*Below left*: **Passing through** Kensington Olympia on 7 September 2001 with an aggregates train are 37248 *Midland Railway Centre* and 37216 in Mainline Freight livery. (*Steve Jones*)

*Below right*: During the West Somerset Railway's 2019 Diesel Gala D6948 approaches Watchet with a service from Bishops Lydeard to Minehead on 22 June 2019. (*Geof Sheppard*)

**37248 (D6948)** (See also 37248 in sub-class 37/0)

## 172 • THE ENGLISH ELECTRIC CLASS 37: CO CO DIESEL ELECTRIC LOCOMOTIVES FROM DESIGN TO DEMISE

**Operational on** the GCR on 8 April 2010 is 37255. (*Tony Hisgett*)

**37255 (D6955)** (See also 37255 in sub-class 37/0)

**37264 (D6964)** (See also 37264 in sub-class 37/0)

**Outside Grosmont** shed, NYMR on 7 April 2019 is 37264 with Class 25 D7628.

**37272 (D6604, 37304, 37272, 37334)** (See also 37272 in sub-class 37/0)

**Passing through** Lostwithiel in Cornwall with a China Clay train on 10 May 1983 is 37272. She was renumbered to 37304 from D6604 in March 1974, then to 37272 and finally to 37334 in September 1994. Even though finally carrying a sub-class 37/3 number she remained unmodified and therefore stayed in sub-class 37/0.

**37278 (D6978)** (See also 37278 in sub-class 37/0)

**Passing Basingstoke** with a Freightliner train in September 1992 are 37278 and 37032. (*Terry Fougler*)

**37308 (D6608, 37274)** (See 37308 in sub-class 37/0)

**At Bescot** on 16 January 2004 is 37308. Renumbered from D6608 during March 1974 she became 37274 in February 1989 and then back to 37308 in August 2000. (*Steve Jones*)

**37331 (D6902, 37202)** (See also 37331 in sub-class 37/3)

**At Fleet**, Hampshire on 6 July 1989 with empty coils is 37202, later to be modified and renumbered to 37331 in September 1994.

Class 37s in Colour • 175

**37350 (D6700, 37119)** (See also 37350 in sub-class 37/3)

**Now preserved** as D6700, 37350 pilots 37220 with a train of oil tanks near Cardiff in the summer of 1990.

**Below left**: Shortly after arriving at Barrow Hill, 37372 is marked up in preparation for conversion to 'the new Baby Deltic'

**Below right**: At Barrow Hill during March 2011, 37372 is being transformed into Baby Deltic number 5910. (*Ashley Dace*)

**37372 (D6859, 37159)** (See also 37372 in sub-class 37/3)

**37401 (D6968, 37268)** (See also 37401 in sub-class 37/4)

*Above left*: **On Scotland's** scenic West Highland Line on 14 August 2005 maroon liveried 37401 *Mary Queen of Scots* leads EWS 37417 between Taynuilt and Connel Ferry near Oban at the head of 'The Orient Express of the North' excursion, Edinburgh to Oban and return. (*Jonathan Allen*)

*Above right*: **Again on** the West Highland Line, 37401 *Mary Queen of Scots* pilots 37410 near Achallader, Bridge of Orchy, on 28 April 2008 heading the Mossend to Fort William 'Alcan' train. (*Jonathan Allen*)

*Right*: **On the** rear of a Rail Head Treatment Train (RHTT) as it passes through York station on 6 October 2021 is 37401 *Mary Queen of Scots*. Operated by DRS as train 315R it ran from York Thrall Europa to York Thrall Europa by way of Scarborough, Bridlington, Beverley, Hull, Selby, Goole and Brough. Leading the train was classmate 37402. After the end of the 2019 Sandite season, the RHTTs which had routinely been hauled by Class 20/3 locos working 'top & tail', the workings were taken over by DRS Class 37s. Regulars in the Yorkshire area also included 37407, 37419, 37422 and 37425, one of which was occasionally accompanied by 37218 or 37716.

37402 (D6974, 37274) (See also 37402 in sub-class 37/4)

**In immaculate** condition in York station Parcels Sidings on 27 June 2013 is 37402.

**At St** Bees on the Cumbrian Coast Line 37402 *Stephen Middlemore 23.12.1954–8.6.2013* heads the 08.45 Barrow-in-Furness to Carlisle service on 12 May 2018. (*Jonathan Allen*)

'**The Easter** Highlander', the Pathfinder Railtours 09.10 Aviemore to Eastleigh led by 37402 *Stephen Middlemore 23.12.1954–8.6.2013* coupled with 37409 *Lord Hinton* passes through Dumfries on 22 April 2019. *(Jonathan Allen)*

**37406 (D6995, 37295)** (See also 37406 in sub-class 37/4)

**On the** West Highland Line at Achallader near Bridge of Orchy on 5 September 2006 EWS liveried 37406 *The Saltire Society* takes the London Euston to Fort William 'beds', 'The Highland Sleeper'. The service is hauled to Edinburgh Waverley by electric loco where it divides into three portions, to Fort William, Aberdeen and Inverness as separate services which are recombined for the return journey. *(Jonathan Allen)*

Class 37s in Colour • 179

**37409 (D6970, 37270)** (See also 37409 in sub-class 37/4)

**At Cummersdale** near Carlisle on 11 January 2019 are 37409 *Lord Hinton* and 37425 *Balchder y Cymoedd/Pride of the Valleys* heading 2Z37, the 09.52 Carlisle to Carnforth '37 Farewell'. (*Jonathan Allen*)

**At Carlisle** with a Network Rail track monitoring train on 28 March 2019 is 37409 *Lord Hinton*. (*Jonathan Allen*)

**37411 (D6990, 37290)**

Passing through Carlisle Citadel station with a south bound 'Silver Bullets' on 14 June 1993 are 37411 and 37670. (Jonathan Allen)

**37414 (D6987, 37287)** (See also 37414 in sub-class 37/4)

Leaving Rhyl on 23 June 1993 is 37414 *Cathays C&W Works 1846–1993* at the head of the 11.33 Crewe to Holyhead. (Jonathan Allen)

**Class 37s in Colour • 181**

**37416 (D6602, 37302)** (See also 37416 in sub-class 37/4)

**On 23 August** 2003 37416 *Sir Robert McAlpine/Concrete Bob* passes Spean Bridge near Fort William with the 21.05 Euston to Fort William 'Deerstalker' sleeper service. (*Jonathan Allen*)

**37418 (D6971, 37271)** (See also 37418 in sub-class 37/4)

**Leaving Holyhead** on 13 August 1994 is Regional Railways 37418 *ELR* while classmate 37408 *Loch Rannoch* waits at the platform with a train for Crewe.

**Passing Dringhouses,** York on 1 September 2022 is 37418 *An Comunn Gaedhealach* with NR Inspection Saloon 975025 *Caroline*. Originally the Southern Region General Manager's Saloon built at Eastleigh Works in 1958 *Caroline* also saw service as a VIP excursion train before being converted in 1999 for NR, and again in the late 2000s after which she would normally be propelled by a Class 37 locomotive, having push-pull controls similar to a Driving Van Trailer.

**37419 (D6991, 37291)** (See 37419 in sub-class 37/4)

**Leaving York** near Shipton by Beningbrough on 23 July 2013 is 37419 *Carl Haviland 1954–2012* in DRS 'Compass' livery propelling NR Inspection Saloon 975025 *Caroline*.

Class 37s in Colour • 183

**Hauling a** train of Rail Head Treatment hoppers past Dringhouses, York on 1 September 2022 is 37419 *Carl Haviland 1954–2012*. (*Rick Ward*)

**37422 (D6966, 37266, 37558)** (See also 37422 in sub-class 37/4)

**Near Ais** Gill on the S&C line, 37422 and 37558 (also carrying number 37424) pass with the 16.21 Carlisle Kingmoor to Carlisle Kingmoor Rail Head Treatment Train on 15 October 2018. (*Jonathan Allen*)

**Approaching York** from the north and passing Shipton by Beningbrough on 18 April 2022 is 37422 *Victorious* leading classmate 37425 *Sir Robert McAlpine/Concrete Bob* with Pathfinder Railtours charter 'The Easter Highlander' (day four of four).

*Below left*: **Standing outside** Crewe Works on 2 March 1986 in 'ex works' condition is 37425 in BR Blue 'Large Logo' livery.

*Below right*: **Passing Kensington** Olympia with train 7L39, the 13.55 Hoo Junction to Temple Mills departmental train on 20 June 2003 is 37425 in EWS livery. (*Jonathan Allen*)

**37425 (D6992, 37292)** (See also 37425 in sub-class 37/4)

Class 37s in Colour • 185

**At Wigton** on 21 June 2016 is 37425 *Balchder y Cymoedd/Pride of the Valleys* heading the 11.40 Barrow-in-Furness to Carlisle service. (*Jonathan Allen*)

### 37427 (D6988, 37288) (See also 37427 in sub-class 37/4)

On 31 May 2005 EWS 37427 *Bont Y Bermo* is at Achallader with the Fort William section of 'The Caledonian Sleeper'. (*Jonathan Allen*)

### 37431 (D6972, 37272) (See also 37431 in sub-class 37/4)

With a loaded coal train at Pwll-Mawr near Cardiff on 16 September 1982 is 37272, later rebuilt as 37431.

**37509 (D6793, 37093)** (See also 37509 in sub-class 37/5)

**Passing Colwyn** Bay with east-bound ballast hoppers on 23 June 1993 is 37509. *(Jonathan Allen)*

*Below left*: **Stabled at York** station Parcels Sidings on 22 December 2012 is WCRC 37516.

*Below right*: **Running 'light** engine' through York station on 11 August 2016 are 37516 *Loch Laidon* and 37669, having brought the Scarborough Spa Express from Carnforth to be steam hauled onward to Scarborough by Stanier 8F number 48151.

**37516 (D6786, 37086)** (See also 37516 in sub-class 37/5)

**188** • THE ENGLISH ELECTRIC CLASS 37: CO CO DIESEL ELECTRIC LOCOMOTIVES FROM DESIGN TO DEMISE

*Above left*: **Stabled with** 33207 *Jim Martin* in York station Parcels Sidings on 21 June 2018 is WCRC 37516 *Loch Laidon*.

*Above right*: **Parked alongside** classmate 6966/37422 at York station Parcels Sidings on 30 July 2022 is 37516 *Loch Laidon*.

*Right*: **With classmate** 37422/6966 at York station Parcels Sidings on 30 July 2022 is 37516 *Loch Laidon*.

Class 37s in Colour • 189

**37517 (D6718, 37018)** (See also 37517 in sub-class 37/5)

**On Rail** Head Treatment Train duty at Eaglescliffe station on 16 October 2004 is 37517 *St Aidan's CE Memorial School Hartlepool Railsafe Trophy Winners 1995*. (*Mark Harrington*)

**37521 (D6817, 37117)** (See also 37521 in sub-class 37/5)

**Passing Kirkby** Stephen on 31 July 2020 is 37521 running as D6817 with 1Z40, Rail Charter Services/LSL 'The Settle & Carlisle Tourist Train', Skipton–Appleby and return (three trains ran each day, virtually every day between 20 July and 22 August 2020), advertised as 'The Staycation Express'. (*Jonathan Allen*)

**At Plymouth** on 8 April 2023 is D6817 heading the Locomotive Services Ltd (LSL) private charter, a six day extended tour from London Euston, through the Midlands to North Wales then to Bristol and on to Devon and Cornwall, mostly in the company of 37667. (*Geoff Sheppard*)

**37601 (D6705, 37005, 37501)** (See also 37601 in sub-class 37/5)

**At Doncaster** on 28 July 2022 is 37601 *Perseus*.

**37603 (D6739, 37039, 37504)** (See also 37603 in sub-class 37/5)

**Viewed from** Arnside Knott, DRS 37603 and 37423 take the Sellafield nuclear waste flasks towards Arnside Viaduct, Cumbria on 23 October 2012.

**37604 (D6707, 37007, 37506)** (See also 37604 in sub-class 37/5)

**At Colton** Junction near York on 2 April 2013 with a Network Rail Track Monitoring Train is 37604. (*Rick Ward*)

### 37609 (D6815, 37115, 37514) (See also 37609 in sub-class 37/5)

**Heading north** from York near Shipton by Beningbrough on 24 July 2013 are 37609 and 37603 at the head of Compass Tours 'The Pennine & North Eastern Explorer', Milton Keynes to Durham and return.

### 37673 (D6832, 37132) (See also 37673 in sub-class 37/5)

**With Pathfinder** Railtours' 'The Cornish Centurian 2' railtour, Manchester Piccadilly to Truro, 37673 pauses at Bugle on 4 May 1991. (*Richard Szwejkowski*)

Class 37s in Colour • 193

**37674 (D6869, 37169)** (See also 37674 in sub-class 37/5)

**Waiting at** Aviemore station on the Strathspey Railway on 30 June 2023 is 37674.

**37680 (D6924, 37224)** (See also 37680 in sub-class 37/5)

**Receiving attention** at St Rollox Works, Glasgow on 4 May 1991 is 37680.

**37681 (D6830, 37130)** (See also 37681 in sub-class 37/5)

**Passing Peak** Forest with a train of empty ICI bogies on 4 April 1990 are 37681 and 37679.

**37684 (D6834, 37134)** (See also 37684 in sub-class 37/5)

**Passing Melton** Ross, North Lincolnshire on 10 September 1997 is 37684 *Peak National Park* with Eggborough to Lindsey Oil Terminal fuel oil empties.

**37686 (D6872, 37172)** (See also 37686 in sub-class 37/5)

**Stabled at** Buxton mpd on 20 January 1991 is 37686 alongside 37679.

**37698 (D6946, 37246)** (See also 37698 in sub-class 37/5)

**At Preston** on 12 April 2003 with 'The Wizard Express' are 37698 and 37712.

# 196 • THE ENGLISH ELECTRIC CLASS 37: CO CO DIESEL ELECTRIC LOCOMOTIVES FROM DESIGN TO DEMISE

**37702 (D6720, 37020. 37702, L30)** (See also 37702 in sub-class 37/7)

**A 'triple-header'** at Cwmbargoed on 20 June 1997 featuring 37702 *Taff Merthyr*, 37897 and 37899 *Sir Gorllewin Morgannwg/County of West Glamorgan*. (*Phil Sangwell*)

**37705 (D6760, 37060)** (See also 37705 in sub-class 37/7)

**Passing through** Ipswich with a train of containers in 1984 are 37060 and 37075. Following refurbishment at Crewe Works 37060 became 37705 in October 1987.

# Class 37s in Colour • 197

**37706 (D6716, 37016)** (See 37706 in sub-class 37/7)

**At Colton** Junction, York on 18 September 2013 WCRC 37706 hauls a convoy from the NRM to the Mid Norfolk Railway, consisting of 'Deltic' 55002 *King's Own Yorkshire Light Infantry*, prototype HST power car 41001 and Class 37 D6700 (37350) in BR green livery.

**37713 (D6752, 37052)** (See also 37713 in sub-class 37/7)

**Passing Lincoln** with a train of oil tanks on 4 April 1996 is 37713.

**37718 (D6784, 37094, 37718, L021, L22)** (See also 37718 in sub-class 37/7)

**At Zuera** (Aragon), Spain on 10 April 2003 is L22 (UK 37718). (*Jean-Pierre Vergez-Larrouy*)

**37884 (D6883, 37183, 37884, L34)** (See also 37884 in sub-class 37/7)

**In EuroPhoenix** livery at Bristol St Phillips Marsh Open Day on 2 May 2016 is 37884. (*Harry Mitchell*)

Class 37s in Colour • 199

**37894 (D6824, 37124)** (See also 37894 in sub-class 37/7)

**With a** train of loaded coal hoppers passing St Mellons, Cardiff on 20 May 1992 is 37894.

**37899 (D6861, 37161, 37899, L022, L21)** See also 37899 in sub-class 37/7

**Working with** 37896, 37899 *County of West Glamorgan/Sir Gorllewin Morgannwg* in Rail Freight Coal livery is heading 'The Bolsover Balladeer' rail tour on 1 September 1991.

**200** • THE ENGLISH ELECTRIC CLASS 37: CO CO DIESEL ELECTRIC LOCOMOTIVES FROM DESIGN TO DEMISE

**At Salillas** del Jalon, Spain, on 24 May 2001 is L21 (UK 37899). (*Jean-Pierre Vergez-Larrouy*)

**37901 (D6850, 37150)** (See also 37901 in sub-class 37/9)

**Having brought** in her train to Ramsbottom, ELR on 8 May 2011 is 37901. (*Robert Wade*)

Class 37s in Colour • 201

**37904 (D6825, 37125)** (See also 37904 in sub-class 37/9)

**Passing through**
Newport South Wales on 15 May 1991 with a train of British Steel bogies are 37904 and 37716.

**37905 (D6836, 37136)** (See also 37905 in sub-class 37/9)

**Passing through**
Craven Arms on 6 September 1990 is Rail Freight Metals liveried 37905 *Vulcan Enterprise* with a heavy steel train from Llanwern. (*Jonathan Allen*)

**202** • THE ENGLISH ELECTRIC CLASS 37: CO CO DIESEL ELECTRIC LOCOMOTIVES FROM DESIGN TO DEMISE

### 97301 (D6800, 37100) (See also 97301 in sub-class 97/3)

**Network Rail's** ERTMS signalling test loco 97301 and train parked at Holgate Sidings, York on 23 May 2014.

### 97304 (D6917, 37217) See also 97304 in sub-class 97/3

**At Stretton** for NR with train 5Z97 Barrow Hill to Derby on 29 October 2008 is 97304. (*Phil Sangwell*)

# Appendix 1
# TECHNICAL DATA

BR Class 37: Original BR Numbers: D6600- D6608, D6700-D6999.
Total: 309 locomotives.
Designer: EE Co.
Builder: Vulcan Foundry, Newton-le-Willows and Robert Stephenson & Hawthorns, Darlington.
Built: 1960-65.
Service: General mixed traffic throughout Britain.
Livery: Originally BR Green with BR crest, later with yellow nose panels.
Then BR Blue with double-arrow symbol.

| | |
|---|---|
| Gauge | 4ft 8½in (1425mm, 'Standard Gauge') |
| Minimum Curve | 4 Chains (80m) |
| Wheelbase | 50ft 8in (15.44m) |
| Bogie Wheelbase | 13ft 6in (4.11m) |
| Bogie Pivot Centres | 37ft 2in (11.32m) |
| Length | 61ft 6in (18.74m) |
| Width | 8ft 10½in (2.71m) |
| Height | 37/0 and 37/3: 12ft 9in (3.89m)<br>37/4, 37/5, 37/6, 37/7 and 37/9: 13ft ¾ in (3.96m) |
| Loco Weight | 37/0 and 37/3: 102t – 108t<br>37/4 and 37/5: 107t<br>37/6: 106t<br>37/7 and 37/9: 120t |
| Fuel Capacity | 37/0 and 37/3: 890 gal (4046l)<br>37/4, 37/5, 37/7 and 37/9: 1690 gal (7682l) |
| Cooling Water Capacity | 160 gal (727l) |
| Lubricating Oil Capacity | 120 gal (545l) |
| Prime Mover | 37/0, 37/3, 37/4, 37/5 and 37/6 and 37/7: EE 12CSVT<br>37/9: Mirrlees MB275T or Ruston RX270T |
| Generator | Main: EE 822-10G, EE 822-13G or EE 822-J<br>Auxiliary: EE 911/5C |

| | |
|---|---|
| Alternator | Main: 37/4, 37/5, 37/6, 37/7 and 37/9: Brush BA10005A |
| | Or, 37/7: GEC G564AZ |
| | Auxiliary: 37/4, 37/5, 37/6, 37/7 and 37/9: Brush BA606A |
| | ETS: 37/4: Brush BAH701 |
| Traction Motors | 37/0 and 37/3: EE 538-1A |
| | 37/4, 37/5, 37/6, 37/7 and 37/9: EE 538-5A |
| Cylinder Size | Bore: 10in (250mm); Stroke: 12in (300mm) |
| Transmission | Diesel Electric |
| Multiple Working | Blue Star |
| Train Heating | 37/0: Steam (removed) |
| | 37/3, 37/5, 37/6, 37/7 and 37/9: Not Fitted |
| | 37/4: Electric |
| Train Brakes | Vacuum (later Air or Dual) |
| Speed | 37/0 (as built) and 37/6: 90mph (145km/h) |
| | 37/0 (modified), 37/3, 37/5, 37/7 and 37/9: 80mph (129km/h) |
| Power Output | Engine: 1,750hp (1,305kW) |
| | 37/9: 1,800hp (1,340kW) |
| | At Rail: 1,250hp (932kW) |
| | 37/4: 1,254hp (935kW) |
| | 37/9: 1,300hp (940kW) |
| Tractive Effort | 37/0: 55,500lb (245kN) |
| | 37/3: 56,180lb (250kN) |
| | 37/4: 57,440lb (256kN) |
| | 37/5: 55,590lb (248kN) |
| | 37/7: 62,000lb (276kN) |
| | 37/9: 62,680lb (279Kn) |
| Brakeforce | 50t |
| Operators | BR |
| Later | Colas Rail, DRS, EuroPhoenix, EWS, HNRC, LSL, Network Rail, ROG, WCRC |
| Numbers | D6700 – D6999 (Later, 37001 – 37308) |
| Route Availability | 5 (37/7 and 37/9: 7) |
| Nicknames | Tractor, also Syphon, Growler or Slug |

# Appendix 2
# LIVERIES

Include:

| | |
|---|---|
| BR | Blue, double arrow logo |
| BR | Civil Engineers "Dutch" (grey/yellow) |
| BR | Departmental (all-over dark grey) |
| BR | Green, double arrow logo |
| BR | Green, lion and wheel emblem |
| BR | Intercity Swallow (As applied to 37152/221/251/505/510/683/685 for working the Inverness and Aberdeen sleepers with generator vans between 1992 and 1994, since carried by 37518 in preservation) |
| BR | Large Logo blue (Applied to all the 37/4s as they underwent conversion, also carried by a number of 37/0s and 37/3s) |
| BR | Mainline (Essentially unbranded Intercity "Swallow" livery) |
| BR | Trainload Freight - Mainline "rolling wheels" branding in blue |
| BR | Two-tone green (As worn by classes 24, 25 and 47. Only carried by 37197 while owned by Ian Riley) |
| BR | Rail Freight "Large Logo" grey/yellow |
| BR | Rail Freight "Red Stripe" grey/yellow |
| BR | Regional Railways two-tone blue |
| BR | Unbranded trainload freight triple grey |
| Colas Rail | orange/yellow/black |
| DB Schenker | red |
| DRS | "Compass" |
| DRS | "Swirly compass" (As applied to the new class 68s) |
| English, Welsh & Scottish Railway | red/gold |
| European Passenger Services | Trainload freight triple grey with the Channel tunnel "polo mint" metal segments |
| European Passenger Services | blue |

| | |
|---|---|
| EuroPhoenix | grey, blue and red |
| GIF (Spain) | light and dark blue |
| HNRC | light grey/orange (Worn by 37087 and 37194) |
| Loadhaul | black/orange |
| Mainline Freight | Aircraft blue with silver decals |
| Network Rail | yellow |
| Royal Scotsman maroon | different permutations - 37428 initially with large yellow numbers, 37401 and 37416 later with small numbers |
| Trainload Coal | black diamonds on yellow background |
| Trainload Construction | blue and yellow squares |
| Trainload FreightGeneral | red and yellow rectangles - carried only by 37104, 37673 and also 37403 for one night only |
| Trainload Freight - Rail Freight Distribution | red 'rhombus' on yellow background |
| Trainload Metals | blue and yellow chevrons |
| Trainload Petroleum | blue and yellow waves |
| Transrail | two-tone grey with blue and red 'T' |
| West Coast Railway Company | maroon |

There have also been a number of permutations and one-offs in addition to the mostly standard schemes listed above, including:

37116 *Sister Dora* carried BR blue livery with the Transrail "Big T" logo during the mid to late 1990s.
37198 is in Network Rail yellow at the GCR.
37501 received a British Steel blue livery in the 1980s.

A few locomotives, such as 37350, 37403 and 37411 have also been returned to BR Green livery at various times from the 1990s onwards.
    37093 was dressed up in a predominantly white "Police" livery for an IC125 advert in the early 1980s.

## Appendix 3
# REGIONAL VARIATIONS

Considering the size of the class and its longevity it is no surprise that variations in the appearance of locomotives have appeared over the years. Those originally allocated to the Western Region could be identified by 'cow horns' on the outer edge of the lamp brackets and by the late 1970s some of this allocation also sported additional brackets to carry the headlights required on the Heart of Wales line. The nose end head-code boxes also showed regional variation with locos bearing the split box design being allocated to northern England and East Anglia while centre box locos were almost all allocated to Wales and the south west, though as time went on the locos were transferred repeatedly around the country.

Some depots got in on the act by adorning their locos with an identifying emblem. These included the Highland Stag (Inverness), the Cockney Sparrow (Stratford) the Cornish Lizard (St Blazey), the West Highland Terrier (Eastfield) and the Kingfisher (Thornaby). The Large Logo blue 37/4s allocated to Cardiff Canton received Celtic Dragons below the driver's window while some Scottish locomotives carried small Saltire flags next to their TOPS data panels or on their noses. Tinsley depot applied a variety of unofficial names to their locos in the late 1980s, including those of well-known volcanoes (suggested to be a reference to the amount of noise and smoke they emitted).

# Appendix 4
# RAIL FREIGHT LOGOS

By the mid-1980s Rail Freight (RF) was established as a semi-autonomous business sector with its own corporate identity, sub-divided into six components, Coal, Construction, Distribution, General, Metals and Petroleum. Each was allocated its own identifying emblem comprising two overlapping rectangles, the lower of which represented a stylised representation of the main freight carried while the upper created a stylised 'F' for freight in the same colour as the lower rectangle.

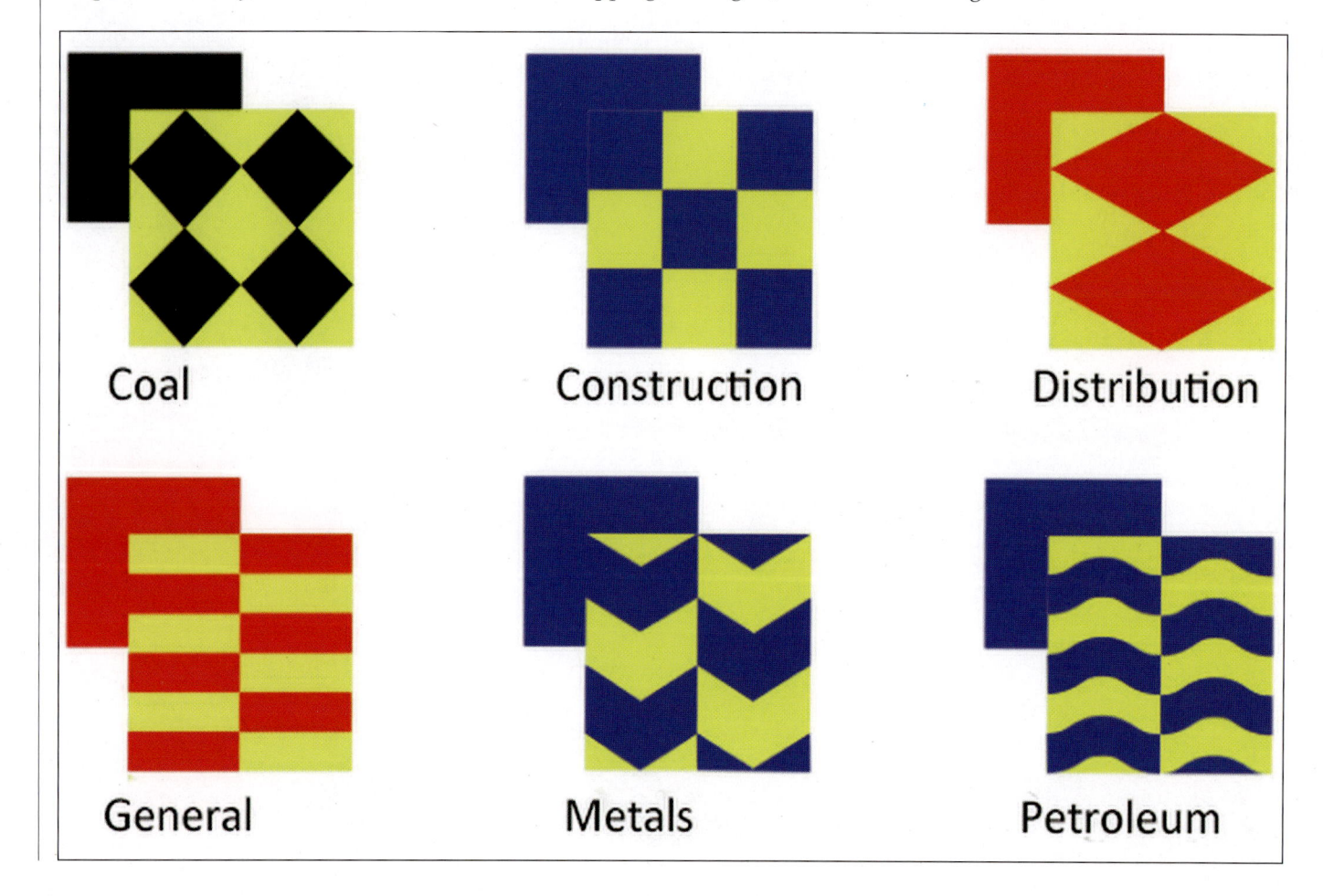

**Rail Freight** logos.

# Appendix 5

# WHERE ARE THEY NOW? (CORRECT TO JULY 2024)

Of the 309 locos built, 210 are listed as having been cut up. Those remaining are:

**In Service: 44** (Available for main line use. Locos may be hired out)

| | | |
|---|---|---|
| D6705 | 37601 | EuroPhoenix, on long-term hire to ROG |
| D6707 | 37604 | HNRC |
| D6722 | 37608 | EuroPhoenix, on long-term hire to ROG |
| D6738 | 37038 | DRS Sold to HNRC, July 2022 |
| D6739 | 37603 | DRS Sold to HNRC, April 2022 |
| D6757 | 37057 | Colas Rail |
| D6759 | 37059 | DRS Sold to LSL, July 2022 |
| D6769 | 37069 | DRS Sold to EuroPhoenix, October 2023 |
| D6776 | 37518 | WCRC |
| D6782 | 37602 | DRS Sold to HNRC, June 2023 |
| D6786 | 37516 | WCRC |
| D6794 | 37716 | DRS Sold to HNRC, March 2024 |
| D6799 | 37099 | Colas Rail |
| D6803 | 37607 | HNRC |
| D6812 | 37510 | EuroPhoenix, on long-term hire to ROG |
| D6816 | 37116 | Colas Rail |
| D6817 | 37521 | LSL |
| D6826 | 37676 | WCRC |
| D6829 | 37669 | WCRC |
| D6843 | 37800 | EuroPhoenix, on long-term hire to ROG |
| D6850 | 37901 | EuroPhoenix |
| D6851 | 37667 | LSL |
| D6870 | 97302 | Network Rail, operated by Colas Rail |
| D6871 | 37611 | EuroPhoenix, on long-term hire to ROG |
| D6875 | 37175 | Colas Rail |
| D6878 | 97303 | Network Rail, operated by Colas Rail |
| D6879 | 37612 | HNRC |
| D6881 | 37610 | HNRC |
| D6883 | 37884 | EuroPhoenix, on long-term hire to ROG |
| D6917 | 97304 | Network Rail, operated by Colas Rail |
| D6918 | 37218 | DRS Sold to EuroPhoenix, October 2023 |

| | | |
|---|---|---|
| D6919 | 37219 | Colas |
| D6934 | 37685 | WCRC |
| D6954 | 37254 | Colas Rail |
| D6957 | 37668 | WCRC |
| D6959 | 37259 | DRS Sold to HNRC, August 2022 |
| D6967 | 37421 | Colas Rail |
| D6971 | 37418 | Privately owned, on hire to Loram |
| D6974 | 37402 | DRS Sold to Sheaf Engineering, October 2023 |
| D6979 | 37424 | DRS Sold to Meteor Power, March 2024. Displays number 37558 |
| D6982 | 37405 | HNRC Sold to Colas, November 2022 |
| D6991 | 37419 | DRS Sold to HNRC, March 2024 |
| D6992 | 37425 | DRS Sold to Meteor Power, March 2024 |
| D6996 | 37423 | DRS Sold to EuroPhoenix, October 2023 |

**In Store: 14** (may be in the process of being sold on)

| | | |
|---|---|---|
| D6605 | 37407 | DRS Sold to EuroPhoenix, March 2024 |
| D6718 | 37517 | WCRC Spares donor |
| D6744 | 37710 | WCRC Partly cut up, April 2021 |
| D6790 | 37508 | DRS Sold to Loram Locomotives, October 2022 |
| D6800 | 97301 | Boden Rail, for component recovery |
| D6802 | 37712 | WCRC Spares donor |
| D6815 | 37609 | DRS Sold to HNRC, April 2022 |
| D6846 | 37146 | EuroPhoenix |
| D6859 | 37372 | BDP, undergoing conversion to D5910 at Barrow Hill |
| D6865 | 37374 | WCRC |
| D6914 | 37214 | Scottish 37 Group, Bo'ness & Kinneil Railway (parts donor) |
| D6966 | 37422 | DRS Sold to HNRC, March 2024 |
| D6968 | 37401 | DRS Sold to LSL, October 2023 |
| D6970 | 37409 | DRS Sold to LSL, July 2022 |

**In Preservation: 41** (Private Owners listed *, with 'home' location, but locos may be loaned out elsewhere or sold out of preservation)

| | | |
|---|---|---|
| D6607 | 37403 | Private Owner* Bo'ness & Kinneil Railway |
| D6608 | 37308 | Private Owner* SVR |
| D6700 | 37350 | The National Collection, NRM York, GCR |
| D6703 | 37003 | Class 37 Group, Mid Norfolk Railway |
| D6709 | 37340 | EE Preservation, GCR, Nottingham |
| D6716 | 37706 | Epping Ongar Railway Sold to WCRC |
| D6717 | 37503 | Private Owner* Shires Removal Group |
| D6723 | 37023 | Pontypool & Blaenavon Railway |
| D6724 | 37714 | Heavy Tractor Group, GCR |
| D6725 | 37025 | Scottish 37 Group Bo'ness & Kinneil Railway |
| D6729 | 37029 | Private Owner* Epping Ongar Railway |
| D6732 | 37353 | Private Owner* North Norfolk Railway |
| D6737 | 37037 | Devon Diesel Society* South Devon Railway |
| D6742 | 37042 | Eden Valley Railway |
| D6767 | 37703 | HNRC* Bo'ness & Kinneil Railway |
| D6775 | 37075 | Private Owner* K&WVR |

| | | |
|---|---|---|
| D6797 | 37097 | Caledonian Railway Diesel Group |
| D6808 | 37325 | Private Owner* Crewe Heritage Centre |
| D6809 | 37109 | ELR Diesel Group |
| D6823 | 37679 | Private Owner* Burton Wagon Works |
| D6836 | 37905 | Watercress Line Sold to UK Rail Leasing (not main line), October 2015 |
| D6842 | 37142 | Bodmin & Wenford Railway |
| D6852 | 37310 | Private Owner* Peak Rail |
| D6869 | 37674 | Private Owner* Strathspey Railway |
| D6890 | 37314 | Midland Railway Centre, Butterley |
| D6898 | 37198 | Darlington Borough Council* Head of Steam Museum |
| D6905 | 37688 | DO5 Preservation Ltd* On long term lease to LSL |
| D6906 | 37906 | Battlefield Line Sold to UK Rail Leasing (not main line), October 2015 |
| D6907 | 37207 | Meteor Power, GCR |
| D6915 | 37215 | Growler Group, Gloucestershire Warwickshire Railway |
| D6916 | 37216 | Private Owner* Pontypool & Blaenavon Railway |
| D6927 | 37227 | Chinnor & Princes Risborough Railway |
| D6940 | 37240 | Vintage Trains, Tyseley Locomotive Works |
| D6948 | 37248 | Private Owner* The Growler Group, Gloucestershire Warwickshire Railway |
| D6950 | 37250 | Private Owner* Wensleydale Railway |
| D6955 | 37255 | Private Owner* Nemesis Rail, Burton Wagon Shops |
| D6961 | 37261 | Scottish 37 Group, Bo'ness & Kinneil Railway |
| D6963 | 37263 | Private Owner* Telford Steam Railway |
| D6964 | 37264 | Private Owner* NYMR |
| D6975 | 37275 | Dartmouth Steam Railway |
| D6994 | 37294 | Embsay & Bolton Abbey Railway |

# BIBLIOGRAPHY

Class 37 Group & Derrick, Kevin, *Syphon Salute. 50 Years of Class 37s*, Strathwood 2015

Dunn, Pip, *Rail Guide 2024*, Crecy 2024

Marsden, Colin, *35 Years of Main Line Diesel Traction*, Oxford 1982

Morrison, B., *The Power of the 37s*, Oxford 1981

Tufnell, RM, *The Diesel Impact on British Rail*, Mechanical Engineering Publications, 1979

Vaughan, John, *Diesel Retrospective. Class 37*, Ian Allan, 2007

Walker, Andrew, et al *Class 37 Locomotives*, Amberley, 2016